Smart Staffing

Wayne Outlaw

Upstart
Publishing Company®
Specializing in Small Business Publishing
a division of Dearborn Publishing Group, Inc.

This publication is designed to provide accurate and authoritative information in regard to the subject matter covered. It is sold with the understanding that the publisher is not engaged in rendering legal, accounting, or other professional service. If legal advice or other expert assistance is required, the services of a competent professional should be sought.

Editorial Director: Cynthia A. Zigmund
Managing Editor: Jack Kiburz
Project Editor: Trey Thoelcke
Interior Design: Lucy Jenkins
Cover Design: S. Laird Jenkins Corporation

Published by Upstart Publishing Company®,
a division of Dearborn Publishing Group, Inc.

Printed in the United States of America

98 99 00 10 9 8 7 6 5 4 3 2 1

Library of Congress Cataloging-in-Publication Data

Outlaw, Wayne.
    Smart staffing : how to hire, reward and keep the best people for
your growing company / Wayne Outlaw.
        p.   cm.
    ISBN 1-57410-095-5 (pbk.)
    1. Employee selection.   2. Employees—Recruiting.   3. Employee
motivation.   I. Title.
    HF5549.5.S38088   1998
    658.3'1—dc21   98-9935
                                                            CIP

Upstart books are available at special quantity discounts to use as premiums and sales promotions, or for use in corporate training programs. For more information, please call the Special Sales Manager at 800-621-9621, ext. 4384, or write to Dearborn Financial Publishing, Inc., 155 N. Wacker Drive, Chicago, IL 60606-1719.

Praise for *Smart Staffing*

"The most important competitive weapon for a growing business in a service economy is people. Wayne Outlaw's expertise in creating competitive advantage through people for emerging enterprises is excellently captured in *Smart Staffing*. Far from theoretical, Wayne has created an incredibly practical guide for any business manager. This book has become required reading nationally for all our people involved in leading and managing our most precious asset."

Jonathan McNeill
Co-President and Chief Executive Officer
Sterling Collision Centers, Inc.

"Comprehensive, throrough, and powerfully effective. *Smart Staffing* is a perfect companion for every business owner—and a valuable reminder for human resource professionals."

Roger E. Herman, CSP, CMC
Author, *Keeping Good People*
Senior Fellow, Workforce Stability Institute

"Wayne Outlaw knows how to find and retain good people. A few hours with *Smart Staffing* will have profound impact on your bottom line."

Alan Weiss, Ph.D.
Author, *Million Dollar Consulting*

"The training we need for life's greatest challenges; marriage, raising children, and recruiting and retaining star employees, is usually left to chance. That's no longer the case. Wayne's *Smart Staffing* is a comprehensive step-by-step guide to hiring and retaining the 'stars' you want for your company. *No one* should fail if they follow his formulas!"

Rosemary Maniscalco
President and Chief Operating Officer
Comforce Staffing Services

"*Smart Staffing* will help with improving 'The Human Asset' side of your balance sheet. Each chapter is filled with ideas that can be immediately implemented. Buy the book and use it, the payoff will be 1,000-fold! You can't grow a business without people, this is an A to Z manual on how to do it right."

Paul E. Berman
President
Val-Pak of Philadelphia

"Wayne Outlaw has written the quintessential book on hiring, rewarding, and keeping top employees for a growing business. Practicing the approach advocated in *Smart Staffing* will take light years off your learning curve and provide you with the peace of mind that comes from knowing you have made the right decisions regarding people. Get it; read it; use it! You'll be glad you did."

George Morrisey
Author, *Morrisey on Planning*

"The largest obstacle to my company's future growth and health is finding, growing, and maintaining human capital. *Smart Staffing* addresses these problems with amazing clarity and direction. It's a must-read for any manager. I distributed five advance copies to my key managers and got instant results. Thank you!"

Mitchell Bender
CEO and President,
Pace American, Inc.

"What a great book! *Smart Staffing* gives the businessperson everything they need to know for managing the critical staffing function. This step-by-step guide is solid and practical, supported by rich background information. It even covers online recruiting and screening. *Smart Staffing* is a must-read."

Wally Bock
Author and publisher, *Briefing Memo*
(www.bockinfo.com/bm.htm)

"*Smart Staffing* is an outstanding resource for all CEOs and business owners trying to understand the challenges of maintaining a stable workforce. I intend to share *Smart Staffing* with my associates, so together we can gain better insight into the *reality-based* staffing process. This book proved very interesting and relevant to my business, and I'm already using some of the ideas in it. Excellent!"

Thomas R. Clarke
President
Creek Pointe

Contents

STEP ONE Think Before You Hire

STEP THREE Interview Candidates and Select Your New Employee

Introduction

It's a good bet that you would like to increase your level of business success. To do this in the past, you may have tried to improve your product and your product's image and visibility (even if you are in a service business and that "product" is *you!*). You may have increased your budget for advertising and/or public relations. You may have joined organizations to network and gain contacts with prospective customers. You've worked hard to outsell and outsmart your competition. But even with all this effort, when you analyze the bottom line at year end, you may still be falling short of your goals.

The most frequently overlooked business asset is the people you employ. The only way a business can produce a satisfied customer and increase success is to have employees who operate at a top level of efficiency. According to a survey done by the School of Management and Labor Relations at Rutgers University, companies with comprehensive programs for employee recruiting, selection, and training combined with sound incentive programs have greater market value, higher annual sales, and higher profits per employee. This is all due to lower turnover and higher employee productivity. Even a great product, service, or innovative approach will not generate these highly desired results without a dedicated, capable staff to make it possible.

If you own a business or assist with hiring, you need to learn the skills of smart staffing, whether you are getting ready to hire your first employee or have been in business for years with a few hundred employees already. Productive people who you and your customers can depend on are the essential ingredient in a successful business. They can literally be termed "human capital," which may be even more important than financial resources, equipment, or technology. Without this human capital, equipment would sit idle, technology would not be used, and products would not move nor services be delivered. Your customers would soon look elsewhere.

Knowing how to find and keep top employees is especially important in smaller businesses for several reasons.

- There is no personnel or human resource department staffed with people trained in the hiring or retaining of employees.
- The quality of each employee more radically affects the functioning of a small business.
- Small businesses are frequently taken to court for employee-related problems. Most personnel laws today, which in the past were directed at large corporations, apply to the small company as well.
- When small businesses expand to multiple locations, they must hire managers to supervise their employees. The quality of these managers affects overall business success.

Smart staffing should also be a priority of small business owners because, according to the U.S. Small Business Administration, small businesses

- provide virtually all of the net new jobs.
- represent 99.7 percent of all employers.
- employ 53 percent of the private work force.
- account for 51 percent of private sector output.
- experience significantly higher turnover than large firms (15.2 percent compared to 9.0 percent).

There is no question that high-performance small businesses need highly skilled, highly motivated employees in the key slots. Small businesses need to be skilled in hiring and retaining employees. Smart business owners know where and how to look for the best employees, and they know how to keep them. Ross Perot, the very successful entrepreneur who started Electronic Data Systems (EDS), had a great idea. But he credits the quality of the employees as the major reason EDS was able to grow into a successful Fortune 500 company. In *On Wings of Eagles* by Ken Follett, Perot describes his method of finding the best people this way: "Eagles don't flock—you have to find them one at a time." This philosophy underscores the importance of taking time to find top employees, a strategy that propelled EDS to a position as one of America's largest and most successful companies. This is not luck. Owners and managers who run successful companies thrive in competitive environments and survive tough times by making staffing a high priority. They know that their people are their most valuable asset and they do not lower their standards or accept lesser-quality employees because of inadequate candidate flow or unskilled, poor hiring practices.

Smart staffing is not a natural skill and it can be difficult to learn as you go. It is not taught in college and is certainly not modeled by most American businesses. Too many companies tend to hire based on feeling, not on a logical, defined, reality-based process. Many small business owners will agonize over the terms of a lease or the wording of a contract, but do not give their full attention to the hiring process. However, losses encountered daily due to bad hiring decisions can make the money saved by negotiating the terms of a lease look almost insignificant. The cost of a bad hiring decision can result in the loss of customers, productivity, profits, and reputation, as well as losses from lawsuits or embezzlement.

The need for smart staffing is especially acute in today's market where there are often more openings than qualified applicants. Many experts forecast that the applicant pool will continue to shrink because the creation of jobs outpaces the numbers entering the workplace. The result of inadequate applicant flow does not mean you must settle for what's available at the moment. A short-term fix to fill positions will turn into long-term employee problems and high turnover.

The solution to the problem of inadequate applicant flow is explored through the first half of this book. But the problem isn't solved when a top candidate has been hired. Getting quality human capital is only half the battle. The second half of this book will show you how to retain and manage this capital. You will learn how to keep quality people by providing an environment where employees feel valuable and needed.

This book is designed to be used frequently to solve the most difficult problems of attracting and keeping top employees. Practical in nature and implementation, it is an invaluable aid in setting up a functional hiring process for an organization. Easy-to-understand directions, how-to charts and guides, and extensive checklists give you the proven tools you need to hire and retain employees. Key concepts that work along with real, adaptable strategies show how to create an environment that not only keeps employees, but keeps them happy and productive.

In Step One of this book you will plan your hiring strategy. You will decide what kind of employee you need and you will establish written job definitions and candidate requirements. You'll then create a job application that will both identify top candidates and keep you out of legal entanglements.

In Step Two you will decide exactly how you will locate the candidates you're after. You will develop a recruiting plan and investigate various creative sources of qualified applicants. Then, you'll learn how to screen applicants and conduct pre-employment evaluations to quickly eliminate unqualified or undesirable applicants.

In Step Three you'll learn how to get the most out of an employment interview and how to use reference checks to their fullest potential. You'll also follow the steps that lead you through the process of choosing and hiring the best candidate.

In Step Four you'll find strategies for rewarding and keeping your employees. This section begins with the orientation and training of a new employee. It then discusses the importance of ongoing communication, career counseling, and esteem-boosting techniques. It concludes with specific methods you can use to offer your employees job enrichment opportunities and financial incentives.

Step Five brings you full circle by giving you a peek at why employees leave a company and how smart staffing strategies can be used to reduce your present level of employee turnover.

The Appendixes offer, for your own personal use, all the forms and worksheets that are used in illustrations throughout the book.

What would it mean to your company to be fully staffed with significantly better employees than you have now and to reduce your turnover by 10, 20, 40 percent, or even more? I have seen some companies with turnover that hits 100, 200, or 300 percent in certain positions. When turnover is at this level, a change to smart staffing will offer a much more dramatic impact on retention and greater savings to your company. Add to this impact improved working conditions, greater customer satisfaction, and increased productivity. What would be the dramatic increase in bottom-line profits? Some successful businesspeople who have learned the smart staffing techniques at Outlaw Group workshops and seminars report bottom-line profits have doubled or quadrupled. Is that improvement worth the effort to implement better techniques in hiring and keeping top employees? I think it is, and so will you when you use the strategies offered in this book and begin to see the difference it makes in your day-to-day operations and your bottom-line profits.

A stable workforce enables you to focus on your product, process, and customers instead of continuously recruiting, orienting, training, and developing new employees. Your goal in business is to grow, to be productive, and to be successful. The goal of this book is to help you do that.

Acknowledgments

The seed for this book was actually planted many years ago. When working as an executive recruiter, I realized that many managers doing the hiring in client companies did not truly understand what they were looking for, nor even how to recognize it once they saw it. They never had been trained to make effective hiring decisions. Because of this, I saw them duplicate their errors and experience frustration in looking for a better way to staff their organizations.

Recognizing this need, and at their request, I created the program *Hiring & Retaining the Winners* that has been presented at annual meetings, conventions, conferences, and workshops. It quickly became popular and has consistently been requested over the years, regardless of the level of employment. As a result of comments at meetings and our consulting experience with clients, I realized that there was a tremendous need for a how-to book on hiring, rewarding, and keeping employees for organizations, especially those smaller ones without the support and assistance of a personnel or human resources department.

Even a great idea doesn't take root and grow without the help of terrific people. I'd like to thank the staff at Dearborn Financial Publishing for having the vision to see this need, and especially my editor, Danielle Egan-Miller, for her assistance in helping to focus and increase the effectiveness of the project.

A special thanks goes to Jeff Herman, my agent, who was invaluable in getting the book published. Also, Theresa DiGeronimo who skillfully assisted in editing the draft manuscript to make it ready for publication.

A special note of thanks goes to Beverly Costello and my wife, Pat, who edited my diction and notes, prepared the original manuscript, bolstered my spirits when my enthusiasm lagged, always had a kind word, and always expressed confidence in the outcome. They helped make the book a reality.

To all the colleagues and friends who have supported and assisted, thank you. To the clients and business associations who have shared specific examples, even if they were painful, and the wisdom and insight, it was greatly appreciated.

And finally, it is to my family that I owe my greatest debt of gratitude. To my wife, who has been my best friend, the love of my life, and my business partner, goes my deepest admiration and appreciation. To my son Michael, who has been an inspiration and who has challenged me to reach new heights, I owe a tremendous debt of gratitude.

Most of all, thank you for your confidence in purchasing this book. I hope it helps you keep your company staffed with top employees to ensure your success.

Think Before You Hire

CHAPTER 1

Determining What You Need

A COMPANY'S REAL ASSETS
ARE NOT MONEY, EQUIPMENT, OR INFORMATION, BUT PEOPLE.

Hiring is routine for anyone who owns or manages a small to medium-sized business. So routine, in fact, that many think the process begins and ends with a quick three-line ad in the Sunday paper that—presto—pulls in many high-quality resumes. Many employers hire the first candidate who "clicks." Yet the casual and quick approach, which lacks depth and skill, is often directly responsible for eventual business failure and/or bankruptcy.

Just look at some statistics from the Department of Labor Statistics, Department of Commerce, and National Institute of Occupational Safety and Health:

- Thirty percent of all business failures result from poor hiring techniques.
- Thirty percent of all employment applications are falsified.
- Forty-five percent of resumes contain false information about job experience, education, etc.
- One out of 20 applicants falsifies a name, Social Security number, and driver's license number.
- Embezzlement is a $4 billion industry, and there is a high correlation between the position sought and the proclivity to the crime.

These are not exaggerated statements thrown out to catch your attention—they're true! Smart staffing is absolutely key to the success or failure of your business.

Use Smart Staffing

Out of hundreds of reasons why the quality of your employees affects the quality and viability of your business, these seven are the most obvious and influential.

3

1. Choosing the Wrong Employee for the Job Costs You Money

This person is not likely to be productive and/or stay long. You will have to fire this wrong employee and find someone new, hire someone to pick up the slack, or hire someone new when this employee leaves. In any case, it will cost you money. In a recent survey of small to medium-sized electronics and appliance stores, the owners pegged the cost of losing a top salesperson at up to $150,000 in revenue and $30,000 in bottom-line profit. Why such a hefty price to pay for each turnover?

Direct costs that can be calculated include the separation or severance pay due to departures, the cost of attracting new candidates, overtime and temporary help to fill in until a new employee is found, conducting interviews and ordering background checks, new training, medical exams and benefit setup, and the cost due to lost and lower productivity during the transition period.

Many companies have found as much as 80 percent of the cost of turnover in what they call "hidden" costs. These include the reduced productivity of employees that remain after the turnover. (Studies by psychiatrists indicate that no matter what the reason for departure, after an employee departs, the remaining employees' productivity declines.) Lower employee morale results in lower sales effectiveness. Customers are lost due to the loyalty factor. Assets and cash may disappear with the departing employee.

Clearly the loss of revenue and profit caused by losing an employee can be significant. It may be even more devastating to a small business with fewer financial and human resources, or companies that have employees spread out in multiple locations.

2. Smart Investment in Human Capital Improves Your Financial Position

When you apply to a lender for capital, you must convince the lender that your organization can make a profit and pay back a loan. A high-quality, stable workforce offers the financial institution confidence about the long-term prospects of the business. Although human capital may not appear as a line item on a balance sheet, it is an important consideration in calculating business success.

3. You Can Be Held Legally Accountable for Your Hiring Decisions

You and your company can be held liable if you have not used "due diligence" during the hiring process. Due diligence is the legal standard for taking reasonable and prudent steps to ensure sound hiring practices. Not only can your company be held liable for damage an individual does as an employee, but also for injury or loss caused off the job and even after the employee has left the job. You can be sued if your delivery person goes back to a house or business after work hours or after leaving the position and robs or injures the occupants. See Chapter 2 for more details about hiring negligence and the law—you'll see clearly why you cannot take lightly your responsibility for hiring.

4. Bad Employees Chase Away Good Customers

We've all taken our business elsewhere because of employee service problems: the sales clerk who acts inconvenienced when you want to buy something while she's talking to her friend on the phone, the computer technician who is impatient and rude, or the receptionist who doesn't deliver your important message. Poor employee performance leads to customer loss, lower sales, and less profit.

5. Good Employees Make Management Easier

Business owners who make good hiring decisions and retain top employees tend to be more successful and less stressed. Their workers know their jobs and fulfill their responsibilities. But when employees do not do their jobs or are absent, someone must take up the slack—often the owner or manager. Thus, those who make poor hiring decisions end up working longer hours in a stressful, chaotic environment.

6. Each Employee Is Critical and Valuable

The small to medium-sized business often requires a lean workforce in order to produce the critical profit to stay alive. Among fewer employees, "bad" hires have a greater negative influence than they might in a Fortune 500 company where their incompetence or poor attitude might be absorbed unnoticed. In very real terms, a new employee in a smaller business can (and usually does) determine a company's height of success or depth of failure.

7. The Time and Effort You Spend on the Hiring Process Protects the Health of the Entire Organization

We all know that given the proper attention and effort, it's much easier to prevent major illnesses than to cure them. Likewise, it's much easier to make good hiring decisions by learning and using the skills presented in this book than to deal with the hassles and legal entanglements that can result from poor hiring decisions and the loss of high-quality employees and customers.

Match the Employee to the Job

Good employees must meet certain, specific job requirements—that's a given. Smart staffing demands you look for more in your employees. You need an employee who not only can do the job, but who fits the job. That means finding someone you believe is a good match.

This is no easy task. An estimated 27 to 40 percent of the workforce is in the wrong job. Neither the employees nor the positions are bad; they simply don't fit together or match. With a statistic like this, such a high rate of turnover is no surprise.

I believe that skilled job matching is one of the most significant factors in creating a tenured and long-term workforce. Because it is so important, you will encounter this subject again and again in this book. The more the individual's intrinsic values, natural behavioral style, and likes or dislikes match the position, the happier the employee will be with the job, the longer he or she will remain, and the more likely that your business will thrive.

Look Beyond the Resume

So how do you make this match? Begin by thinking of what does not appear on a resume but is important to the success of your company. These include values, attitude, and capability.

Values

Looking for certain intrinsic values in a job applicant may seem a bit picky or idealistic, but in fact, it's an employee's values that keep businesses afloat. Think about what values you'd like employees to possess. Of course, you want them to be honest and trustworthy—you know what a dishonest employee can do to your balance sheet. But what else? What about persistence? Integrity? Loyalty? Flexibility? Will this employee have the strength of character to stick by a tough decision? Will he be truthful and candid no matter what the personal price? Will she bad-mouth the firm to outsiders? Will he give up on tough assignments? Will she be able to adapt to a new computer system or program? Will this applicant pitch in to help others? Such questions help you determine if you've made a good match between an applicant and the job.

Think about the position you need to fill and the values you would like the employee to bring to that job. Imagine you're hiring sales clerks, for example. What values should they have? Perhaps they'll need a sense of pride in their work to clean up after patrons without being told. Patience would help them appease screaming children and exhausted parents. A sense of teamwork may encourage them to work late when other employees call in sick. Flexibility will enable them to work without complaint in a different department when you're short-staffed. Once you know what values you want your employees to bring to the job, then you can create interview questions to tap into these areas. Chapters 10 and 11 provide some specific ideas about creating questions that dig into values during an interview.

Attitude

You need employees who have a good attitude for two reasons: (1) a person with a positive attitude is pleasant for other employees to work with, and (2) a pleasant attitude will attract and please customers. A successful sales clerk smiles naturally, greets customers pleasantly, offers advice and puts 110 percent effort into the job. In contrast, the sales clerk who is very competent at ringing up sales, taking inventory, unpacking merchandise, and fixing displays does not help your company grow if he or she wears a persistent scowl, grunts at customers, and frequently calls in sick.

Looking for a positive attitude during the hiring process is imperative because you can't make employees pretend to be positive once they're hired (even the best incentives will only produce short-term results). Your job is to bring positive people into the company. Many people resign or are terminated, not because they couldn't do the job, but because of their attitude—they didn't want to invest the time, energy, and effort needed to help the company become successful. Chapters 9 and 10 will help you isolate the attitude factor during interviews. You will learn how to distinguish the person who wants to work for you from the person who only wants a paycheck.

Capability

Capability is, first, the natural, innate ability to mentally and/or physically handle circumstances. If you're hiring for a sales position that requires hours of cold calling, for example, you must consider if the new recruit can not only dial the phone but also deal with daily rejection. A person with a high need for acceptance is not suited for this job.

Secondly, capability is the potential for growth beyond today's specific needs. If you hire a receptionist, can he or she move into a position of greater responsibility, perhaps as a customer service representative? Can he or she grow in the business, learning new tasks and skills? Is this a person who has management potential?

When you interview an applicant for a position, always look for capabilities. A strong business promotes from within, but you can't do that if none of your employees has the capability to grow with the company's needs. Remember: You can teach almost anything to a person who really wants to do the job and has the capability of quickly learning the tasks required, but there's little you can do with someone who hasn't the inner resources or personal potential to do more than he or she does today. As you build your job descriptions in Chapter 3 you will see how to include an analysis of an applicant's growth capabilities.

Seek "A" Level Employees

The "A" level employee is someone who meets the needs of your company today, tomorrow, and beyond. Of course, this employee is on the top of everyone's wish list, but is rarely found through the standard, surface-level hiring practices often used in smaller businesses. It takes time, effort, and thoughtful planning to find the person who has the virtues, attitudes, and capability to fit into your organization and help you meet your business goals. If you take the time to go through the smart-staffing process outlined in this book, you will have an impressive collection of A level employees who all bring winning qualities to their jobs. Level A employees

- know the responsibilities and duties of their jobs and have the skills, experience, and personal drive to meet these requirements.
- are extremely productive. They look for work that needs doing rather than waiting for the next assignment.
- don't try to do the least amount of work in the greatest amount of time.
- perceive customer needs and act on them.
- have the insight and creativity to solve problems they may never have faced before.
- are versatile. They can fill in wherever they are needed.
- care deeply about the business. They think like an owner.
- have a pleasant attitude and are a pleasure to be around.

You may ask yourself, "Who can afford the time, effort, or money to find and reward these A level people?" The question you should be asking is, "Who can afford not to?" Time and again the most successful companies are those that have a logical step-by-step process for identifying and hiring top people. They invest time and resources to get the best match between the position and the applicant. As a result, their organizations have high productivity, are more responsive to their customers, and are better able to adapt to changing market needs.

Use the Five-Step Hiring Process

To ensure that you have an ample supply of quality candidates, make hiring a systematic and logical procedure. The hiring process is mapped out in this book in five steps.

Step One: Think Before You Hire (Chapters 1–5)

At this stage, you take a good look at your company's needs, review the laws that govern hiring and firing, carefully define the job you want to fill, and determine what kind of employee can best fill the position. You also create job applications.

Step Two: Locate Qualified Applicants (Chapters 6–7)

In Step Two you develop a recruiting plan and determine where you can find the best applicants, from traditional and nontraditional sources.

Step Three: Interview Candidates and Select Your New Employee (Chapters 8–13)

In Step Three, create a step-by-step interviewing process that brings you from decisions about screening applicants to choosing the best candidate. You will find out if applicants have the attributes and characteristics that cannot be presented on the resume, but are vital to the success of your business. Create interview questions that give you the information you really need, contact references to determine past performance, and conduct pre-employment evaluations, background checks, and skill testing. You will select your candidate and make an offer.

Step Four: Reward and Keep Top Employees (Chapters 14–18)

Step Four includes proven strategies for retaining good employees. You create a plan for welcoming your new recruit with orientation, mentors, and training. You establish programs that build employee self-esteem and open the lines of management/employee communication. You implement programs for career counseling, job enrichment opportunities, financial incentives, perks, and tenure.

Step Five: Learn from Your Losses (Chapters 19–20)

In Step Five you consider how to learn from the inevitable loss of a valuable employee to prevent future losses. Use carefully planned techniques to uncover the reasons for the resignation, and examine the cost of the loss in terms of insurance, severance, unemployment, disability, etc. You will learn valuable business lessons from each lost employee.

The Value of Human Capital

The skills and methods needed to improve hiring techniques and retain top employees take time and effort to acquire, but the payoff is tremendous. Whether you're responsible for a factory floor or a restaurant kitchen, you can't serve your customers without employees. It's time to look at these employees as your most precious resource—as the human capital that allows your business to function and grow.

*F*REQUENTLY *A*SKED *Q*UESTIONS

Q. *What is the real impact of a bad hiring decision?*

A. According to statistics from the Department of Labor, the Department of Commerce, the National Institute of Occupational Safety and Health, and the Small Business Administration, 30 percent of all business failures result from poor hiring techniques, and embezzlement is a $4 billion industry taking money out of all businesses, especially small business owners' pockets.

Q. *As a small business owner I feel it is almost impossible to keep up with laws and do a great job of hiring and retaining top employees. I don't have the time to become a personnel manager. Is this really something to worry about?*

A. It is true that it takes a lot of effort and energy to keep up with all the laws and to ensure an organization is staffed with top people, but it is much more difficult to fix problems resulting from poor hiring and the turmoil of turnover. All staffing improvements are rewarded with reduction of stress and an improved bottom line.

CHAPTER 2

Establishing a Job Definition and Hiring Criteria

YOU MUST HAVE A CLEAR PICTURE
OF THE JOB IN ORDER TO FIND THE BEST CANDIDATE.

Stories of the disastrous results of hiring unqualified friends or family members are common, like the shop owner who makes his mother-in-law cashier, or the restaurant manager who lets his nephew make deliveries. Only after beginning work is it evident that the person doesn't have the skills, temperament, or work ethic needed to do the job well—then it's too late to go back and explain what you really want in an employee and ask the person to adapt.

In order to properly fill a position, it is critical that you and your prospective employees understand all aspects of the job. Without establishing the job definition and the necessary qualifications of an applicant, you cannot expect to match the applicant to the job. You must clearly identify and define the requirements of the job and what is to be required of a candidate before you can hire anyone.

Job Definition

Before you begin the hiring process, you need to establish a specific job definition with the following elements:

- Job responsibilities and duties
- Essential job functions
- Expected level of performance
- Growth potential
- Compensation

Job Responsibilities and Duties

You must look closely at the responsibilities and duties required by the position in order to create an effective and practical job definition. The *responsibilities* of a job are the end results the individual is charged with producing, such as bringing in new clients, publicizing your service, or handling phone communications. The *duties* of a job are the physical actions or activities that enable an employee to carry out the stated responsibilities. To meet the responsibility of bringing in new clients, the employee might have the duty of cold calling. To publicize your service the employee might write business brochures and weekly press releases. To handle phone communications, the employee might answer with a pleasant voice before the phone rings three times.

For each job, determine the responsibilities, then establish the methods for achieving them. Employees can better accomplish the responsibilities of a job if they know their duties up front. In Figure 2.1, you'll find a complete job description for a sales clerk. Take a look at how the responsibilities and duties are closely tied together.

FIGURE 2.1 • Sample Job Definition

Sales Clerk

Job Responsibilities

- Greet customers and sell merchandise
- Receive customer's payments and input transactions
- Handle incoming phone calls
- Assist in merchandising sales floor
- Work hours assigned
- Make outgoing telemarketing calls
- Complete and file paperwork

Job Duties

- Greet customers as they enter the store
- Assist customers to identify needs and sell merchandise
- Explain purchase and rental pricing
- Complete sales order
- Calculate the cost and payment due

- Take payment in cash or check and post accurately on computer
- Assist customer with questions and resolve customer problems
- Assist store manager by making suggestions and helping to merchandise sales floor
- Work from 9:30 AM to 7:30 PM Monday through Saturday
- Make effective telemarketing calls using provided script
- Fill out and file paperwork
- Count down drawer to account for all cash

Essential Job Functions

- Lift 40 pounds unaided and move 40 feet
- Answer the phone politely and courteously by the third ring
- Visually see customers entering the store and move quickly to greet them

Expected Level of Performance Standards

Within 90 days of employment, the employee should be able to:

- Sell at least 50 percent of the potential customers.
- Calculate, receive and post payments with 95 percent accuracy.
- Complete the four types of sales orders with 100 percent accuracy.
- Make 40 telemarketing calls per week with at least a 20 percent sales rate.
- Know all account pricing and promotions.
- Account for all cash 100 percent of the time.

Compensation

- $7/hour salary
- Up to 5 hours of overtime pay per week

Growth Opportunities

- Potential to become assistant store manager

Essential Job Functions

Essential job functions identify minimum levels of capability, such as lifting, mobility, hearing, communication skills, or mental capacity necessary to perform the job. These requirements help determine a candidate's ability to do the job.

A shuttle bus driver, for example, knows it will be his or her duty to carry a guest's bags, but job functions specify the minimum weight, carrying distance, and assistance from another person or device such as a hand cart. A receptionist knows to answer phones quickly and pleasantly, but you may also want him or her to be able to communicate in a clear, easy-to-understand voice. Or, if you are hiring someone to stock your store room, applicants are aware that they must lift and place merchandise on the shelf, but you may want to add the essential job function of intellectual competence to read the inventory sheets and record information.

Detailing essential job functions can help you avoid disagreements and misunderstandings, and ensure your compliance with the Americans with Disabilities Act, which may require reasonable accommodations (see Chapter 4). The sample job definition in Figure 2.1 shows the essential job functions and more clearly defines the actions of a sales clerk.

Expected Level of Performance Standards

Establishing an expected level of performance creates a standard by which the responsibilities and duties of the job can be measured. If you expect a data programmer to input information into the computer with 95 percent accuracy within one month of hiring, it should be stated as an expected level of performance for that job. If a sales employee must reach a budgeted sales volume of $20,000 per month in six months and consistently exceed that amount each month thereafter, the individual should know this before accepting the position. It is a mistake to not tell a candidate the standard against which the employee will be evaluated. If a candidate knows in advance the job performance required, you have a much better chance of hiring someone who will meet your standards and stay for the long term.

Creating expected level of performance standards also forces you to evaluate the reality of your expectations by analyzing how long it would take a qualified candidate to reach a certain level of performance. You can't expect a new sales representative to sell $50,000 worth of merchandise the first month, if the expected level of performance is $20,000. This also ensures you don't oversell the earning potential of the position if based on commission.

Expected level of performance standards also set the guidelines for a qualified candidate (as described later in this chapter). If the job requires being able to type 50 words per minute, that will be the performance standard and you will only consider candidates who can type at that speed.

Expected level of performance standards state clearly what it will take for the employee to do the job successfully. Both the employer and the employee need this information. These measurements should be shared with a prospective employee once you've decided to offer this person the job.

Compensation

You need to define the compensation range and makeup of the position before you set out to find a candidate. If the vacant position can only be filled by candidates who earn $50,000/year, but you have budgeted $30,000, you'll waste time and effort in your hiring process. You may also make painful compromises such as lowering your standards or hiring someone who will soon leave due to low compensation. There are a number of ways to determine the competitive rates for your vacant position:

- Find out what companies in your area are paying employees in similar positions.
- Analyze the classified ads for the pay scale of similar jobs advertised.
- Put a trial ad in the newspaper asking for a salary history from all applicants.
- Contact business associations like trade organizations or the local chamber of commerce for hiring statistics. (Be wary of national average statistics because they may not give you an accurate picture for your market area.)
- For less skilled labor, find out what other employers in your area, regardless of the business, might offer that same applicant. If you're looking for a receptionist, for example, keep in mind that your pool of candidates might also be applying to the unionized automotive plant in the next town—you have to compete with this wage to get employees.

You'll also need to decide if the job will pay a salaried or hourly wage. Labor laws require that certain conditions be met for a wage to be salaried and exempt from overtime pay. These conditions are complex—they change over time, and vary from job to job and state to state. To help you make this determination, you'll need to get input from an attorney or consultant who specializes in labor and employment law.

You also need to consider the makeup of compensation, which may consist of incentives such as a commission or bonus in addition to an hourly or salaried wage. Decide if you will offer incentives or perks such as car allowances, travel expenses, entertainment allowances, educational benefits, stock options, or profit sharing. The compensation must be designed to reward the person for meeting the expected level of performance. This will play an important part in motivation and retention (see Step Four: Keep and Reward Top Employees).

Growth Opportunities

When formulating your job definition, you need to ask yourself, "How do I see the ideal candidate for the position growing over the next five years?" The answer to this question will help you determine the candidate requirements you seek. It also helps you create interview questions that reveal if the applicant shares your view of the future.

To determine growth opportunities you need to look at the organization of your business and ask:

- Are there enough positions in the organization for this employee to advance?
- Can the person in this job ever be promoted to a supervisory position?
- If the person is not promoted, can the job lead to different pay levels?
- Can this person be given a pay increase and additional responsibilities without changing positions?
- Can the job be enriched to provide challenge and fulfillment over an extended period?

Let's say you own an office equipment repair business and need to hire a new computer printer repair technician. If you need someone who will repair printers and nothing more for the entire tenure of the individual's employment, you and job applicants need to know this. You can rule out the candidate who is looking to leave present employment because there is no "room to move up." Realistically, you will not be able to keep this person long term.

On the other hand, if you see potential growth in this position, you should incorporate that fact in your hiring process. You want to look for an indication that a potential employee has the capability to learn how to repair other equipment. During the interview, you can ask if the candidate is willing to take training courses, or has a desire to move into management or administrative work. You can look at a candidate's employment history for signs of initiative and the ability to take on new responsibilities.

When you are aware of your current needs and future expectations, you can better measure a candidate's skills and experiences. These factors are important considerations when you want to hire for the long haul.

Using Your Completed Job Definition

When you have compiled a list of the job requirements, you have an accurate and very useful job definition. For the employer, it is the sifting pan you will use to separate the worthless sand from the precious metal that will become the human capital for your growing business. To the prospective employee, it is a clear outline of what is required to be successful in the position.

The details of the job definition should only be discussed with the candidates in very brief and general terms during the hiring process. Revealing too many details early on will allow the candidates to tailor their responses to match your needs, rather than giving you a true picture of their experience and abilities. But once you decide to issue an offer of employment, the candidate should be given the written job definition so that the person has a complete understanding of the position before accepting your offer.

Hiring Criteria

After you've created the job definition for the position you want to fill, you can determine the specific qualifications required to be a candidate for the job. Qualifications might include level of education, experience, skills, intelligence, values, attitudes, and capabilities. Figure 2.2 lists the requirements for the Sales Clerk position. By establishing the requirements before you begin interviewing, you can avoid setting standards so high that you never find the perfect candidate. It will also keep you from setting standards too low and settling for anyone who can "fog a mirror."

Define the Musts and Preferreds

The most reasonable approach to determining the qualifications you seek in a candidate is to divide them into two groups—the *musts* and the *preferreds*.

Musts. The qualifications you need a candidate to possess are called the *musts*—the criteria absolutely necessary to perform the job. Musts cannot be compensated for by relying on other strengths, learning new skills, or getting assistance from others. The lack of these musts will seriously impair a person's ability to do the job. For example, if a sales clerk is required to use a fairly complex, computerized point-of-sale system during very busy peak periods, the candidate must be keyboard literate. Familiarity with a keyboard is a must. It is frustrating for everyone involved to screen an applicant, conduct an interview, and then find out in the second interview that this person cannot use a keyboard with any degree of speed. Without a stated list of musts, you might find yourself with an employee who meets the qualifications in education, skills, and experience, but can't perform the basic functions of the job.

FIGURE 2.2 • Sample Hiring Criteria Form

Sales Clerk

Musts

- Strong friendly voice with a pleasant smile
- Excellent verbal communication skills
- Keyboard or typing skills
- Basic mathematical ability to calculate payment amounts and handle cash accurately
- Good general clerical skills and legible handwriting
- Ability to lift 40 pounds and move it 40 feet unaided
- Ability to work with a variety of people
- Flexibility and ability to adapt to changing situations
- Willingness to pitch in to help others
- Ability to work independently
- Ability to solve problems
- Willingness to work for entry-level salary
- Ability to work from 9:30 AM to 7:30 PM Monday through Saturday as assigned

Preferreds

- One year experience as a cashier
- Two years previous sales experience
- Natural aptitude for working with customers
- One year previous office or clerical experience
- Excellent organizational skills with attention to details
- Bilingual with written and verbal abilities in English and Spanish
- Ambition to move into management

Unless a candidate has all the must qualifications, the individual should not be considered for the position. If a person does not have the musts, continuing the hiring process would not only be a waste of time, but could lead to a bad hire.

Use caution when creating a list of musts because you may eliminate a lot of good candidates if the musts are unreasonably demanding. Some musts may also be illegal. Several years ago a large utility company was challenged by an applicant for requiring employees to have a high school diploma. That job requirement was struck down by the court because the company could not prove the job could not be done by a person without a high school diploma.

When you create your must list, use the job responsibilities and duties to determine what requirements a candidate must possess. Also, you may sabotage your own hiring process if the musts don't match the position. For example, don't require ten years experience if you are only offering minimum wage. Or, why seek exceptional math skills, if the job requires customer communication, not complex computation. Your list of job responsibilities and duties will help you clearly see what skills and characteristics an employee truly must have.

Preferreds. Once the musts have been identified, the balance of your requirements are grouped into a category called the *preferreds*. The preferreds form your basis for comparing the attributes of candidates who seem in all other ways equal. For example, you might not require that a candidate have a year's experience with a cash register, but you would prefer it. You might also prefer that a candidate be bilingual. Consider the preferred items your ideal wish list after all the musts have been satisfied.

It's More Than Paperwork

In a small organization it is very tempting to say, "I really can't define the job." Or, "I can't write down all the tasks for this job because they change frequently." Or, "Please, I can't deal with any more paperwork!" If this is the case, you're asking for performance problems down the line. How can anyone be expected to conscientiously perform the duties of a job without knowing what the duties are? The more varied and complex the job, the more important it is to establish the qualifications an employee needs to have to perform the job. See Appendix A for a Job Definition Form and Appendix B for a Hiring Criteria Form that you can use.

You can increase your ability to find the best employee for the position if you take time to think through the job and determine what is required to accomplish the job.

FREQUENTLY ASKED QUESTIONS

Q. *Once I have written the job definition and filled the position, do I have to rewrite the job description when I rehire for the same position?*

A. If little time has elapsed since the original job definition was created, you do not need to rewrite the job definition. But it is still a good idea each time you hire to review the information to make sure the requirements are still applicable, and the expected level of performance is still accurate.

Q. *What do I do if I can't find someone who meets all the musts?*

A. First evaluate your requirements to see if the musts are accurate—can the job be done without the skills, background, and experience listed? If the musts are accurate then continue to recruit applicants to fill the position properly rather than compromise.

Q. *What do I do if I have two musts that are in conflict, such as requiring a specific amount of experience or skill for a salary that is less than what qualified candidates will work for?*

A. Occasionally, two items listed as musts will be in conflict and unless it is resolved, the job will never be filled. Evaluate both of the musts and determine which should be changed, or consider other adjustments such as the hours worked or duties.

Q. *Isn't the expected level of performance just a guess?*

A. In some cases it will be difficult to clearly define the expected level of performance and determine how long it will take an individual to reach that level. You can make an educated guess based on past experience with others performing the same or similar work. It is an important consideration, however, in helping you and the applicant make an informed decision about the position.

CHAPTER 3

Considering Smart Staffing Options

THERE'S MORE THAN ONE WAY TO FILL A POSITION.

What type of employee do you need? You have several options—full-time, part-time, work-at-home, or temporary employees. You can also outsource the work to independent contractors who bring their specific expertise to a specific project or business function. While you need to match the candidate's qualifications to the requirements of the job description (see Chapter 2), you must also determine what type of employee you really need. Even an A level employee can inhibit the successful growth of your company if you hire the individual full-time, when all you need is a temporary fill-in. This will create a financial drain on profits and cause a talented employee to be underutilized.

What Type of Employee Do You Need?

When choosing the type of employee, you need to consider

- the amount of help you need. Do you need someone 40 hours a week or only 20?
- the length of time. Will you need this employee on a regular basis (full time), only during peak hours (part time), or only during peak periods (temporary)?
- the variability of demand. Do you need one person 40 hours a week (one full-time employee), or two people to work together 20 hours a week during your busiest hours (two part-time employees)?
- the level of expertise required. Does the project or business function require special knowledge or training that you cannot provide?
- the frequency of the requirement. Do you need someone for a one-time project, fairly frequently, or on a consistent basis?

- the security of the business or position. Are you certain about the job's future? Should you hire someone full-time and invest in business cards, training, and an office, or would it be best to test the waters with a temp or outsourced person?

Once you answer these questions, you will have a good idea of the type of employee you need. The rest of this chapter will help you solidify your decision.

Full-Time Employees

Full-time employees are the core workers that keep your business alive. These experienced workers, professionals, technicians, and managers are indispensable. They should be staffed at a level that allows the company to function without outside assistance during normal periods. Maintaining a staff of full-time core employees requires your time, attention and training. They usually receive full medical benefits, sick days, personal days, holidays, an office or work area, and the supplies and utilities needed to perform their jobs. They are indispensable—and expensive. That's why more companies are taking a second look at the staffing levels they've created to find places where they can minimize payroll costs by taking advantage of today's flexible options.

If you can't afford to hire a full-time employee or aren't certain that an additional staff member is best for your business, you should consider the options of part-time or temporary employees, or outsourcing.

Part-Time or Temporary Employees

Part-time and temporary employees are members of a fast-growing segment of the employment market today. After calculating the cost of down time and overtime, many companies have found that it is far more profitable to bring in a temporary or part-time person instead of hiring another full-time worker or having existing staff work overtime.

When you have a vacancy to fill, consider these hidden costs of full-time employees:

- Mandatory payroll taxes (FICA, state unemployment insurance, workers' compensation, disability insurance)
- Benefits (pension, profit sharing, medical insurance, bonus programs)
- Down time (vacations, holidays, sick leave, personal days, rest periods, lunch, shift changes)
- Administrative costs (recruiting, hiring, training, payroll, and recordkeeping)

Temporary employees fill an employment need for a prescribed period. Temporary help is especially useful for seasonal requirements, special projects, staff absences and family leave, and jobs that require special skills that you are not equipped to handle. Rosemary Maniscalco, president and chief operating officer of Comforce/Uniforce Staffing Services in Boca Raton, Florida, names these common special skills or temporary positions:

- Customer service representative
- Data entry/order taker
- Marketing representative
- Survey taker
- Telemarketer
- Product development
- Research and development

Ms. Maniscalco suggests that when hiring a temporary employee, use a staffing agency that offers prescreened, knowledgeable, and highly effective professionals who have the attitude and communication and listening skills you desire, while also meeting the requirements of your written job description. See Figure 3.1 for information on choosing a temporary agency.

Outsourcing

Through outsourcing you employ independent contractors to perform specialized functions or tasks that your own personnel cannot complete. Outsourcing may mean sending work to be done off premises, or it may involve hiring an individual or outside company to come into your business and work on a particular project, much like a temporary employee. Either way, these employees work short-term on specialized projects that you do not have the skilled personnel to handle. You do not pay for sick days, personal days, medical benefits, social security, or unemployment insurance. You pay them a set fee for a specific job—period. Outsourcing allows your business to expand its capability to handle tasks and projects that arise infrequently.

According to a study by Coopers and Lybrand reported in the *Sacramento Business Journal,* "More than eight in ten of America's fastest growing companies now contract out some portion of their day-to-day management." For years personal computer companies have been masters at outsourcing manufacturing. It might surprise you to know that many computers have been created and assembled by a virtual army of individuals not employed full-time by the company. Large organizations like IBM, Compaq, and Hewlett Packard have found outsourcing an excellent strategy; smaller businesses are now joining this movement.

FIGURE 3.1 • Guide to Selecting a Temporary Service

You will get the best temporary employee by finding the best temporary employment agency. When selecting an agency, the National Association of Temporary Services recommends that you consider the following:

- *reliability.* Is the agency well established with a good reputation in the community?

- *recruiting.* Is the agency's recruiting program aggressive? It is important that agency have a competitive recruiting program to get the best employees, especially in areas of low unemployment.

- *testing and evaluation.* What are the agency's testing and evaluation requirements?

- *retention program.* How long do employees stay with the agency? The tenure of the employees may be directly related to the quality of the workers.

- *professional staff.* What are the agency's staff like? Are they experienced in your field?

- *knowledge of your needs.* Do you have confidence that the agency understands your specific needs?

- *prompt service.* How quickly can you get a temporary worker to your company? Many times these immediate needs are critical.

- *quality control.* What type of quality controls are in place? Does the agency follow up to see how the employee performed? Have references been checked thoroughly?

- *insurance protection.* Does the agency have adequate insurance to protect you against workers' compensation claims or any other problems that might arise?

- *guarantee.* Does the agency offer any guarantee? What recourse do you have if you are dissatisfied with the temporary?

Coopers and Lybrand recently surveyed the 392 fastest growing companies in the United States concerning their use of outsourcing. The following are the percentages of outsourced personnel used by these companies:

Payroll services	68%
Tax compliance	48%
Employee benefits/claims administration	46%
Maintenance/equipment services	35%
Manufacturing/processing/assembling	33%
Sales reps or brokers	27%
Internal auditing	21%
Account services	19%

Not listed in this survey are three functions that many small to medium-sized businesses also outsource: (1) the creation of marketing materials like brochures and sales letters often farmed out to a PR firm, ad agency, or a freelance copywriter, (2) special research or product development frequently handed over to R&D consultants or companies, (3) advice and assistance with personnel, management and finance often provided by consultants. Especially in a small business, it is much easier to hire an outside expert for a project than an employee you would need to train. For some projects, outsourcing provides a better quality output at a more reasonable price, and usually requires less management effort to ensure it is completed.

The driving force behind the popularity of outsourcing is its positive impact on the bottom line. Savings are accrued not just from reduced wages, but also the elimination of additional cost associated with employees. For example, if a job is outsourced, the company does not have to provide the office space, utilities, telephone, or equipment needed to get the job done. This helps you increase margins, reduce expenditures, and improve operating performances. The economics of hiring out for expertise has made outsourcing a hit. According to an article in the *Mississippi Business Journal*, one ad agency saved fifty to seventy-five thousand dollars per year through outsourcing because they didn't have to pay for more office space, staff salary, and benefits.

Advantages of Outsourcing

Here are a number of reasons you might consider outsourcing instead of hiring an employee:

- Creates less overhead investment or debt.
- Provides an economic and efficient way to increase sales.

- Saves you from paying additional benefits and administrative costs.
- Allows expansion of capacity during peak times.
- Eliminates the need to find fill-in work for employees during off-peak hours.
- Expands capability in areas where staff is not skilled.
- Provides expert assistance when needed.

Disadvantages of Outsourcing

There are also several inherent disadvantages to outsourcing:

- There is a natural resistance to turning over key functions to outside companies or individuals.
- You may worry about loss of control.
- You may lose continuity from one project to another.
- Outsourcing affects your ability to manage the situation.
- Your own in-house expertise is not developed.
- You are not building skill/knowledge equity in your company.
- You have to pay to "educate" an outsourcing agency about your company.
- You have less control over deadlines, project changes, and shifting priorities.
- The outsourced person may not be willing to do small projects or update their work as often as needed.
- You must learn specific skills (outlined in the next section) to manage outsourcing.
- You may worry about security and confidentiality.

Making the Advantages Outweigh the Disadvantages

Those who have used outsourcing successfully have learned that managing non-employee resources requires special techniques. Even though you probably are not writing up a complete job definition for outsourced personnel (as explained in Chapter 2), you still need to communicate exactly what is expected. The biggest problems of outsourcing are unclear expectations at the beginning of a project, no schedule of feedback to monitor progress, and a disagreement about the end results.

These problems can be eliminated by employing the following techniques:

- Clearly outline what you expect the end result to be.
- Set a deadline.
- Explain how much assistance you can offer and/or who else in your business they can contact for input.
- Explain what milestones need to be met and set a schedule for meeting them.

- Establish a review for quality and content at certain milestones.
- Provide clear, detailed and candid feedback at the milestones.
- Clearly define what constitutes completed work and the timing and payment at each stage or milestone.
- Use nondisclosure agreements to protect company confidentiality as to customer lists, trade secrets, copyrights, patents, etc.

Finding Sources for Outsourcing

If you decide to outsource some of your work, there are a number of ways to find good independent contractors.

- Start in the yellow pages. Look under the heading that describes your needs—printers, public relations, accounting, payroll services, etc.
- Ask for referrals from other businesses. Call printers, for example, and ask which graphic artist they would recommend to work on a project like yours.
- Tap into your personal network. Call people you know personally that have similar needs. Ask them for recommendations. They will not only know who can do the project for you, they may also have had personal experience with someone and can vouch for the quality of work provided.
- Use networking. Contact your local chamber of commerce, professional organizations, or your peers in a company similar to yours. These sources will help you build a resource list that you can refer to when you need assistance.
- Consider job applicants. If you find an exceptional job candidate, but can't hire the individual for a full-time position, ask if that person might be interested in working independently on a per-project basis. You never know!

The IRS Side of Independent Contractors

Using temps or outsourced personnel makes smart business sense in many circumstances, but it is also a sure way to attract the attention of the Internal Revenue Service (IRS). The IRS has been aggressively attempting to reclassify independent contractors as employees to increase collection of unemployment taxes, social security, payroll tax, and even penalties. If you use self-employed workers to keep books, take dictation, do secretarial work, deliver materials, conduct research, or the like, the IRS might target your firm for an audit.

During an audit, the IRS reviews the type of relationship that exits between an employer and the worker. The following questions may raise red flags for the IRS:

- Is the person's work controlled by the employer?
- Did the employer maintain the right to fire the worker?
- Did the employer specify the number of hours in which the work must be completed?
- Did the employer demand the work be done on the premises?
- Was the worker required to report to the employer?

If you decide to use outsourcing, make sure you carefully examine your relationship with the worker to be sure it can stand up to the IRS test. According to the *Pittsburgh Business Times,* "This agency [the IRS] estimates that 94 percent of all independent contractors are in fact mis-classified employees. The agency says it loses more than $1.6 billion annually as a result of the mis-classification of independent contractors." As you can see, the IRS is very interested in capturing a portion of this $1.6 billion for themselves. To make sure your outside contractors are classified correctly, refer to the IRS rules in Figure 3.2.

There are "statutory employee" and "statutory nonemployee" status workers who may qualify as independent contractors. You should ask your attorney about this.

Smart staffing is critical to your company and its success. How well and how creatively you do this not only affects the cost or expense of running your business, it also affects overall productivity and future growth.

*F*REQUENTLY *A*SKED *Q*UESTIONS

Q. **How can I be sure that information about my organization will not leak out when I use outsourced personnel?**

A. There is always a possibility that confidential information will leak out, even from your own employees. To minimize the risk with outsourced work, first ask to see a statement of ethics by which the provider agrees to abide. Most associations, such as the Institute of Management Consultants, to which I belong, have a strict ethical policy that all members in good standing ascribe to. This protects the client from disclosure of their information. If this is not sufficient you might also consider including in your agreement a statement of confidentiality. In this statement define the circumstances, situations, and information to be kept confidential.

FIGURE 3.2 • IRS Common-Law Rules

The Internal Revenue Service has adopted the common law rules to help employers classify workers. Generally, workers are employees for tax purposes if they

- must comply with employer's instructions about the work.
- receive training from or at the direction of the employer.
- provide services that are integrated into the business.
- provide services that must be rendered personally.
- hire, supervise, and pay assistants for the employer.
- have a continuing working relationship with the employer.
- must follow set hours of work.
- do their work on the employer's premises.
- must do their work in a sequence set by the employer.
- must submit regular reports to the employer.
- receive payments of regular amounts at set intervals.
- receive payments for business and traveling expenses.
- rely on the employer to furnish tools and materials.
- lack a major investment in facilities used to perform the service.
- cannot make a profit or suffer a loss from the services.
- work for one employer at a time.
- do not offer their services to the general public.
- can be fired by the employer.
- may quit work anytime without incurring liability.

Q. If I outsource my work, what is to stop the individual I contract with from working with competitors and using it to benefit them?

A. Part of your agreement can stipulate the organizations with which your outsourcing partner cannot do business. In our organization, as independent contractors, we even include the length of time after the work is done before we are eligible to work with a competitor. In the event a situation not covered in the agreement occurs, we use good business judgment and ethics.

Q. How do I determine if I can classify a person as an independent contractor rather than an employee?

A. Review the IRS Common Law Rules in Figure 3.2, check the statutory rules with your lawyer, and also check with your accountant. You can also file Form SS-8 with your IRS district director—it's called "Information for Use in Determining Whether a Worker Is an Employee for Purposes of Federal Employment Taxes and Income Tax Withholding."

CHAPTER 4

Hiring Within the Law

HIRE ABILITY WHILE AVOIDING LEGAL ENTANGLEMENTS.

You must hire within the law. Following the rules and regulations that govern hiring will not only allow you to avoid legal entanglements, it can also increase hiring effectiveness by giving you a framework in which to gather logical and sound information about your applicants.

The intent of this chapter is not to give you legal advice, but to provide you with information on federal laws that apply to you as an employer. However, keep in mind that many state and local regulations prohibit actions that the federal law may allow. That's why I recommend that before you implement your hiring plan you speak with a competent attorney or consultant. You should either find an attorney specializing in labor and employment law or use an accredited consulting organization specializing in the legal aspects of employment.

You should know from the start that the size of your company is no defense against breaking the laws that govern the process of staffing your business. Even small businesses are subject to a great deal of legal regulations pertaining to the dos and don'ts of hiring. That's why it makes good business sense to understand the rules and regulations governing this part of your operation before you set your hiring plan into action.

Laws Business Owners Should Know

The law books are filled with labor laws far too numerous to detail in this book. The following is a quick overview of the laws that most concern the small business owner.

Discrimination Laws

Federal and state laws prohibit discrimination against protected classes of people. The protected status categories are: age, sex, race, color, marital status,

31

national origin, religion, disability, Vietnam veteran, citizenship, and pregnancy or other related medical conditions. It is important to note that the law does permit discrimination if it is based on legitimate business needs. For example, if you are shooting a television commercial for a product marketed to teenagers, you could specify the age of the actors hired, thus legally discriminating against a 50-year-old applicant based on a legitimate business need.

Title VII of the Civil Rights Act of 1964

Title VII of the Civil Rights Act of 1964 led to the establishment of the Equal Employment Opportunity Commission (EEOC). Applicable to companies with 15 or more employees, this act prohibits discrimination in hiring, firing, compensation, terms and conditions, or privileges of employment on the basis of race, color, religion, sex, pregnancy, or national origin. In other words, unless a specific criteria is job-based and reasonable, it cannot be used in determining who you hire.

Equal Pay Act of 1963

The Equal Pay Act of 1963 applies to companies with two or more employees and it prohibits pay differentials on the basis of sex. It requires that there be equal pay for equal work regardless of sex. The term *equal work* means equal use of skills and effort, as well as equal responsibility and working conditions. Those covered under this act are employers engaged in interstate commerce and subject to the Fair Labor Standards Act, which requires employers to pay a minimum wage and overtime after 40 hours a week. (Executive, administrative, professional, and outside sales employees are exempt from the Fair Labor Standards Act.)

The Vietnam Era Veteran's Adjustment Assistance Act

The Vietnam Era Veteran's Adjustment Assistance Act established affirmative action for disabled and qualified veterans of the Vietnam era, and prohibits discrimination against veterans in all employment practices by certain contractors and subcontractors holding federal contracts. This law pertains to Vietnam vets who were on active duty for more than 180 days from August 5, 1964 to May 7, 1975 and were discharged or released with other than a dishonorable discharge. Also covered is anyone discharged or released from active duty for a service-connected disability during the same period.

This act invites veterans to identify themselves and requires employers to maintain records of veteran placement.

Age Discrimination in Employment Act

The Age Discrimination in Employment Act (ADEA) applies to businesses with 20 or more employees. It prohibits discrimination based on age of employees who are at least 40 years old. Under the law, age cannot be a reason for paying one employee more or less than another, nor can age be used as a reason for giving one person a job over another.

It would not be unlawful under the ADEA, however, to use age as a deciding factor in employment, pay, or promotion if age were a bona fide occupational qualification that is reasonably necessary to the normal operation of the business. The ADEA also does not make it unlawful to observe the terms of an established seniority system.

Section 503 of the Rehabilitation Act of 1973 and
Title I of the Americans with Disabilities Act

Section 503 of the Rehabilitation Act of 1973 requires federal contractors and subcontractors with government contracts in excess of $10,000 to take affirmative action to employ and advance in employment qualified individuals with disabilities. Far more relevant to most small businesses is the Americans with Disabilities Act (ADA), which prohibits job discrimination, by employers with 15 or more employees, against qualified individuals with disabilities. Both acts cover persons with a wide range of mental and physical impairments that substantially limit or restrict a major life activity such as hearing, seeing, speaking, walking, breathing, performing manual tasks, caring for oneself, learning or working. Both acts also cover those who have a record of such impairment or are regarded as having such an impairment. AIDS, mental illness, drug addiction (not current users of illegal drugs), and alcoholism are also considered disabilities.

Keep in mind, however, that only job-qualified individuals with disabilities are protected by Section 503 and the ADA. The person must have the necessary education, skills, or other job-related requirements. The person also must be able to perform the essential functions of the job—with or without reasonable accommodation. (Reasonable accommodation involves making adjustments or modifications in the work, job application process, work environment, job structure, equipment, employment practices or the way the job duties are performed so that an individual can perform the essential functions of the job.)

Under these laws, you may be required to reasonably accommodate a physical or mental disability, unless the accommodation would pose an undue hardship. The determination of hardship is based on the size of the organization and the amount of cost and effort required to accommodate the disability.

The Civil Rights Division of the U.S. Justice Department explains this law in the publication "A Guide to Disability Rights Laws" as follows:

> Title I of this act requires employers with fifteen or more employees to provide qualified individuals with disabilities an equal opportunity to benefit from the full range of employment-related activities available to others. For example, it prohibits discrimination in recruitment and hiring. It restricts the questions that can be asked about the applicant's disability before a job offer is made, and requires that employers make reasonable accommodation to known physical and mental limitations of otherwise qualified individuals with disabilities, unless it results in a hardship.

In short, no questions can be asked of an applicant to determine disability. It is unlawful to use medical examinations to screen applicants or to ask an applicant with a disability about the nature or severity of such disability.

You may make pre-employment inquiries into the ability of an applicant to perform job-related functions and ask an applicant to describe or demonstrate how, with reasonable accommodation, the individual will be able to perform the duties of the job. This is another reason it is wise to have a written job description that outlines all responsibilities and duties. (See Chapter 3 for more information about creating a sound job description.) You may also require a medical examination or make an inquiry after extending an offer of employment or a conditional employment offer based on the results of such examination—if ALL employees entering the same job category are subjected to the same examination or inquiry.

For more information about the Office of Federal Contract Compliance Programs (OFCCP) contact any of the OFCCP's regional or district offices. The offices are listed in telephone directories under U.S. Department of Labor, Employment Standards Administration, Office of Federal Contract Compliance Programs. For information on how to comply with the ADA regarding job descriptions, employment applications, tests, drug-testing, medical examinations, training, safety programs, employee handbooks, disability compliance procedures, and contracts, see *The Upstart Small Business Legal Guide,* 2nd edition, by Robert Friedman (Upstart Publishing Company, 1998).

Immigration Reform and Control Act of 1986

The Immigration Reform and Control Act of 1986 affects all employers. It prohibits the hiring of illegal aliens and imposes sanctions on employers who fail to comply. It is essential that you hire only citizens and aliens lawfully authorized to work in the United States. You should advise all job applicants of your policy to follow this law, and within three business days of the first work day you should require new employees to complete and sign Form I-9 (Employment Eligibility Verification) to certify eligibility for employment. When Form I-9 is completed, you should examine the documentation presented by new employees, record information on the form, and sign it.

This form should be retained for at least three years or for one year past the end of the individual's employment period, whichever is longer. If requested, Form I-9 must be presented for inspection by the Immigration and Naturalization Service or Department of Labor.

Failure to ask a new employee to verify eligibility, even if the person hired is a U.S. citizen, subjects you to civil penalties that range from $100 to $100,000 per violation. It is easy to require a signed Form I-9 and authorization documents from all new hires. Unfortunately, this bit of paperwork is often overlooked by small business owners.

Personal Responsibility and Work Opportunity Reconciliation Act of 1996

This act requires you to report certain information on your newly hired employees to the designated state agency. This report is then matched against the state's records in an effort to locate people who are fraudulently collecting unemployment insurance, welfare, Medicaid, or food stamps. This report is also matched to orders of child support to locate parents, establish an order of payment, or enforce an existing order. Contact your state government and find out what agency (usually the Health and Human Services Agency) handles new hire reporting.

Negligent Hiring

Court decisions on negligent hiring have proven that what you don't know about an applicant can hurt you. These decisions have held that you, as the owner or manager of a business, are responsible for implementing a hiring process that assures the applicant can safely fill the position.

Negligent hiring can be claimed when an employer knows (or should have known by conducting a reasonable pre-employment investigation) that an employee is not competent to perform the job or is in some other way deficient. (See Chapter 11 for the details on pre-employment investigation.)

For example, if an applicant has a previous conviction for a violent crime such as assault, it would be reasonable to assume an employer would have uncovered this information and would not employ this person to deal with customers. But if the employee's felonious background is not uncovered and that individual later harms another employee or customer, the employer can be held liable.

This liability can be imposed even on the acts of an employee outside the scope of employment or after the employee has been discharged. Let's say your delivery person, previously convicted of theft, returns after work hours to rob a house that he had delivered your goods to earlier in the day. The homeowner could sue you because your employment relationship provided the thief initial access to the home.

Examples abound of employers held liable for injury or loss caused by their employees.

- An owner of a laundromat hired youths from a residential treatment program to work in his business. One of the juveniles attacked a customer with a hammer, causing severe injuries. The court held that the victim could maintain a cause of action for negligent hiring, finding that the employer did not fulfill his duty to properly screen for competent employees.
- A small furniture store in Florida was held liable for damages to a person injured as a result of a criminal assault by an employee of the store. The jury awarded $2.5 million in damages to the victim.
- Domino's Pizza was sued by the parents of two boys—a three-year-old and a six-year-old—allegedly molested by a pizza delivery person. An out-of-court settlement was reached in each case, one for $95,000, and the other $28,000. At the time of the delivery person's arrest, it was revealed that he had been previously arrested for burglary and grand theft.

On the other hand, proper hiring practices can be your defense in negligent hiring claims. In a case where a trucking company's on-duty employee sexually assaulted a motel clerk, the court found that the company was not guilty of negligent hiring when it was determined that an adequate pre-employment background check had been performed, verifying the information supplied by the employee and asking for criminal conviction information.

While the law may limit methods or even the extent to which certain information can be used (as explained in Chapter 11), it does not limit normal "due diligence" or prudent fact checking to ensure you hire an individual who is not only a productive employee, but is not a known threat to others. Because of the importance of due diligence, over half the states have enacted statutes that give employers a qualified privilege when checking employment references.

Create Legally Sound Job Applications

The first place to begin when hiring within the law is to use a well-written, detailed employment application. If you haven't reviewed your company's job application recently, now is the time to examine it carefully to make sure that it is legally compliant and tailored to the needs of your company. The next chapter tells you exactly how to do this.

Store Employment Documents Carefully

Take good care of all employment documents. You may need them down the line to support or defend claims of incompetence or unfair employment practices. Make it a rule to never write on an employment document provided by an applicant. If the information on a resume or application is incorrect or incomplete, give the document back to the applicant to complete or correct it. Remember, the certification of truthfulness signed at the bottom of an application does not apply to anything not written by the applicant.

Be sure to establish an organized method of storing all employment documents. Applications, interview notes, pre-employment evaluations, physical examinations, and even the advertisement used to recruit the applicant can be used to defend against a claim of discrimination. Keep this information on candidates you've interviewed but did not hire for three to five years to be sure you're covered on any claims of discrimination. Keep these records on your employees for the full term of their employment plus an additional three to five years after they leave.

Know Your Legal Responsibilities

You are responsible to hire within the guidelines of the law. This should not be a burden to the employment process you develop for your company, but a helping hand. Any hiring decision you make will have a significant effect on your organization's success and profitability. If you are not prudent in investigating those you hire, you may not only face a negligent hiring claim, you are jeopardizing the future of your company. Hiring within the law does not mean abdicating your responsibility or taking on burdensome legal tasks. It simply means knowing your rights, knowing the rights of the applicants, and staying within the law while diligently looking for the best candidate to fill the position.

*F*REQUENTLY *A*SKED *Q*UESTIONS

Q. *We are a small company. How many employees would I have to have before I worry about the laws of hiring?*

A. Different laws apply to different size companies. Many use the magic number of 15, but that is not always the case. The Immigration Reform and Control Act, for example, applies to all employers regardless of the number of employees, and the Equal Pay Act applies to companies with two or more employees. It is a good practice to hire within the law regardless of your size; then, as you grow, you won't have to worry about former noncompliance.

Q. *Are applications and resumes equal in the eyes of the law?*

A. No. You cannot control what an applicant writes on a resume. He or she may voluntarily give you information about age, marital status, and sex. But your company's application is considered a legal document that you require your applicants to complete and sign. This is the employment document that must adhere to labor and discrimination laws.

Q. *What if I do not want my interview notes to be reviewed at an audit for discrimination?*

A. Because interview notes can be used as evidence in discrimination suits, it is best to keep them on separate sheets of paper so they may be removed from the official document. Many interviewers scribble notes regarding the resume or application on sticky notes that can be discarded at a later date. If you've already written discriminatory notes on your employee's application there's nothing you can do except learn from this mistake.

Q. *What do I do if someone admits having a felony conviction?*

A. You have to ensure that you are exercising diligence in hiring to protect employees, customers, and the general public from someone who might be in your employment. If the felony conviction does not have any relation to the person's ability to perform the job and does not reasonably indicate that the individual, if employed, would pose a threat, you should consider the individual for employment. However, if there is any indication of problem behavior, such as violence or sexual abuse, that might be a threat to employees, customers, or the general public, you should refrain from hiring.

Q. *I'm tired of having to refill a position every time a female employee has a baby or relocates with her husband. Can I hire only males or single females?*

A. No. Discrimination laws protect applicants from discrimination based on marital status, sex, or pregnancy. You cannot even ask a female applicant if she plans to have children in the future or if her husband's job might require relocation.

Q. I have had trouble getting employees who can get to work without relying on public transportation (which in my area is very unreliable). Can I require new hires to have their own car?

A. No. You can require that employees have a car only if that car is needed to perform daily job duties, such as driving to sales calls. If a car is not required in the performance of daily duties, you cannot require an employee to have a car. You can, however, ask them to demonstrate that they have reliable transportation to and from work at the assigned times.

Q. I am starting a small business on the second floor of an old building. It is not handicap accessible. Is this a problem?

A. It depends. If you hire 15 or more employees, you are bound by the Americans with Disabilities Act which requires that you make reasonable accommodations for employees with physical disabilities. If you can prove that making your business handicap accessible would cause undue hardship, however, you would not be required to hire a person in a wheelchair who was qualified for the job but in need of a ramp and elevator. However, the ADA requires that owners or tenants of commercial facilities (office buildings, factories, and warehouses) make them handicap accessible if they are remodeled or renovated.

Q. Do I have to hire a qualified applicant who has a history of drug abuse?

A. Drug abuse is considered a disability and is protected from discrimination by the ADA. However, it does not cover a person currently abusing drugs. If the person has not undergone treatment and cannot prove freedom from addiction and use, you could be guilty of hiring negligence if you did hire him or her.

CHAPTER 5

Creating Customized, Legal Job Applications

ASKING THE RIGHT QUESTIONS WILL LEAD YOU TO THE RIGHT CANDIDATE.

An application is one of the most useful tools in the hiring process—if you tailor it to fit your company's needs and it is legally sound. If you are currently using a standard blank application form that you purchased from an office supply store, I advise you to throw it away and begin again from scratch. Create your own applications on a word processor that reflect the responsibilities of the job and the needs of your company. The information needed from an applicant for an outside sales representative position is slightly different than what is needed for a receptionist position. A well-constructed application will help you obtain the information you need to find the right person for the job.

Creating the Base Application

There is certain information that you need from all applicants regardless of the position. This information becomes part of your base application.

Date

Always include a space for noting the date the application is completed. This will allow you to know how current the information is or how fast people move through the employment process.

Contact Information

This part of the application provides full information on the applicant's name, address and phone number. You may want to ask for current and permanent addresses or alternative phone numbers to assist you in contacting the applicant.

Preferences

An applicant's preferences should state the position and type of employment (full time, part time, temporary/seasonal) sought, as well as desired location and salary requirements. Also ask when the applicant is available to work.

Personal

You should ask the applicant to state: (1) Social Security number, (2) eligibility to work in the United States, and (3) any felony convictions.

Education

All relevant education should be noted. Ask for the name and location of all schools attended, the course or field of study, the extent of study (such as the number of years attended), the diploma received or credits earned, and any special training classes attended. Do not ask for dates of attendance or graduation—this may open the door to claims of age discrimination.

Past Employment

Past employment is one of the most neglected resources. A good rule of thumb says that at least one-third of the application should focus on past performance. Ask for information from at least the last five jobs. You'll need to know the companies' names, addresses, and phone numbers; the dates of employment in each position; the starting and ending salary of each position; the name, title, and phone number of the direct supervisor at each position; a description of duties for each position; and the reason for leaving. Give instructions to begin this section with the most recent job and work backward.

References

It is critical that the application ask for references and permission to check them. Professional references are the most valuable because they offer job-related information you can use. Personal references can be biased and lead to discriminatory information. Ask the applicant to provide at least five references who are not already listed as supervisors in the past employment section. For each reference, you will need the person's name, company, job title, and phone number. Also ask the applicant how long and under what circumstances the reference has been acquainted.

Customizing the Application

With the base application on file, you can easily customize it to focus on the needs of specific positions.

Driving Information

If driving is a job function, it is essential to determine an applicant's qualification for insurance. You will need the driver's license number, state of issue, and expiration date. You should also ask:

- Has your privilege to drive ever been suspended or revoked?
- Have you ever been denied a license, permit, or privilege to operate a motor vehicle?
- Have you had any accidents in the last five years? If so, list them.
- Have you had any traffic convictions in the last five years? If so, list them.

Be sure to leave space for full explanations if the applicant answers yes to any of these questions. Ask for complete details on the dates, actions, and results. (Then, double-check all answers as directed in Chapter 8!)

Additional Skills

After the Past Employment section, include questions that can be objectively measured to determine if the candidate meets the "must have" requirements. If the job requires the employee to be able to type 50 words per minute, ask the applicant to state typing speed. If your employee must be verbally bilingual in English and Spanish, ask the applicant to state all languages spoken. Take a look at the sample application in Figure 5.1 and see how questions customized for a sales clerk position are incorporated into the base application. Answers to these questions are necessary in choosing an A level employee who can do the job, and more importantly, they are legal because they are relevant to the job and candidate requirements.

Age Information

You cannot ask an applicant's age unless age is necessary in fulfilling the requirements of the job (see information on the Age Discrimination Act in Chapter 4). If you are hiring a sales clerk in a liquor store, for example, in some states you must ask for the candidate to confirm that he or she is at least 21 years old. Or, if you are hiring senior citizens to participate in product research, you can ask candidates to verify their age.

Essential Job Functions

The job description you created in Chapter 2 established a list of essential job functions. This now should become a supplement to your application.

FIGURE 5.1 • Application for Employment

We encourage applications from qualified individuals with disabilities.

Name of applicant

First name   Middle name   Last name   Date of application

_____   _____   _____   _____

Current mailing address   **Telephone number**

Number and street   City   State   Zip   Area   Number

_____   _____   _____   _____   ____-____-____

Permanent mailing address   **Telephone number**

Number and street   City   State   Zip   Area   Number

_____   _____   _____   _____   ____-____-____

Type of work for which you are applying   **Type of employment you want**

First choice   Permanent ☐

_____   Part-time ☐

Second choice   Summer   ☐

_____

Any preference or restriction regarding work location

_____

Minimum salary requirements   Date available for work

_____   _____

Personal

Social Security Number   Are you eligible to work in the   Are you at least 18 years old?
                              United States? Yes ☐ No ☐   Yes ☐ No ☐
_____

Are you able to work flexible hours?   Have you ever been convicted of a felony? If yes, list
   Yes ☐   No ☐   date and place   Yes ☐ No ☐

Do you have a relative   _____
employed with ABC Company?
   Yes ☐   No ☐   Have you applied before, if so when?
                                           Yes ☐   No ☐   _____

Military

Branch of U.S. Service   Date entered   Date discharged   Highest rank attained

_____   ____/____   ____/____   _____

Do you have U.S. Armed Forces Reserve obligations?   Yes ☐   No ☐

List any special training received: _____

FIGURE 5.1 • Application for Employment (continued)

Education

Last high school and address   Highest grade completed

_____   _____

Did you graduate   Yes ☐   No ☐   Course or field of study _____

Business or Technical school and address   Years completed   Certificate obtained

_____   _____   _____

College   School location (city & state)   Major field of study   Credits   Degree

_____   _____   _____   _____   _____

_____   _____   _____   _____   _____

Employment Record

List most recent employment first. Include all former employers and self employment.

Employer's Name and Phone number   Supervisor's name   Supervisor's job title

_____ _____   _____   _____

Employer's Address, City, State   Start pay / End pay   Reason for leaving

_____   _____   _____

Describe duties _____

_____

Job title _____ From _____ / _____ To _____ / _____

Employer's Name and Phone number   Supervisor's name   Supervisor's job title

_____ _____   _____   _____

Employer's Address, City, State   Start pay / End pay   Reason for leaving

_____   _____   _____

Describe duties _____

_____

Job title _____ From _____ / _____ To _____ / _____

Employer's Name and Phone number   Supervisor's name   Supervisor's job title

_____ _____   _____   _____

Employer's Address, City, State   Start pay / End pay   Reason for leaving

_____   _____   _____

Describe duties _____

_____

Job title _____ From _____ / _____ To _____ / _____

FIGURE 5.1 • Application for Employment (continued)

Employer's Name and Phone number	Supervisor's name	Supervisor's job title

Employer's Address, City, State — Start pay / End pay — Reason for leaving

Describe duties _____

Job title _____ From ____ / ____ To ____ / ____

Employer's Name and Phone number	Supervisor's name	Supervisor's job title

Employer's Address, City, State — Start pay / End pay — Reason for leaving

Describe duties _____

Job title _____ From ____ / ____ To ____ / ____

References

Please provide the names of five references who know you in a work environment who are not listed above as supervisors.

1 Name — Telephone number — Occupation or position

Company, institution, or organization _____

How long has reference known you? — Under what circumstances has reference known you?

2 Name — Telephone number — Occupation or position

Company, institution, or organization _____

How long has reference known you? — Under what circumstances has reference known you?

3 Name — Telephone number — Occupation or position

Company, institution, or organization _____

How long has reference known you? — Under what circumstances has reference known you?

FIGURE 5.1 • Application for Employment (continued)

4 Name   Telephone number   Occupation or position

_____   _____   _____

Company, institution, or organization _____

How long has reference known you?   Under what circumstances has reference known you?

_____   _____

5 Name   Telephone number   Occupation or position

_____   _____   _____

Company, institution, or organization _____

How long has reference known you?   Under what circumstances has reference known you?

_____   _____

I certify that the above information is true and complete to the best of my knowledge. I understand that misrepresentation or omission of facts requested on this application is cause for rejection of this application or for subsequent dismissal from employment. I authorize an investigation of any of the facts set forth in this application. I give permission to check my educational background, references, professional license, criminal record, driving record, and credit record and release any and all persons, companies, or agencies responding to such investigation from any liability for any damage due to releasing information pertaining hereto. I understand I will be required to provide information for compliance with the Immigration Reform and Control Act. I understand that I may be required to have a physical examination, drug test, and pre-employment evaluation. I understand and agree that my employment with ABC Company is entered into voluntarily and I may resign at any time.

Signature _____ **Date** _____

Application will be active for ninety (90) days.

FIGURE 5.1 • Application for Employment (continued)

If driving required:

Driving Information

Driver's license number   State   Expiration date

_____   _____   _____

   A. Is the above a valid driver's license?   Yes ☐   No ☐

   B. Have you ever been denied a license, permit or privilege
      to operate a motor vehicle?   Yes ☐   No ☐

   C. Has any license, permit or privilege ever been suspended or revoked? Yes ☐   No ☐

If the answer to either B or C is YES, attach a statement giving details.

Have you had an accident in the past 5 years? (Attach sheet if more space is needed.)

                    Nature of accident (head-on, rear-end, etc.)

Last accident date _____   _____

Injuries Yes ☐ No ☐   Fatalities Yes ☐ No ☐

                    Nature of accident (head-on, rear-end, etc.)

Next previous date _____   _____

Injuries Yes ☐ No ☐   Fatalities Yes ☐ No ☐

Traffic convictions and forfeitures for the past five years (other than parking violations)

Location (city and state)	Date	Charges	Penalty
_____	_____	_____	_____
_____	_____	_____	_____
_____	_____	_____	_____

Additional Information for Sales Position:

Describe your typing or keyboard skills.

_____

_____

Explain situations where you have had to demonstrate your mathematical ability such as calculating payments and handling cash.

_____

_____

Are you able to lift 40 lbs. and move it 40 feet?   Yes ☐   No ☐

Can you reach and answer the phone by the third ring
from any place in the store? Yes ☐   No ☐

Making It Legal

You must be sure your job application does not contain questions that might be unlawful. The Equal Employment Opportunity Commission and state agencies assume that job applications include only relevant questions. You must be able to demonstrate that the answer to each question is related to the job for which the applicant is applying. Any questions referring to race, color, marital status, age, sex, religion, national origin, or disability are prohibited. Think carefully about how each question might unintentionally discriminate. Asking for high school or college graduation dates, for example, could lead to an age discrimination complaint.

If you are an Equal Opportunity Employer be sure it is stated on the application and in all other documents. You should also include a statement saying that you encourage applications from qualified individuals with disabilities.

Certification and Agreement Clauses

A very important part of an application is the certification and agreement clauses. These eight clauses are often recommended by employment lawyers. (Look for them on the sample application in Figure 5.1.)

1. The applicant certifies that the information given is true and complete to the best of his or her knowledge; the applicant also agrees that if employed and false statements are uncovered, he or she may be dismissed without recourse.
2. The applicant authorizes an investigation of any of the facts set forth in the application.
3. The applicant gives permission to check his or her criminal and/or driving record, credit, educational background, professional license, and references. Without a signed authorization, you face the potential for a claim of invasion of privacy by the applicant. (See Chapter 11 for information about how to make these background checks.)
4. State a reminder that the applicant will be required to provide information for compliance with the Immigration Reform and Control Act.
5. Include a statement that the employer may require physical examinations, drug tests, and other types of pre-employment evaluations.
6. If allowed in your state, include an employment-at-will statement. This statement may read, "I understand and agree that my employment with the company is entered into voluntarily and I may resign at any time." This is recommended by lawyers to clarify that the application is not a contract.

7. If state law allows, it can be beneficial to add, "My employment may be terminated for any reason at any time without previous notice."

8. Notify the applicant that any offer of employment is conditioned upon certain specified events, such as the completion of a criminal background check.

These clauses may seem like legal mumbo jumbo, but they can save you time, stress, and potential legal fees. Each one protects you, the employer, from various types of legal entanglements. There's an owner of an apartment complex in Minnesota who wishes he had included clauses 2 and 3 in his employment application. In 1983, a tenant in one of his apartments was raped by the manager of the complex. The tenant brought suit against the owner alleging that he was negligent in hiring the manager. The manager had a criminal record including burglary and armed robbery. In his most recent job as a bus driver, the manager had been fired for drinking on the job and fighting with his supervisor. In the hiring process, the manager revealed that he had been convicted of a crime, but he described the crime as "traffic tickets." The owner did not inquire further. At trial, the manager testified that if he had been required to sign an authorization releasing his criminal record, he would have refused and not sought the job. Protect yourself by making sure your application includes certification and agreement clauses.

FREQUENTLY ASKED QUESTIONS

Q. *Can I create one application and use it for all positions?*

A. While it might be tempting to create an application that covers all positions, it is not wise. It is reasonable to assume, for example, that knowing an applicant has a bad driving record (even though the job requires no driving) may affect your hiring decision, leaving you open to charges of discrimination. Use your word processor to edit the application to match the information needed for each specific position.

Locate Qualified Applicants

CHAPTER 6

Developing a Recruiting Plan

ANY IMPORTANT BUSINESS UNDERTAKING
BEGINS WITH A PLAN—HIRING IS NO DIFFERENT.

You would never consider beginning a trip to deliver products to customers without careful thought and planning. You would ensure nothing was left behind, plan a well-defined route, strive to use the least amount of time and effort, and plan to have the products delivered on time. You should approach the key task of hiring an employee with the same forethought, preparation, and commitment. Some employers simply put an ad in the paper and hire the first applicant with which they are comfortable. With this approach, is it any wonder performance is low, management's stress significant, and turnover high?

Any important business undertaking begins with a plan. Hiring is no different. If you want to ensure your business is staffed with A level employees, you must begin with a recruiting plan. This plan maps out exactly how you will fill a position before the situation arises. Will you keep the same job description for a new employee? How long will you allow for filling the new position? Can the position be left open for any length of time? Will the new employee need a training period? How many applications will you need to solicit? How will applicants apply? Who will screen and interview them? All these questions should ideally be answered before the position becomes open, and definitely, before you begin your search for applicants. If your company has recurring needs or is growing rapidly, you can apply these principles to create an ongoing recruiting plan. The sample recruiting plan in Figure 6.1 will give you an overview of the kinds of things you need to consider. (This form also appears in Appendix D.)

Define the Position

There are two circumstances in which you'll find yourself in need of a recruiting plan: (1) if a current employee vacates a position, and (2) if you create a

FIGURE 6.1 • Sample Recruiting Plan

Position: _____

Date of projected opening: _____

Reason position open: _____

Date the position must be filled: _____

Staffing Options:

____ full-time   ____ part-time

____ permanent   ____ temporary

____ outsourcing   ____ work-at-home

____ professional employee organization

Job Description:

current one: ____ accurate   ____ needs revision

new position: ____ create one

Candidate Requirement List:

current one   ____ accurate   ____ needs revision

new position   ____ create one

Compensation:

hourly: _____   salary: _____

commission: _____   bonus: _____

incentive perks:

_____

_____

Applications:

No. needed: _____

Submission form: ____ mail   ____ e-mail   ____ fax   ____ in-person

Locations to apply: _____

Telephone calls (time/day): _____

FIGURE 6.1 • Sample Recruiting Plan (continued)

Action	Individuals Responsible	Target Date
Creating/placing ads	_____	_____
Networking	_____	_____
Other applicant sources	_____	_____
Screening applications	_____	_____
Screening interviews	_____	_____
In-depth interviews	_____	_____
Pre-employment evaluation	_____	_____
Reference checking	_____	_____
Creating and making offer	_____	_____
Sending reject letters	_____	_____
Orienting new employee	_____	_____
Training new employee	_____	_____

Post-Hiring Evaluation:

What did I learn that can apply in the future to get a higher-quality candidate, reduce the effort needed, or shorten the time required? What valuable lesson did I learn?

_____

_____

_____

_____

_____

_____

new position. In either case, you need to take a good look at the job itself before you look for someone to fill it.

The recruiting plan begins with the need for the position itself. Make a record of the position title and the date you expect it to become open. You might want to also note why the position is open. If you have a definite vacancy coming up, record the date by which the position must be filled.

What Are Your Staffing Options?

The next step is to review the decisions made in Chapter 3 about the the level of need for the individual. Will this need be long-term and filled with a full-time employee? Or, is this an occasional or seasonal need that a part-time or temporary employee could accomplish? Can two part-time employees, at twenty hours each, fill the need better than one-full time employee due to the diverse skills required or work schedule? Is this a job that can be handled by an employee working at home? A good look at the job requirements you created in Chapter 2 might indicate that a better alternative is to outsource a portion of the work and reduce the requirements in terms of hours or competence for a part-time employee. Decide what you need and record it on your recruiting plan.

Examine the Job Definition

It is unlikely that you will find a top rate candidate to fill a position that you do not clearly understand. That is why you must clearly define the job duties, job responsibilities, essential job functions, and level of performance (outlined in Chapter 2) before you attempt to create a recruiting plan.

If an employee is leaving, take a good look at the job definition and hiring criteria for that position. Do they still match your needs? Do you want to revise or update any of the qualifications? This is an excellent opportunity to fine-tune the job definition to better match your business needs. Keep an open mind and re-examine the situation each time a position is filled. Don't just replace a person. Use your creativity and staff the position smartly.

If you don't have a written record of these requirements, or if you are creating a new position, now is the time to write down the responsibilities and duties of the job and the qualifications of the employee. You can't effectively advertise for a position if you can't clearly state what the job entails and what qualifications are needed to perform the work.

Note the status of your job definition and hiring criteria on your recruiting plan. Are you going to use the current ones? Revise them? Create new ones?

Determine the Compensation

Think about the position and ask yourself these two questions to determine compensation

1. What is this job worth?
2. How much can I afford to pay?

Your job definition will give you an objective look at what you have budgeted for this position. Put this figure, and any incentive perks, in your recruiting plan. This information, written down in black and white, will be invaluable to you later in the hiring process. Too often employers get into a bidding war or negotiation and offer a candidate more money than the position warrants or they can afford. Write it down in your recruiting plan and use it as your guide during the process.

Where Will You Find Potential Applicants?

Think about where you will find the best applicants while expending the least amount of time and money. (Chapter 7 will show you the many ways you can recruit and advertise.) Write in your recruiting plan how you will reach these applicants. Note: In this book *applicant* refers to anyone who has forwarded information to the company in pursuit of employment, and *candidate* is an applicant that meets the musts.

Then consider how much time you will need to gather applicants through these sources. For example, if you choose to advertise the job in print media, you'll need time to create the ad, place it in the newspaper, and give individuals time to see the ad and respond. You can expect at least one week to pass from the time you decide to advertise until you begin to see responses. In most instances, the best response will occur shortly after the ad appears.

How Many Applicants Do You Need?

How many applicants will you need to assure a quality pool of candidates? Most business owners vastly underestimate the number of applications required. In my experience working with small and medium-sized businesses, the number of applicants can be as few as five or over one hundred. The reason for this wide range is the variability of position types and location.

You must plan to solicit a significant number of applicants if

- experience has shown that it is hard to find a quality individual to fill this position.

- this is the first time you'll be hiring for this position.
- the hiring criteria is very specific.
- unemployment rates in your area are low.

In many instances, as the pool of qualified applicants decreases, the response to advertisements for general recruiting, such as want ads, still remains relatively high. The effect of low unemployment is not a reduced quantity of applicants, but a reduced quality. You may get almost as many applicants, but fewer qualify as A level candidates. Be sure to account for difficult conditions and allow yourself extra time in the hiring process.

Many employers wrestle with the question of how long they should continue accepting applications. You don't have to set a cutoff date. Once you have a number of candidates you can begin moving them forward through the hiring process. Never stop accepting applications because you might turn away a "superstar." Until you have made a hiring decision, allow anyone interested to complete an application. Compare these new applicants to those already moving through the hiring process. If their background and capability appear to be better than those you are considering, add them to the process. If they do not meet your standards, you can reject them when you notify others not selected.

Decide how many applications you need to adequately fill the position and record that number on your recruiting plan.

How Will the Applicants Apply?

Now it is time to determine how you will accept resumes and applications for the position. The decisions you make will affect the time you invest in the process and quantity and quality of applicants.

The easier it is to respond without formal letters and resumes, the more responses you will receive, especially from applicants who are already working and don't have much time to respond. The drawback to making application easy is that more unstructured responses will be generated and going through them will be time-consuming. It is important to strike a balance between flexibility and structure so that you still get quality candidates without wasting too much of your time.

You can accept responses to your job opening via

- *mail or fax.* These allow you to get a high volume of responses quickly from different locations that you can screen on your own schedule.
- *hand delivery.* This requires the applicant to visit your place of business. This is often inconvenient for working people and can eat up your time as

well. If you choose this method, don't "interview" people who come in to apply. If their background and skills don't match your needs, you've wasted precious time.

- *e-mail.* This medium of communication will be especially effective if you plan to use online recruiting or electronic networking. Some organizations are creating homepages that include a simple input document. You can offer an online application that can be e-mailed directly to your company. If you choose this option, be sure to include your e-mail and/or website address in your ads and recruiting materials.

- *telephone.* A telephone call is an easy way for the applicant to respond to your recruiting material or request an application. This will increase the quantity of responses, and also cause significant interruptions during your day that can be very time-consuming.

The method or combination of methods you choose should be recorded in your recruiting plan.

Screening: Who? When? For How Long?

You will use your job definition and hiring criteria list to sort out the qualified from the unqualified resumes and applications you receive. (Methods of screening are detailed in Chapter 8.) On your recruiting plan you will decide in advance who will do the screening and how long this task should take. (The timing depends, of course, on how many applications you are soliciting.)

After the resumes or applications have been screened, you will conduct another level of screening by interview, either on the phone or in person. You should allow approximately 30 minutes for in-person screening interviews, but less time for phone screening. Schedule these steps into your recruiting plan.

Scheduling Interviews

Certainly you will want to interview the top candidates for the position. Decide now how many interviews you will require of each candidate, who will conduct them, and how long you will allocate for each one. A good rule of thumb is to allow 90 minutes for each in-depth interview. Most in-depth interviews are approximately one hour; this extra time will give you room to review the applicant's background before the interview and then complete the interview worksheet afterwards. Record this information on your recruiting plan.

Consider the Types and Timing of Pre-Employment Evaluations

Pre-employment evaluations you can conduct include criminal and credit checks, physical exams, skill tests, behavioral style instruments, drug tests, and reference checks. Before you recruit for your open position, read through Chapter 9 to decide what kind of pre-employment evaluations you require for this position and how long it will take to schedule, conduct, and evaluate them. Put this information in your recruiting plan.

What's Your Timeline?

Timing is always a critical issue in hiring. In many instances, employees quit without notice and positions open without warning. Many employers vastly underestimate the time it takes to generate quality applicants and make a good hiring decision. The pressure of a hiring deadline compounded with the day-to-day pressures of running a business can prompt a business owner to reduce his or her standards and hire the first able body available to fill the position. If your timing is hurried, you might check fewer references, skip a needed interview or background check, or compromise your list of musts. Easing your standards or short-cutting your recruiting process will have detrimental effects on your business in the long run.

Your recruiting plan will keep this from happening. Before you need an employee, you should take a careful look at how long each step of the hiring process will take to determine how long it will take to fill the position. To set a realistic timeline, begin with the date you would like the employee to be on board and productive, and then work backward through the steps. This will show you how much has to be done and how long it will take to get your new employee settled.

Work backward through each of these milestones:

- Completes training.
- Completes orientation.
- Reports to work.
- Accepts offer.
- Makes hiring decision.
- Selects final candidates.
- Checks references.
- Completes interviews.
- Completes pre-employment evaluations.
- Begins interviews.

- Activates applicant recruiting.
- Creates a recruiting plan.
- Defines job and hiring criteria.

Once you have determined how long it will take to bring a quality individual on board, you can compare it to the amount of time that you have available. In some instances, the time required to hire will be longer than the time you can live with the position open. Don't panic and hire the first warm body that walks in the door. Instead, develop strategies to compensate during this transition period. Outsourcing, temporary workers, and redistribution of responsibilities are the typical ways to cope with the open position.

Your recruiting plan is a document that should be prepared before you have a hiring need, with an objective view of the position and your needs. Its purpose is to keep you on track when you're in the thick of the hiring process and can easily be swayed to cut corners, rush, lower your standards, or forget important hiring procedures. Of course, changes may be made along the way as expected schedules or circumstances change, but at least you'll have a tool to navigate with. And if you find that the recruiting plan had unrealistic guidelines, you should make note of that at the end of the form and make the necessary changes for the next time you need to fill that position.

FREQUENTLY ASKED QUESTIONS

Q. *Isn't it easier to begin recruiting and make up a recruiting plan as you go along?*

A. It is tempting to begin work before the plan is complete; however, if you were planning a trip you would make sure you had all your planning done before you departed to make it as easy and trouble-free as possible. The amount of time planning before you begin recruiting will pay significant dividends in time saved and stress reduced.

Q. *What do I do with the recruiting plan after the employee is hired?*

A. You have a lot of valuable information at your fingertips. Be sure to evaluate what you learned during the process and file it away. The next time you begin recruiting, that file will make your job easier.

Q. *The recruiting plan considers only one position. Since we hire a lot more, what should we do?*

A. The process and techniques work whether you are filling one position occasionally or many positions on a continuous basis. Simply build a recruiting plan for the entire organization from the individual recruiting plans.

CHAPTER 7

Identifying Sources of Qualified Candidates

YOU HAVE TO DIG IF YOU WANT TO FIND GOLD.

To avoid settling for an unqualified candidate, companies (especially growing ones) must find and utilize a variety of applicant sources. You can run an ad or turn to an employment agency, but to find the best candidate you may have to be more creative and think beyond the obvious. Sometimes you have to dig deeper to find things most valuable.

In this chapter you'll explore ten possible applicant sources.

1. Print advertisements
2. Employment firms
3. Networking
4. Employee referrals
5. Customer referrals
6. College campuses
7. Internships
8. Career nights
9. Online recruiting
10. Creative ideas

The planning of your recruiting strategy has already been spelled out in your recruiting plan (see Chapter 6). Having determined how long you want to solicit candidates and how long you'll be accepting applications, you can move on to preparing your soliciting campaign.

Take a close look at each one of the strategies in this chapter and use them to be bold and aggressive while recruiting applicants. Go after the sources that you think will lead you to the very best applicants in the business. Whether you're looking for a receptionist, sales clerk, or computer operator, you want an A level employee who matches your needs and is driven to be successful. Finding this person takes time, effort and sometimes creativity, tenacity, and courage.

Print Advertisements

The most common source for finding job applicants is print advertisements. Although this can be an effective way of generating applicants, it's sometimes called the "pay and pray" method—you create an ad, pay to run it, and pray for a good response.

To make your investment worthwhile, you should create an accurate, compelling ad that will generate the response you need from qualified candidates. Consider your ad for an employee no different than ads for your product or service. You need to identify the benefits and attributes of your product—the company and the job—then zero in on a target audience, and create an appealing, can't-resist advertisement.

Targeting Your Ad

The cost of print advertising varies greatly. An in-column ad in the classified section of a newspaper can range from $25 for a two-inch line ad in a small suburban paper to nearly $5,000 for a six-inch, two-column display ad in a major metropolitan paper. The cost depends upon the size and shape of the ad, and the circulation of the publication in which it appears. (Many papers give multiple-insertion discounts to get you to increase frequency, but this also increases the cost.) Because the cost to run a poorly designed ad is the same as running a great ad, it's vital that you put time and thought into your ad before placing it.

To ensure that you effectively spend advertising dollars and attract the best candidates, carefully read your detailed job definition. Now envision the perfect candidate who fulfills your hiring criteria. Create and place the ad to generate response from *this* person.

What publications does this person read? This is where you want to advertise. Where would this person look if he or she was thinking about finding a new job? Put your ad there. Consider a variety of the publications that follow.

Newspapers. This is the traditional source for classified ads, but think before you advertise. If you want a local person to be a sales clerk, use local papers with wide circulation over the surrounding area—the suburban presses and penny shoppers tend to be good for this kind of relatively unskilled position. If you want a highly trained and experienced technician or professional, consider a metropolitan paper's Sunday edition (this is when employed professionals are more likely to have time to read!). Remember to keep location in mind. Unless you're expecting someone to relocate for the job, don't waste money advertising in *The New York Times* for a position in your Los Angeles company. You can request a press kit that details circulation figures and demographic information to help you determine your best targets.

Magazines. Because magazines are carefully marketed to a very specific audience, you can use them to reach applicants who match the magazine's target. Trade publications are especially good at reaching individuals in a certain business. If you need a skilled assistant in your video production business, place your line ad in the back of *Video Magazine.* If you are looking for someone to join your travel agency, try *Travel Holiday.* Business journals are most useful for filling professional, sales, and management positions.

College papers. If a college student or upcoming graduate would be a good candidate, place your ad in a college paper. This is a very receptive market for all types of employment including full-time (for graduates), part-time (for students), temporary (during semester breaks), and even outsourcing (for work that students can do at home). And don't forget that faculty and staff read the paper too and may be looking for extra work.

Newsletters. There are thousands of business and trade newsletters published in this country, and many of them carry classified ads. These newsletters will deliver your ad directly to individuals interested in a very specific area of their business. If you look at the newsletters you receive, you will find they are generally focused on your business.

A visit to the reference section of your library will help you find the publications most likely to get results. In addition to the library's own collection, review references such as *Standard Rate and Data Service,* which not only identifies thousands of publications, but provides the geographic area served, a readership profile, and advertising rates.

Designing Your Ad

Step One: Analyze similar ads. Before you place your advertisement, take a good look at the ads running in your target publications. Look at the ads from a distance to see which ones grab your attention first. As a general rule, larger ads or those with unusual shapes and higher contrast get more attention. Look at the ads for the type of position you are trying to fill. You will want to make your ad different—more compelling. Look at the headings under which your job offer can be printed. If you need a copywriter, for example, you can place that ad under "Writer," "Editor," or "Copywriter." Look at ads already listed and then choose the most advantageous position.

Step Two: Decide on the type of ad. Most ads can be divided into two types: (1) classified, in-column, line ads, or (2) display ads. Line ads are the small ads in newspapers and in the back of some magazines. Cost is generally determined by the number of words or lines. (A tip: These ads are often arranged alphabetically based on the first word of the ad. An ad that begins with "advertising sales" will precede "sales position.") Display ads are the larger boxed ads that often include a logo, picture, and bold heading. These are more expensive than line ads because price is based on the column inch and sometimes you pay a premium for placement—top right corner is a favored, more expensive position).

Most employers first try line, or in-column, ads because they are almost always less expensive. If they are not successful at generating enough quality applicants, they will change to display ads. The message may be the same but the design, graphic and format are different. The choice between line ads and display ads also depends on what your competitors are doing to attract applicants. If all competing ads are in-column ads, a display ad may not be necessary. But if all competing ads are large display ads, an in-column ad would probably be a waste of money and valuable time. See Figure 7.1 for typical advertising rates of line and display ads.

Step Three: Create the content. Your ad must give information that will make the reader want to respond. The words of the ad should "sell" the job, company, opportunity, location, industry, income, education potential, benefits, and anything else that makes it a great position. You can also try to use the ad as a screening device by including the musts of a candidate (as outlined in Chapter 2). I say *try* because, unfortunately, print advertisements usually generate a large number of unqualified applicants because anyone with the price of a stamp can respond.

When writing your ad, use words that will grab the reader's attention, and focus on the hot buttons of the candidate based on your list of job and candidate requirements (outlined in Chapter 2). For a sales position, some typical grabber words are *opportunity, income,* and *earnings.* For other positions you might use:

- *Professional development*
- *Benefits*
- *Work as a team*
- *Job security*
- *Travel*
- *No travel*
- *Consistent work schedule*
- *Flexible schedule*

FIGURE 7.1 • Advertising Rates

	Charleston Post & Courier	Atlanta Constitution	Chicago Tribune
(obtained 12/17/97)			
		(14 lines=1")	(14 lines=1")
Classified weekday rate	$31.84/col. in.	$15.82/line ($221.48/col.in)	recommended Sunday paper
Classified Sunday rate	$35.33/col. in.	$7.42/line ($103.88/col. in)	$27.00/line $378.00/col. in)
Classified Friday rate* *Constitution recommended		$16.41/line $229.74/col. in)	
2 col. × 6" display (single insertion) weekday	$532.80	$3,474.32* *half price if also run on Sunday	$2,856.00
2 col. × 6" display (single insertion) Sunday	$602.40	$3,414.32	$4,536.00

- *Training provided*
- *Paid vacations*
- *Management opportunities*
- *Career growth*

Be sure to include how you want applicants to respond. In your recruiting plan, you have already determined if you'll take an application in person, by phone, or by mail, e-mail, or fax. Communicate this decision in your ad.

Lastly, it's a good idea to note at the bottom of your ad if you are an Equal Employment Opportunity Employer. The words quickly communicate that fact that you hire without discrimination based on age, gender, race, national origin, religion, disability, or veteran status. Some organizations simply include the initials "EEO/M,F,H,V" which stands for "equal employment opportunity/minority, female, handicapped, veteran."

Be Legally Correct

Because our language responds to societal change, your ad should too. Jobs that used to be male-only and carried male-only designations are now filled by both men and women. To be sure you do not discriminate, use inclusive job titles that are gender neutral. For example:

Instead Of	*Use*
salesman	sales clerk, sales rep or salesperson
businessman	business executive
foreman	supervisor
spokesman	spokesperson
waitress	waiter
repairman	technician
manpower	workforce

The sample ads in Figures 7.2 and 7.3 illustrate the techniques suggested in this chapter. Note they use grabber words, emphasize job benefits and musts; advise how to respond; and use legally correct language.

FIGURE 7.2 • Sample Line Ad

> **SALESPERSON**
> **Looking for a Career?**
> A local retail company that dominates the market and is experiencing great growth offers professional training, promotion and advancement, excellent salary, benefits, including medical.
> To qualify you must have excellent verbal communication, strong keyboard/typing skills, able to handle cash transactions, able to lift 40 lbs. and move it 50 feet.
> Bilingual in English and Spanish, one year cashier, two years sales a plus.
> Results-oriented and looking for a career opportunity with a growing company, we want to talk to you.
> Send resume and salary history by e-mail to wayne@ yourcompany.com, by fax to 803-555-1212, or call Michael Heyward between 9:00 and 11:00 a.m. at 803-555-1213.

FIGURE 7.3 • Sample Display Ad

SALESPERSON
Looking for a Career?

Want an excellent starting salary and the opportunity to grow with a success-oriented organization?

We are a local retail company that dominates our market and is experiencing great growth.
We offer:
- Professional training
- Promotion and growth
- Excellent salary
- Benefits, including medical

To qualify:
- Excellent verbal communication
- Strong keyboard/typing skills
- Able to handle cash transactions
- Able to lift 40 lbs. and move it 50 feet

A plus:
- Bilingual in English and Spanish
- One year experience as cashier
- Two years sales experience

If you are results oriented and looking for a career opportunity with a growing company, we want to talk to you.

Send resume and salary history by e-mail to wayne@yourcompany.com, by fax to 803-555-1212, or call Michael Heyward between 9:00 and 11:00 a.m. at 803-555-1213.

Your Logo

Tracking Your Ad

Once you've placed your ad, your job is not over. Like any expenditure of significant size and strategic importance, the results of your advertisement should be tracked. You can use the Employment Ad Placement Log found in Appendix E to keep a written record of each ad. It will help you track where and when you placed the ad, the ad number and costs, the quantity and quality of responses, and how you can improve the ad if you run it another time.

Print advertising is a critical part of filling many positions today. The better you get at creating compelling ads that generate positive responses, the greater the number of quality applicants your ads will produce.

Employment Firms

Outside employment firms can be a viable source for applicants. However, before approaching an employment firm it is important to be aware of the different types of firms and their strengths and weaknesses.

Retained Search Firm

Retained search firms generally focus on hard-to-fill or high-level management positions. These firms provide professionals who operate as partners with your company to ensure the best candidate gets the offer, even if the candidate is already a current employee. But as the term *retained* indicates, the firm earns its fee whether it fills the position or not, as long as it delivers the contracted assistance. The fee for search firms can be expensive—often 30 percent of the candidate's total targeted compensation for the first year, plus the firm's expenses.

Contingency Search Firm

This search firm's success is contingent upon finding a candidate to fill a job vacancy. The firm will help you locate a candidate for almost any type of position and there is no fee unless the candidate is hired. (Be aware that if the position is filled, the fee can be as high as a retained search—30 percent but without the firm's expenses.) On the down side, contingency search firms tend to focus only on "fillable" positions. If the position appears difficult to fill, they may not give it their full attention because they depend on getting their candidates hired to earn their fee.

Employment Placement Agencies

There are many types of employment placement agencies that do not operate on a search basis. Instead, they create a stable or data base of people actively looking for work and then find jobs to fit these candidates. These employment agencies focus on mid- or lower-level positions that do not usually require highly specialized skills.

You can find these agencies in the yellow pages of the phone book. You can also ask owners of businesses similar to yours if they have used or can recommend an agency. Figure 7.4 details the pros and cons of employment agencies.

FIGURE 7.4 • Pros and Cons of Employment Agencies

PROS

- No financial risk unless you hire the candidate.

- Agency usually refers a number of people right away.

- Saves time and effort in generating applicant flow.

- Applicants are prescreened.

- Agency schedules the interviews.

CONS

- Agency is motivated to fill the position and may take quantity over quality approach when suggesting interviews.

- Agency will usually not give time and effort to a position that is difficult to fill.

- Quality of prescreening varies from firm to firm.

- Receive many of the same applicants that would respond to a newspaper ad.

Networking

Job applicants have used networking for years to find positions. You, as an employer, can also use networking to find the best applicants.

Networking does not mean haphazardly asking everyone you meet if they know someone looking for a job. It is a conscious, deliberate strategy that enlists friends and associates as sources for excellent candidates. You can network through professional associations, such as your local chamber of commerce or trade associations, or contact civic and religious groups in your town and put out the word that you are looking for an employee.

Here are six steps to networking effectively.

1. Identify people and organizations who might refer you to suitable candidates.
2. Call or write your contacts and inform them of your vacancy.

3. Ask questions to generate better response from contacts. "Who do you know who might consider a better career opportunity?" Or, "Who do you know who is dissatisfied with his or her career position?"
4. Describe your job and the applicant requirements you're looking to meet.
5. Ask for phone numbers and addresses of potential applicants. Don't expect applicants to call you.
6. Follow up with a thank-you letter to your contact, stressing your appreciation and emphasize that making a referral does not make them responsible for the applicant.

When networking, it is especially important that you clearly relate the job definition and the required qualifications of the applicant. Without this understanding, your contact may refer anyone who happens to be available, rather than someone who fits the job.

When someone does make a referral ask a few questions before contacting the potential candidate.

- How do you know this person?
- How long have you known this person?
- Do you know why this person would consider this opportunity?
- Do you know what this person's career goals are?
- Tell me about this person's work background.
- What is your opinion of this person?
- Who else, that I might know, knows this person well?

This preliminary research or pre-interview can save you the trouble of contacting someone who is clearly not suited for the position. If the referral does not meet your needs, be honest and explain that to your contact. On the other hand, if the person does appear to meet your requirements, thank the individual and follow up promptly.

You can make your request for a referral informally at a social gathering, professionally at a trade or civic meeting, or formally in writing. I once received a letter from the sales manager of an insurance company who was looking for qualified representatives. Although I didn't personally know this person, he contacted me because we graduated from the same college—an automatic networking bond. The adaptation of his letter in Figure 7.5 gives you an idea of how you can present your employment needs to others who may be in a position to help.

Such a thorough and detailed networking approach paid off for this man because I took the time to identify several people who might fit the situation. Networking is like anything else in life—your returns are in direct proportion to your efforts. Networking is an excellent way to identify quality candidates.

FIGURE 7.5 • Letter Asking for a Referral

Mr. John Doe
999 Any Street
Pleasantville, US

Dear Mr. Doe,

   I would like to ask for your help. I am looking to hire a sales representative for our company. I am particularly interested in a person who is not satisfied with the future of his or her present position. A career as a representative of our company offers the right individual:

- *An exceptional compensation plan.* The average income in our office is over $50,000.
- *Training Programs.* We offer an individualized training program in various aspects of the insurance business.
- *A rewarding career.* This position offers the opportunity to be in business for oneself selling a variety of insurance products.
- *Management opportunity.* After a proven track record of selling, an individual could qualify for management.

   I am particularly interested in making this opportunity available to someone associated with, and/or recommended by, an alumnus of the Citadel, such as yourself. I would appreciate it if you would search your mind for someone you consider qualified for this work. Then, if you will jot his/her name, address, and phone number at the bottom of this letter and return it to me in the enclosed envelope, I will contact him/her personally and let you know the outcome of our interview.

   For whatever help you can give me, my sincere thanks.

Sincerely,
Bill Smith

_____

Dear Bill:
I recommend
Name _____
Address _____
Phone Number _____

Whether the referral is a qualified candidate or not, be sure to thank the person who made the referral. It takes time and effort to reply to your request for help. If you respond poorly, or not at all, you greatly diminish your chances of getting any help in the future. It is also a good idea to send a thank-you note or small gift, especially if a referred candidate is eventually hired. A gift certificate at a favorite restaurant, theater passes, or something for the office are nice gestures of your appreciation. The gift does not need to be large or expensive; it should simply express appreciation.

Employee Referrals

An effective employee referral system should encourage employees to generate referrals to assist in staffing the company. A well-thought-out program can turn employees into "headhunters" for the company. This is an especially effective strategy for organizations that are growing and have satisfied employees. It is hard to get employees to refer friends and family members unless they feel the company is a good place to work.

One of the keys to a successful employee referral program is a monetary reward. This incentive encourages employees to only refer potential candidates who are qualified, and therefore, likely to be hired. The amount of the reward depends on your business and your budget. It is important to make the reward large enough to keep employees focused on this very important task, but not so large that it disrupts work schedules or encourages poor referrals from individuals who only want the reward.

The first step in implementing this kind of program is to let your employees know you need their help. If you have only a few employees, you might simply talk to each one and explain your needs. In a larger company, you can distribute a letter that details your plan, as shown in Figure 7.6. Either way, you need to communicate exactly what you desire.

Customer Referrals

Customers are often overlooked as a source for employee candidates. Customers themselves may be looking for a career change, or they may know someone who would make an excellent employee. Customer referrals can be especially valuable when filling sales or service positions.

You've seen this tactic in action if you've ever eaten at McDonald's. They have been a leader in using daily restaurant traffic to identify workers for years. The company periodically uses a place mat on a serving tray with a catchy head-

FIGURE 7.6 • Sample Employee Referral Program Announcement Letter

Dear Employee:

I would like to ask your personal assistance in a very important task. I need to identify and attract top-notch, talented people to work with us to grow this business. I have found that many of the best people I have hired in the past have been referred by our own employees. Winners tend to attract winners.

Over the next week, I'd like for you to observe those you come in contact with in all aspects of your life. When you see an energetic person with the skills and drive for success that make them a natural fit in our organization, I'd like to know about them. All I ask is that you identify them and I'll do the rest.

I've attached a referral sheet to this letter. All I really need is the individual's name and phone number (preferably home number). If you have any additional information, such as why you think the person will be an excellent employee, or details about past work experience, it would be helpful.

To reward your efforts, I will pay a cash bonus of _____ for any individual who is hired as a result of your referral. The first half of this payment will be made after the person has been hired; the second half will be paid when the person has been with the organization for ___ days.

As you can see, I'm serious about hiring the very best people to help us grow. In order to do that, I need your assistance.

[The referral form mentioned in this letter is found in Appendix F.]

line like, "Join the McDonald's team. All that's missing is you." It shows customers a picture of a diverse group of smiling employees with the caption, "Earn extra money, set your hours, meal benefits, free uniforms, and job variety. McDonald's is now hiring." Every customer is a potential candidate or source of referral.

There are many ways you can tap into this source. One gourmet coffee shop in my area proudly displayed a typed ad for employment in a picture frame next to the cash register. A large video chain made up preprinted business cards advertising a vacancy and handed them out to selected customers. Many businesses put a help-wanted sign in the window. Others print up help-wanted flyers and put one in every customer's bag. You might include a flyer in your monthly mailings or bills. If you have a waiting room, keep referral forms and a pencil on the table. If your product is delivered to your customers, send an employment flyer as well. You can also choose to be more selective by only giving your flyer to those customers you would like to recruit. Any method used to keep in touch with your customers can be used to remind customers of your need and personally invite them to refer job applicants.

College Campus Recruiting

Recruiting on college campuses was once thought to be only for Fortune 500 companies, but today it is a major source of highly qualified candidates for smaller businesses. As corporate downsizing continues to reduce the workforce, fewer new college graduates are hired by large companies. Not only has downsizing reduced the number of companies recruiting on college campuses, it has also reduced the attractiveness of Fortune 500 companies. Many of today's college grads are very eager to explore opportunities with entrepreneurial companies and small-to-medium-sized businesses where they can grow with the company. This recruiting method is a useful strategy if you have several similar positions open and will need candidates over a period of time. For filling one specific position, it may not be effective.

To recruit on a college campus, begin by contacting career services or the career placement center. Tell them you would like to set up a recruiting opportunity on campus for the students and provide information on your company, the job, and the candidate requirements (from Chapter 2). They will usually publicize your visit and schedule a day for interviews. When students sign up, the career center generally handles all the details. In fact, if the career center has a clear idea of the kind of applicant you're seeking, the staff will screen out individuals who do not fit your hiring criteria.

Campus interviews are usually tightly scheduled one after another. It's important to adhere to the schedule so you don't lose the opportunity to meet with students who need to leave for their next class. These interviews allow you to meet potential candidates and determine which ones you would like to interview again in depth. With so many applicants, you need to keep accurate notes on each person you meet and which ones you'll contact at a later date.

Internships

Internships let you preview top-notch college candidates and provide them with real world experience in business. Today most top candidates have had at least one internship while looking for full-time employment. The Charleston, South Carolina, *Post and Courier* reported that a 1995 study showed 33 percent of U.S. college students participated in an internship compared to 26 percent in 1980. Obviously internships are becoming more popular because they allow job candidates to test the waters while employers test the candidates.

An internship gives you a talented, motivated, short-term employee at a very reasonable rate without having to pay benefits. Some internships are completely unpaid, but to attract the highest qualified, most productive candidates, you may have to offer at least entry level compensation. (Be aware that the U.S. Fair Labor Standards Act restricts the kinds of tasks that unpaid interns or trainees may perform.) If the intern is someone you would like to hire permanently, you can get a jump on the competition before he or she even starts looking for full-time employment. Many interns accept positions even before campus interviewing starts. If the intern is not the kind of employee you're seeking, you have no long-term commitment to this person.

To investigate possible internships, contact the career placement service at your local college or university. Give specific details of the job such as hours, duties, compensation and length of internship. Your offering will be advertised to the students through department heads, flyers, radio announcements, and ads in the school paper. Be sure to check your recruiting plan in advance to help you decide how and when students should respond.

Career Nights

Career nights, or open houses, can be useful in recruiting personnel, especially in industries that require specific training, such as insurance or real estate. They are also effective when you need to fill a significant number of positions within a short time, such as opening a new location. Conducting a career night requires a great deal of planning, but in just a few hours, you can find and screen a large number of potential applicants.

Objectives of a Career Night

At a career night you want to

- create an awareness of career opportunities in your company or industry.
- generate significant applicant or candidate flow.
- allow large numbers of individuals to be screened at one time.
- easily coordinate quick follow-up interviews with potential candidates.
- best utilize time to speed up the hiring process.

Publicity for a Career Night

The key to the success of a career night is publicity. The task is to get the message to a large group of potential applicants and persuade them to invest thirty minutes to an hour to investigate career opportunities. It is essential to use many publicity sources because any one source will not generate sufficient response. You might try the following.

Newspaper ads. An ad in the local paper's Sunday classifieds will draw a group of attendees. However, it may be the same group that would apply if you ran a help-wanted ad. You will need to be more creative by putting the career night announcement in the upcoming events section or advertising in the sports or business section.

Radio ads. Radio ads aired during morning and evening commuting times will usually reach people not actively looking for a new job, thus producing results you cannot get from newspaper advertising. In a subtle way, these ads also promote your business.

College placement centers. Career centers will help you publicize your career night on their bulletin boards. Don't overlook community colleges, junior colleges, or technical schools—they may also have candidates who match the job as well as students from four-year colleges. Sometimes schools will also volunteer to hold your career night on campus and assist in the preparation and presentation.

Preprinted invitations. Invitations can be distributed by employees in your store or office, or they can be mailed to individuals who are identified as potential candidates. The invitation should request an RSVP, and invite interested candidates who cannot attend to call for a Career Opportunities Packet (described later). Invitations can either be created on your computer or by your local print shop.

Job services. Local agencies and organizations devoted to assisting individuals in securing employment, such as the Employment Security Commission, will help publicize your event.

Posters. An inexpensive way to advertise to a very small geographic area, a poster can be put into a store or office window. It can also advertise a business that is going to open soon and needs employees. Local print shops and graphic art studios can help you design and print your poster.

In-store notices. Place in-store notices that advertise your career night in an area of your business where there is customer and employee traffic. Put them up at least two weeks before your career night.

Employee referrals. You can use employees to help you draw attendees to your career night by giving each one invitations to distribute and offering a prize to the employee who draws in the most people. This can be tracked by coding the invitations.

Customer referral. Your own customers are a good source of potential attendees for the career night. Ask them to identify people with a job similar to the one you are trying to fill. This information can be used to send invitations or call the referrals directly and invite them to the career night. Not only are your customers likely to identify excellent candidates, but you will make them feel important.

Timing

The best time for a career night is generally late afternoon until early evening—about 4:30 to 7:30 (Specific times will depend on work and traffic patterns.) Your career night can be held on one night or two consecutive nights. Tuesday is the best day, Wednesday second best, then Thursday. Stay away from Mondays and Fridays. A typical agenda will take 30 to 45 minutes to complete so you can offer it two to four times in one evening.

Support Materials

You will need a career opportunities packet to hand out to each attendee. This information packet is a versatile tool that can be used not only at a career night, but also to mail to referrals, or to present to interviewed applicants. The packet can be a simple pocket folder that contains

- a letter from the company president about career opportunities.
- the history of the company.
- positive and informative quotes from employees.
- a list of company locations (if any).
- a sheet defining positions available and opportunities for career advancement.
- the method for applying for a job.

Make sure contact information for your company is on each packet.

Career Night Agenda

The following agenda for a career night or open house will give you an idea of what to do, but don't hesitate to create a program tailored to your company's needs.

1. Greet your guests at the door and ask them to sign in with their name, mailing address, phone number, and if desired, their current employer. Give each person a name tag.
2. During your introduction
   - thank participants for coming.
   - give an overview of how career night works.
   - summarize the history of your industry.
   - talk about opportunities and challenges in your business.
   - explain the basics of the open positions.
   - briefly share the opportunities.
3. Have an experienced employee or promising new hire share his or her success story.
4. Mention the training and support available to assist new employees. Have a display table with sample training materials.
5. Answer questions.
6. Thank attendees for participating and invite them to have some refreshments, review the career opportunities packet, and talk to you individually if they wish.

By the end of the night you should have identified a few qualified individuals and invited them to return for an interview. You can also expect to receive resumes from several attendees that you can review at a later time. Be sure to send a follow-up note to each attendee within two or three days to thank them for coming.

Online Recruiting

The computer age has made it possible to find qualified candidates online. In a 1997 survey conducted by the Olsten Forum, 17 percent of the companies surveyed accept resumes online and 30 percent were considering this option. Online recruiting is definitely an employment tool of the future for companies of all sizes.

Searching for Applicants Online

The Internet opens a whole new world to the recruiting process. But unfortunately, the Internet is not as neatly organized as a newspaper's classified section. It is vast, complex, and ever-changing. But with some creativity, you can make it an active part of your recruiting efforts. If you plan to recruit online, consider these five approaches.

1. Create your own Web page on which you describe your company and list your employment needs. This is not a very effective way to find qualified candidates, however. Kurt Wagner, reference librarian and online specialist at William Paterson University in New Jersey, feels that this method is like tacking your ad to a tree in the park—you're not targeting the audience you're trying to reach.

   Company Web pages are more useful as a public relations tool to spread information about your company and your employment needs to applicants you have already found through your other advertisements. For example, you can post your online address on a flyer to draw applicants to your Web page. Then provide a link on your Web page that will take applicants straight to a section that lists employment opportunities. This method is similar to print advertising, but can contain more details because you're not paying by the word. Advertisements placed on your own Web page can also be easily and quickly changed to match your changing needs.

2. Use online headhunters for specialized or hard-to-fill positions. You can locate these companies by using a search engine to find the term *headhunter*. You can also try terms like *job placement, recruiting,* or *personnel*. Keep in mind that what you find may not necessarily be reputable or reliable. Anybody can go online and claim to be a nationally famous accredited headhunter.

3. Use search engines to locate applicants. You can, for example, type in "sales clerk seeking employment." However, this may lead to a very time-consuming task. A recent search of this term yielded 2,661,366 pages of possible applicants.

4. Post your job listing on a Usenet newsgroup. Many of the large sites, like Career Mosaic, have a newsgroup searching function that allows potential applicants to look for a job using keywords to narrow the field. A person looking for a job as a sales clerk can search by category (retail sales), state, job qualifications, job title, and even a specific company name. You can post your job opening in a newsgroup for a fee. Career Mosaic charges from $40 to $150 per job listing. (See Figure 7.7 for more job sites.)

5. Communicate with applicants through listservs. These highly focused electronic mailing lists have subscribers interested in a specific topic. There are literally thousands of these lists in all subject fields, especially profes-

FIGURE 7.7 • Online Databases

CareerWEB (www.cweb.com)
phone: 757-446-2757
fax: 757-627-2175
CareerWEB benefits human resource managers and recruiting managers by providing a cost-effective method to run job listings worldwide for $40 to $65 per job listing per month.

Cors. Inc. (www.cors.com)
phone: 800-323-1352
fax: 708-250-7362
With over 8,000 clients and the most extensive employment database, Cors continues to be the largest resource offering a full range of recruitment research products.

Global Intelligence Network (www.gi-network.com)
phone: 800-52-GLOBE
fax: 312-684-5623
Global Intelligence Network's all-encompassing and comprehensive recruitment programs include receptions, outsourcing, 800-Response management, recruitment research, private receptions and recruitment advertising.

Career Mosaic (www.careermosaic.com)
phone: 650-812-9851
Career Mosaic is a large recruiting site with ads from more than 200 employers. The service draws from hundreds to thousands of job seekers each month.

Remote Job Listings (ww2.wilpaterson.edu/wpcpages/career/joblinks.htm)
This site offers you an index of a dozen or more resources.

America's Talent Bank (atb.state.nj.us/atb/seeker/index.html)
This is an excellent site to view resumes posted by users looking for employment.

FIGURE 7.7 • Online Databases (continued)

Other Sites of Interest

America's Job Bank (www.ajb.dni.us/index.html)

Career City (www.careercity.com)

Career Mart (www.careermart.com/main.html)

CareerPath (www.careerpath.com)

Employment Services by Field (www.jobweb.org/catapult/jfield.htm)

High Tech Careers (www.hightechcareers.com)

JobTrack (www.jobtrak.com)

Monster Board (www.monster.com)

TOPjobs (www.topjobsusa.com)

sional and academic areas. Interested individuals subscribe to a listserv for free by placing their e-mail address into the subscriber pool. Subscribers then talk to each other about topics that interest the targeted group and also advertise open positions. It's like gaining the advantages of both advertising and networking. Your online provider may have a Web resource called "electronic discussion groups" that summarizes, categorizes, and provides access to hundreds of different listservs. You can also find listservs at www.tile.net or www.liszt.com to help you fine-tune your search in your employment field.

The Internet offers vast possibilities to the business owner looking for qualified employees. But before you grab your mouse, keep in mind Wagner's words of caution: "There's no one, best, sure-fire way to use the Internet for employment recruiting; that's one of its inherent weaknesses. Still, it's certainly a great place to advertise if you can get your ad in a place where the people you're after will see it."

Creative Ideas

Over the years I've noticed that companies continually come up with creative ways to recruit job applicants. This list highlights some innovative techniques that may work for your company:

- A Val-Pak franchisee in Atlanta inserted a help-wanted coupon in its regular mailing to all the homes in Atlanta.
- A rental organization offered customers a certificate for free rent if they referred an individual who was later hired. This strategy created a great deal of response and filled the position.
- A regional pharmacy created an 8½" by 11" help-wanted flyer and distributed it in the Sunday paper along with the sale catalog.
- For entry-level or unskilled positions, state and federal organizations such as your state's Job Service can be helpful.
- Direct mail has been used when the job has a tightly targeted market, such as a technical position. By purchasing a list from a professional organization or mailing list company, you can literally put your message in the hands of potential employees.
- Organizations like the Welcome Wagon or Newcomers' Club are a source of talented people who have recently moved to the area.
- Look for layoffs or a business closing in the area. Human resource departments are usually very helpful in directing qualified individuals to potential employers.
- Alumni associations actively help graduates find employment. They usually focus on graduates who have been in the workforce for several years.
- Senior organizations are a good source of reliable, motivated workers for full and part-time positions.
- Bankers are a good source of referrals when you are seeking professional people. They have many contacts in the community, are able to get the word out that there is an opening, and may generate a referral.
- Contact a local college professor who teaches a course to potential employees. Suggest speaking to the class about a topic of interest. Later, the professor can direct you to the best candidates before campus recruiting begins.

The key to good applicant flow is to utilize all sources of candidates. You need to look beyond the obvious, beyond what jumps to mind. Think carefully and creatively about where you can find the A level employees for your business. Then go after them.

Frequently Asked Questions

Q. When income is listed in an ad how realistic does it have to be?

A. Like anything else stated in an ad, the salary information stated should accurately portray what the company offers. If income is exaggerated or stated inaccurately, it is a poor basis for a relationship. If the income is based on bonuses, commissions, and other incentives, it should be clearly labeled as "potential" so you don't mislead the applicant or create an implied contract if the individual takes the position based on the information in the ad.

Q. My business is located in an "undesirable" location so the response to my ads is low. What can I do?

A. You can use a "blind box" ad that asks applicants to send their responses to the publication (such as the newspaper), which, for a fee, forwards them to you. Or, you can rent a P.O. box in a more desirable town and have respondents send their resumes there.

Q. How often should I change the ad copy?

A. Any advertisement begins to lose its effectiveness after it has been used and becomes familiar to readers. It is especially true of employment ads because repeat ads lead people to believe that the company has a hard time attracting applicants or there is a great deal of turnover—both warning signs of a bad employment opportunity. If you run your ad continually, it's a good idea to re-examine it as soon as the responses begin to taper off. If you run your ad only when you need a new employee, you can change the ad each time it runs, by simply changing the lead.

Interview Candidates and Select Your New Employee

CHAPTER 8

Screening Applicants

LEARN TO READ BETWEEN THE LINES
TO SEE THE REAL APPLICANT.

If you've successfully solicited candidates for your position, you now have a pile of responses to sift through—looking for gold. A rule-of-thumb says you should continue to look for candidates until you have a number that meets your "must" requirements and you are comfortable that you can make a selection without compromise. Now you are ready to begin the screening process.

This first step in the screening process should be quick because you're separating the good from the bad based on objective facts alone. Use the process outlined in this chapter to efficiently increase the likelihood of retaining the most qualified candidates for the more in-depth interview process that follows

Telephone Screening

Telephone calls are frequently used by business owners and hiring personnel as the initial screening. Phone calls allow you to quickly get necessary information and listen to the applicant's ability to communicate verbally. You have to be careful with these interviews, however. An applicant may feel that a phone screening doesn't give ample opportunity to present credentials and pursue employment if it is not done well. You should make it clear that this is not a formal interview, but rather a screening to determine which candidates to pursue further.

If you have asked candidates to apply for the job by calling your company, you must be prepared before the phone starts ringing. Your goal is to arrange a system for answering the phone that will not disrupt your daily business, yet will provide the information you need to determine if you want the caller to come in to fill out an application.

Decide who will receive applicant calls. Whether you take them yourself, or delegate the responsibility to someone else, all incoming applicant calls should be forwarded directly to the designated person. This person should have a scripted greeting and a list of questions that quickly zero in on key information—the job and candidate requirements listed in the job definition.

If you are looking for a sales clerk, for example, you might use this script.

Hello. Yes, this is XYZ Company. We are looking for a new sales clerk. I would like to ask you a few questions if you have time to talk.

1. *What is your current job?*
2. *How much experience do you have as a sales clerk?*
3. *How many words per minute do you type?*
4. *How much experience have you had in calculating the correct dollar amount of cash transactions?*
5. *How much weight can you lift without help from someone else?*
6. *How would others describe the legibility of your handwriting?*
7. *What are your salary expectations?*
8. *What days and hours are you available to work?*

That's all the questions I have right now. Thank you very much for calling. What is your phone number and mailing address? We will notify you of the status of your candidacy shortly.

If you find that the applicant meets your job and candidate requirements, you can invite him or her to fill out an application (if not done so already).

Resume Screening

If you have asked applicants to forward resumes to your company, you need to screen them to select candidates. Most often resumes are used for management and skilled positions only, but if you've requested an employment history for any position you can also use the following criteria to evaluate your candidates.

There is no singular criteria that can be used to evaluate a resume, because they come in so many styles, formats, and even colors. You may receive traditional resumes that list background and experiences in chronological sequence, usually starting with the most recent job. This tends to be straightforward, including dates of employment, positions, companies, locations, and a description of each job. You may also receive functional resumes that group the specific activities in which the candidate has experience. These activities are generally grouped into functional areas of business such as marketing, sales, or management, and place all the applicant's abilities under a heading. A functional resume makes it difficult to understand where a candidate's expertise was gained or job stability, but conversely, it offers an easy-to-understand snapshot of the applicant's capabilities.

Depending on the submission possibilities you presented in your ads, you may receive resumes in person, by mail, by fax, or online. Whatever the form or method of delivery, each one will first be evaluated by its appearance—it's human nature to make judgments on the way things look. Some resumes will be long, others a single page. Some will be presented conservatively on white paper with black ink and traditional font; others will be presented creatively on day-glow purple paper with orange ink in varying type styles. Your personal reactions to the appearance will immediately influence your screening. If you need a creative personality who can "think out of the box" you may jump at the purple one. But if you're looking for someone who can strictly follow a conservative company policy on dress and manner, you may not even give this one a second glance. This is a very subjective, but real, way to weed through the pile.

Next, you look at the content. Be aware that what you read on a resume is not necessarily what you get. Applicants view resumes as a marketing tool to get a foot in the door—not a factual document. They often claim to have competence in areas with which they are only vaguely familiar. They may confuse the real meaning of the words *resign* and *terminated*. They may use selective memory to relate work history. With thorough investigation you can uncover many inaccuracies and even outright lies in any batch of resumes.

Each year the firm of Jude M. Werra & Associates of Brookfield, Wisconsin, publishes a Liars Index. Year after year, the firm reports that almost 15 percent of management and executive level candidates misrepresent their academic credentials, despite the ease with which they can be verified. It is interesting to note that in a recent update Werra found 72 percent of the executives caught lying about their education were sales management candidates. Apparently many of these candidates view resumes as just another marketing tool designed to sell rather than represent the truth. (Background checks will be discussed in detail in Chapter 11.)

Once you've discarded resumes that fail the appearance test and you're prepared to keep a skeptical eye on the remaining resumes, you can evaluate each using the same criteria for judging applications described in the next section.

Application Screening

The selection process moves into high gear when the candidate fills out an application. This may be the second step after a resume has been submitted, or it may be your first contact with an applicant, depending on the application process you've determined in your recruiting plan (see Chapter 6). Job applications require applicants to list exact dates of employment, duties, responsibilities, salary, reason for leaving, and other key information. They also provide a uniform record of the credentials of all candidates. (See Chapter 5 for detailed information about job applications.) With completed job applications stacked in front of you, begin to sort them to create a pool of applicants to interview. The following tips will give you criteria to use while sifting through your pile. Figure 8.1 also outlines red flags to look for on an application.

Tips for Sorting Applications

Reject sloppy or incomplete applications. If the individual does not consider the application important enough to neatly complete it, he or she will prob-

FIGURE 8.1 • Application Red Flags

- Information not complete or areas omitted

- Application illegible or sloppy

- Gaps in employment record

- Short tenure in positions without logical reasons

- Vague information, such as salary stated in round numbers as in $8/hour or $20,000 per year

- Lack of expected progression in job responsibility and title

- Lack of valid reason for leaving job

- Inconsistent career moves such as into and out of sales several times

- Description of job duties not consistent with title

- Lack of supervisors' names at past employment

- Past experience inconsistent with position applied for

- Work history or education would logically not provide experience or skill to meet musts

ably not give the job proper attention and effort. It is unreasonable to expect every qualified candidate to have beautiful handwriting, but the overall appearance and completeness of an application is a key factor to consider in the screening process. Keep in mind that some foreign-born applicants may lack English language skills, but judge their applications as you would others, making exceptions for suspected language-based problems.

Look for specific information. Based on the job definition and candidate musts, look for the skills, training, and experience that are needed. Quickly determine if the candidate meets your musts.

Look for reasons not to hire. At this point in the selection process, it is easier to look for limitations or liabilities, rather than strengths. If you eliminate those who cannot do the job, only qualified candidates are kept for consideration.

Note what is not on the application. Consider the information that is provided, but also look for what's not there. Omissions in education or job experience, for example, may be more telling or important than what is included.

Look for progression and growth. Can you see evidence of career progression as the candidate moves from job to job? Or, are all the jobs at the same level? Or, has the candidate begun to slide backwards? All of these things can give you insight into the candidate's track record and success pattern.

Check the applicant's pay history. Is the candidate's previous pay in line with what your job offers? If you are offering less, you can eliminate the candidates who are already making much more. If you are offering much more than the candidate is presently making, does the candidate have the experience and skills to warrant a large pay increase?

Look for gaps. Go to the end of the employment history and find the first job the candidate held. From there, move forward developing a chronological picture of the applicant's background. Compare the ending date of one job to the starting date of the next. Are there any lengthy time gaps between jobs? Be suspect of employment dates that list only the year because they can camouflage employment gaps. Make a note to probe any gaps if you ask the candidate to return for an interview.

Look for career jumps. Does the candidate move from one industry or type of position to another? This can be reason for concern—the candidate may not have any career goals or motivation.

Look at reasons for termination. If the candidate says he or she left a job for a better career opportunity, you would expect the next job to reflect that step up. If you see no upward movement, question the honesty of the information.

Examine tenure. People tend to establish predictable patterns of behavior in all areas of life, and employment is no different. Applicants who have a history of less than one year at a job will probably continue job hopping. A consistent record of short-term employment is a predictor of future employment instability.

Identify potential interview questions. As you read through each application, record questions that need to be answered if the candidate is selected for an interview. You might want to ask about such things as gaps in employment history, reasons for termination, or missing pieces of information. Remember to make your notes on a separate piece of paper. As explained in Chapter 5, the application is a legal document that can be used to defend or prosecute claims of discrimination.

Online Screening

Increasing automation in the screening process is inevitable. Many companies are looking into using online resources to more efficiently screen the applicants they eventually invite for the traditional face-to-face meeting.

Firms such as Coopers & Lybrand are starting to hold initial screening interviews for college students on an Internet site. Students answer about 40 questions, including some requiring essay responses, to find out whether they qualify for an interview. Brinker International tried a similar approach when it opened two restaurants in California. Applicants first answered a 20- to 30-minute computerized interview that asked, among other things, how they would respond to common service mishaps presented in a video clip. Resumix Inc. of California, one of the pioneers in resume scanning services, offers another high-tech look at the future of hiring—new software that allows managers throughout a company to search through resumes from an internal pool. These companies are using cutting edge systems too expensive and impractical for most small businesses today. But they give you a good idea of where the hiring process is headed.

Screening Practice

The application in Figure 8.2 is an adaptation of an actual resume provided by a client. (The information has been altered slightly to protect the identity of the individual.) Read it and use the worksheet that follows to practice the screening process. Whether screening a resume or an application, you should be aware of the red flags that you'll find in this example.

Would you ask this candidate to come in for an interview? Let's analyze the application to decide.

- Is it sloppy or incomplete?
- Does the candidate meet your standards defined as musts?
- Do you see any glaring reason not to hire?
- Are there any omissions that concern you?
- Can you see evidence of career progression as the candidate moves from job to job?
- Is the candidate's previous pay in line with what your job offers?
- Are there any gaps in the employment history?
- Does the candidate move from one industry or type of position to another?
- Are you satisfied with the stated reasons for termination?
- Does the applicant seem to have employment stability?
- Identify all red flags.

Through this analysis, you should have noted that this is a problem candidate who will go no further in your hiring process.

This kind of screening analysis will give you a pretty clear impression of an applicant's fitness for the job. As you finish each application, you can sort them into rated piles. Some use adjectives for their piles such as *excellent, good,* and *poor.* Others prefer *no, yes,* and *maybe.* You might want to use numbers: (1) does not meet criteria, (2) meets criteria, and (3) exceeds criteria. Using these three levels of differentiation are more objective and can help move the process forward quickly. If you find that there are not enough candidates who meet or exceed hiring criteria, don't lower your standards and reach into the pile of excluded candidates. Instead, return to Chapter 7 and consider how you can attract more candidates.

FIGURE 8.2 • Sample Application

We encourage applications from qualified individuals with disabilities.

Name of applicant

First name	Middle name	Last name	Date of application
Leslie	*Chris*	*Johnson*	*July 1, 1998*

Current mailing address

Telephone number

Number and street	City	State	Zip	Area	Number
101 Oak Street	*Charleston*	*SC*	*29401*	*803*	*727 - 9186*

Permanent mailing address

Telephone number

Number and street	City	State	Zip	Area	Number
same as above					- -

Type of work for which you are applying

First choice
Retail sales clerk

Second choice
_____

Type of employment you want

Permanent ☑
Part-time ☐
Summer ☐

Any preference or restriction regarding work location
Local area

Minimum salary requirements
Open

Date available for work
a.s.a.p

Personal

Social Security Number
251-78-4961

Are you eligible to work in the United States? Yes ☑ No ☐

Are you at least 18 years old? Yes ☑ No ☐

Are you able to work flexible hours? Yes ☑ No ☐

Have you ever been convicted of a felony? If yes, list date and place Yes ☐ No ☑

Do you have a relative employed with ABC Company? Yes ☐ No ☑

Have you applied before, if so when? Yes ☐ No ☑ _____

Military

Branch of U.S. Service	Date entered	Date discharged	Highest rank attained
_____	____/____	____/____	_____

Do you have U.S. Armed Forces Reserve obligations? Yes ☐ No ☐

List any special training received: _____

FIGURE 8.2 • Sample Application (continued)

Education

Last high school and address

Wanda H.S. Mt. Pleasant

Highest grade completed

12

Did you graduate   Yes ☑   No ☐   Course or field of study _____

Business or Technical school and address   Years completed   Certificate obtained

College   School location (city & state)   Major field of study   Credits   Degree

Employment Record

List most recent employment first. Include all former employers and self employment.

Employer's Name and Phone number   Supervisor's name   Supervisor's job title

Acme Rentals   851-7157   Ed Smith   Store Manager

Employer's Address, City, State   Start pay / End pay   Reason for leaving

2408 Rivers Ave. Charleston, SC 29405 $8⁰⁰/$8⁰⁰   Employed

Describe duties   daily and monthly reports, deposits, rental of merchandise, telephone, inventory, office duties

Job title   Retail Specialist   From 8 / 97 To 6 / 98

Employer's Name and Phone number   Supervisor's name   Supervisor's job title

Coastal Exterminators   791-8888   Terry Sharpe   Owner

Employer's Address, City, State   Start pay / End pay   Reason for leaving

481 Coast Highway, Charleston SC 29407 $8⁰⁰/$8²⁵   back to retail

Describe duties   Deposits, telephone, accounts receivable, posting, warranties and contracts.

Job title   Admin. Asst./Bookkeeper   From 7 / 94 To 7 / 97

Employer's Name and Phone number   Supervisor's name   Supervisor's job title

Royal Rentals   487-5999   Michael Wayne   Store Manager

Employer's Address, City, State   Start pay / End pay   Reason for leaving

1787 Ashley Ave. Summerville, SC 29407 $7.⁷⁵/$8.⁵⁰   better job

Describe duties   Rental of merchandise, contracts, telephone, office duties

Job title   Secretary   From 7 / 93 To 7 / 94

FIGURE 8.2 • Sample Application (continued)

Employer's Name and Phone number | Supervisor's name | Supervisor's job title

James Insurance — *779-4344* | *Susan Marks* | *Office Manager*

Employer's Address, City, State | Start pay / End pay | Reason for leaving

8716 Palm Drive, Tampa, FL | *$7⁵⁰/$8⁰⁰* | *better position*

Describe duties *Posting, payments, deposits, typing policies, telephone, office duties*

Job title *Office Clerk* From *10* / *93* To *10* / *94*

Employer's Name and Phone number | Supervisor's name | Supervisor's job title

SC Highway Dept. — *741-5757* | *Gus Beck* | *Counter Supervisor*

Employer's Address, City, State | Start pay / End pay | Reason for leaving

$7⁰⁰/$8⁰⁰ | *relocation*

Describe duties *Telephone, general office duties*

Job title *Clerk 1* From *4* / *85* To *4* / *87*

References

Please provide the names of five references who know you in a work environment who are not listed above as supervisors.

1 Name | Telephone number | Occupation or position

Ted Edwards | *781-4861* | *Clerk*

Company, institution, or organization *Highway Dept.*

How long has reference known you? | Under what circumstances has reference known you?

13 years | *Worked at Highway Dept. with me.*

2 Name | Telephone number | Occupation or position

Mark Summers | *418-7944* | *Account Mgr.*

Company, institution, or organization *Royal Rentals*

How long has reference known you? | Under what circumstances has reference known you?

4 years | *He was account mgr. at Royal for several months*

3 Name | Telephone number | Occupation or position

Ralph Peterson | *?* | *Account Mgr.*

Company, institution, or organization *Royal Rentals*

How long has reference known you? | Under what circumstances has reference known you?

4 years | *Worked at Royal*

FIGURE 8.2 • Sample Application (continued)

4 Name

Allen Reeves

Telephone number

856-0896

Occupation or position

Asst. Mgr.

Company, institution, or organization *Royal Rental*

How long has reference known you?

4 years

Under what circumstances has reference known you?

Worked at Royal with me

5 Name

Sean Hightower

Telephone number

886-6169

Occupation or position

Account Mgr.

Company, institution, or organization *Royal Rental*

How long has reference known you?

4 years

Under what circumstances has reference known you?

Worked at Royal with me

I certify that the above information is true and complete to the best of my knowledge. I understand that misrepresentation or omission of facts requested on this application is cause for rejection of this application or for subsequent dismissal from employment. I authorize an investigation of any of the facts set forth in this application. I give permission to check my educational background, references, professional license, criminal record, driving record, and credit record and release any and all persons, companies, or agencies responding to such investigation from any liability for any damage due to releasing information pertaining hereto. I understand I will be required to provide information for compliance with the Immigration Reform and Control Act. I understand that I may be required to have a physical examination, drug test, and pre-employment evaluation. I understand and agree that my employment with ABC Company is entered into voluntarily and I may resign at any time.

Signature *Leslie C. Johnson* Date *July 1, 1998*

Application will be active for ninety (90) days.

Additional Information for Sales Position:

Describe your typing or keyboard skills.

Type 20 - 30 words per minute. Familiar with Word Perfect, Lotus, and Data Base.

Explain situations where you have had to demonstrate your mathematical ability such as calculating payments and handling cash.

Calculate payments in all of last four jobs. Handled cash at rental companies

Are you able to lift 40 lbs. and move it 40 feet? Yes ☑ No ☐

Can you reach and answer the phone by the third ring from any place in the store? Yes ☑ No ☐

FIGURE 8.3 • Screening Analysis—Practice

1. The application is relatively neat and complete.

2. The candidate meets the musts.

3. There is no glaring reason not to hire.

4. There is no significant omission that can be detected other than military service; however, there is a high probability that the individual did not have any military service and simply failed to mark "not applicable."

5. The candidate has moved from job to job. There is a general lack of progression. Beginning as a clerk working for the state of South Carolina, the individual performed clerical duties in an office with the exception of two positions. These positions involved retail customer contacts and tenure at each was very short.

6. Her pay rate is in line with what this job offers; however, she has not shown normal or expected progression.

7. There are gaps in the employment history. The applicant began with the state of South Carolina on 4/85 and stayed two years until 4/87. From 4/87 until 10/93 is a gap of six years and six months. There may be a reasonable explanation for the gap and it should be clarified if interviewed. Of potentially greater concern, however, is that it appears the dates of employment are inaccurate. There is a consistent pattern of employment starting and ending in the same month, which is suspicious. The last date of employment at James Insurance is in 10/94, but a starting date at Royal Rentals of 7/93 indicates an overlap in employment, which is impossible because the jobs are in different locations.

8. The candidate bounces between industries and types of positions frequently. Administrative positions are the most common, but they are not in the desired area of retail sales.

FIGURE 8.3 • Screening Analysis—Practice (continued)

9. The reasons for termination of employment are not clear nor do they appear to be candid and accurate.

10. The applicant does not demonstrate employment stability. If you decided to pursue employment, the circumstances surrounding her frequent job changes would need to be explored thoroughly through interviews and reference checks.

11. Few references are provided that appear to know candidate in last two positions. Most are from one position. This may indicate a desire to limit information about those two positions.

The Screening Interview

The screening interview refines the sorting process. Now you will talk with the candidates you selected to further weed out those who do not meet your qualifications. A quick screening interview saves you time and money by eliminating unqualified candidates before in-depth interviews begin.

The screening interview can be conducted on the phone or in person. If you contact applicants by phone, remember that you may be interrupting at a time when it is not convenient or possible for them to concentrate on an interview. When you call, always ask if it is a good time to talk for a few minutes. If not, schedule a better time to call.

The screening interview is the time to verify that the applicant meets all the requirements of the job description and candidate musts. Not all of these are listed on a resume or application and some that are, like years of experience, should be double-checked. An applicant may list the skills you require on the resume but that doesn't mean that he or she is actually trained or experienced. You can also take this opportunity to pursue your "preferred" list. Through screening interviews you can quickly eliminate those who are not candidates by asking focused, to-the-point, close-ended questions.

The sample screening interview for a sales clerk position in Figure 8.4 gives you an idea of how these interviews can very quickly get to the point. The questions are drawn from the list of candidate musts and preferred found in Chapter 2.

FIGURE 8.4 • Screening Interview Form

Name: _____ Current Job: _____

Date: _____ Phone: _____

1. What is your reason for looking for a job at this time?

2. Tell me about your current job.

   a. Do you greet customers?

   b. How many words per minute do you type?

   c. How often do you handle cash?

   d. Are you responsible for keeping any written records?

   e. How would you describe your customers?

   f. Can you lift boxes of merchandise that weigh about 40 pounds and carry them 40 feet without any help?

3. Sometimes I have to ask my sales clerks to help out in my other store or fill in for absent employees. Would you be willing to do that?

4. What is your salary requirement?

5. Do you speak any other languages?

6. What are your career goals?

NOTES:

Strengths:

Weaknesses:

Areas to be probed further:

Candidate yes_____ no_____

If you determine that the individual is a qualified candidate by the conclusion of the screening interview, you can say, "I would like to talk with you further. Can you come into our office for an interview on (date)." Or, "Someone will be contacting you in the near future to schedule the next step in the employment process."

In the event the person is not considered a viable candidate or if you are undecided, the response might be, "Thank you for talking with us; however, we have a number of other candidates to talk with so we will notify you of the status of your candidacy at a later time. If you have any questions please give us a call at (phone number)." Later, if you want to interview this person further, call back and arrange a meeting. If you decide not to pursue employing the person, send a letter of rejection as shown in Figure 8.5.

An effective, well-planned screening interview identifies all those who meet the musts in the hiring criteria to become candidates, and screens out those who

FIGURE 8.5 ▪ Letter of Rejection

Date

Mr. Bill Edwards
678 Popular Avenue
Mt. Pleasant, SC

Dear Mr. Edwards,
    Thank you for taking the time to apply for the position of salesperson.
    We have carefully reviewed your credentials and unfortunately do not find a suitable match between your background and experience and current or projected openings in our company.
    Thank you for your interest in our company. Good luck in your job search.

Sincerely,

Name
Title

are not qualified. It is important to determine early if an individual is a true candidate so you can focus your time only on those who will best fit the job.

Contacting Candidates

When you've finished sorting and screening your resumes and applications, you have two kinds of letters to write. One invites qualified candidates to come in for an interview to continue through the hiring process (Figure 8.6). The other notifies applicants that their qualifications do not meet your needs (Figure 8.5). You can copy these samples directly, or adapt them to fit your needs. Even if you

FIGURE 8.6 • Letter of Invitation to Interview

Date

Mr. Bill Edwards
678 Popular Avenue
Mt. Pleasant, SC

Dear Mr. Edwards,
   Thank you for taking the time to explore employment opportunities with our company. I was impressed with your background and experience.
   I would like to schedule a time to meet with you to continue exploring a match between our employment needs and your career interests. Please call me to schedule a time to visit our office for about one to two hours.
[Or: I would like to meet with you at our office on Tuesday the 15th at 9:00 AM for about one to two hours.]
   I am looking forward to meeting you. [Please call me or Beverly to confirm this appointment.]

Sincerely,

Name
Title

contact the applicants by phone or e-mail, you should use these letters as scripts to give each individual clear and accurate information without miscommunicating the message.

FREQUENTLY ASKED QUESTIONS

Q. *If I find a small error on a resume, such as an incorrect employment date, is that a problem?*

A. It is not uncommon for typos to occur on resumes, especially with dates. If the error was unintentional and not designed to cover a gap in employment, it is not a problem. However, once an error is detected, a resume should be checked very closely because there is a high probability it contains more erroneous information.

Q. *How can I tell if a person used a professional service to create the resume?*

A. It is very difficult to tell. If you want a better indication of a person's writing and organizing abilities, take a good look at the cover letter or the application.

Q. *What does it mean if a person says he or she left a job for a better opportunity, but the next position is at the same level and income?*

A. There are a number of things that can be considered opportunity. Examine carefully the reasons for leaving other positions. If there is a consistent pattern of leaving for better opportunity, but the next position doesn't reflect advancement or increased income, that may not be the real reason for leaving. If the applicant appears to be qualified and is offered an interview, this fact should be probed further at that time.

Q. *Once I see resumes or applications of several top candidates do I really need to screen all the other applications and resumes?*

A. Yes. Experience has shown that it is a good idea to screen all responses to avoid having a superior candidate go undetected or choosing a group of candidates that doesn't live up to your expectations in interviews.

CHAPTER 9

Preparing for the Interview

BUILDING A SOLID FOUNDATION
BEGINS WITH PREPARATION.

Preparing for the employment interview is essential. Too often the busy business owner or manager schedules an interview and doesn't think about how to conduct the interview until the applicant arrives. This is one more reason many small-business owners hire unqualified people who cost them money down the line.

To prepare for your interviews, you'll need to first think about the logistics of when, where, and for how long. Then consider what style of interview you want to use and what questions you want to ask.

Styles of Interviews

Over the years several different styles of interviews have been developed to fit specific needs. Keeping in mind that no one style is perfect nor addresses every need, your job is to know your options and adapt them to fit your situation.

Patterned Interview

The patterned interview forms the basis of all other interview styles. The objective of a patterned interview is to make sure all the important areas are covered. It prevents interviewers from beginning the interview with no notion of what information they must gather from the applicant. To prepare a patterned interview, take out your written job definition and hiring criteria forms (as prepared in Chapter 2). Use these facts as your guide to create the questions you will ask in the interview. Later in this chapter you will learn how to write effective questions that will be the backbone of the patterned interview.

The patterned interview allows you to compare your candidates. When they each answer the same questions, you have an objective comparative tool. This style of interviewing is especially useful in the initial screening process where you need a great deal of information quickly to determine if the applicant is a serious candidate.

The patterned interview will keep you on track so you do not forget to ask for vital information. Some interviewers feel uncomfortable about using a written list of questions because they feel it robs the interview of spontaneity and conversation. You must be comfortable with your method, of course, but the patterned interview is definitely the best way to make sure you've covered all the bases before the applicant leaves your office.

Serial Interviews

This technique is a series of interviews designed to build on the information gained from each previous interview. Information learned during each interview is compiled on an interview evaluation form and passed to the next interviewer, along with any concerns, questions, and areas to be probed. The next interviewer prepares by considering notes and concerns of the previous interviewer.

The questions used in serial interviews cannot be preprinted on a standard form. Only you know how many people will be involved in each serial interview, how many questions each will ask, how the questions will be formulated to probe deeper with each interview. You want to formulate questions based on what is learned in each successive interview, so be sure to allocate time for each interviewer to review the evaluation form and create questions in advance. Without a progressive plan of questioning and a record of the previous interview questions and concerns, you will end up with several people asking each candidate the exact same questions.

A serial interview style is useful because it connects one interview to the other, creating a progression of deeper and more meaningful conversations. But it has its drawbacks too. First, serial interviews require that you have several people qualified and available to give interviews. And secondly, it often takes more time than other types of interviews. There must be time between each interview to allow the next interviewer to analyze the results of the previous interviews and prepare to use that information in the next interview.

As you begin to set up your interview structure, consider the serial interview only if you have the time and assistance from others qualified to interview.

Panel Interview

This style combines the best of the patterned interview and the serial interview—several interviewers using a prepared set of questions. The difference is that the interviewers sit together to hear the candidate answer the questions. This is most useful in companies where there are several supervisors and/or managers who can sit on the panel. It is advantageous to you because it saves time and also gives all those involved in the hiring decision the same opportunity to see and hear the candidate's responses. The applicant gets to meet with several decision-makers at once and is saved the time and effort of coming back for serial interviews.

The major drawback of this style is that it can be stressful for the candidate who may feel "ganged up on." If you choose to use a panel interview, make sure you advise the candidate of the format, don't let it run too long, and be sure to designate an effective panel leader.

Electronic Telephone Interviews

Electronic interviews are becoming more popular in businesses of all sizes and certainly will become more common in the future.

Pick & Pay Shoes uses an electronic method of interviewing provided by an outsourced company that creates and implements computerized telephone interviews. After an individual has been screened by the store manager, the applicant is given a toll-free telephone number to call for an interview. The telephone interview consists of a series of questions designed by management at Pick & Pay. The questions focus on honesty, work attitudes, drug use, candor, dependability, and self-motivation. Applicants answer yes or no to the questions by pressing keys on a telephone. The total interview takes seven minutes. There are 57 standard questions with a subset of questions to be used based on responses to previous questions. Not only does the computer record the response, it also measures the time it takes the applicant to answer. For example, if the question, "Are you willing to take a drug test today?" causes a long delay, the computer will continue to ask related questions.

Immediately after the applicant hangs up, his or her responses are faxed to the interviewers at Pick & Pay who interpret them. Each applicant receives a follow-up phone call from one of the interviewers to probe questionable responses more thoroughly. If satisfied with the candidate the interviewer calls the store manager and makes a hiring recommendation. According to Pick & Pay, since the new interviewing strategy began in 1991, turnover has been cut in half, and shrinkage, mostly caused by employee theft and shoplifting, has been cut by 39 percent.

If you're interested in this type of interview you will need to hire a computer consultant to set up the program. This initial investment will cost several thousand dollars. You will also need to use a personnel consulting firm that can design the interview process and advise the computer consultant to ensure the interview works. This option is most appropriate for businesses that do a significant amount of hiring, but it may be too costly for those that hire for only a few positions each year. Remember, the goal is not simply to have an automated interview process, but to improve your hiring process.

The Logistics of an Interview

Before you pick up the phone to schedule an interview, think about the details of time and place. Many job applicants can tell stories about the interview that was delayed while the interviewer scurried around looking for a place where they could both sit down. Some interviews have been held in noisy restaurants, others while standing on the shop floor, and others in the middle of a busy day with constant phone and personal interruptions. This is not the way to conduct an effective interview—but it happens too often to be omitted from this discussion.

When planning your interview schedule, look back at your recruiting plan (see Chapter 6). Here you outlined who will be in charge of interviews and when you plan to begin. Use this information to select a location. It should be a quiet place free of distractions and interruptions. You want to be able to concentrate on the interview and you want the applicant's full attention. When you've chosen a spot, double check to make sure it's a clean area with chairs and that it's available when you need it.

Next, as you begin to schedule your interviews, decide how long each interview will run. Try to be realistic so that you have plenty of time to ask all necessary questions without rushing anyone and without having a backup of applicants in your waiting area. A typical screening interview usually takes about 15 to 20 minutes. An in-depth interview requires 45 minutes to an hour and a half. On-campus screening interviews are usually scheduled every 30 minutes.

After you've conducted several interviews, you'll have a better idea of how long it takes. You can then call the remaining applicants to schedule their time. Remember, if you plan to ask open-ended questions, like those discussed later in this chapter, allow time for the applicant's responses and your follow-up.

Preparing the Interview Questions

The outcome of your interview depends on the information you draw from each candidate. The quality of this information will depend on the quality of your questions. This point in the interview preparation stage has the most long-lasting effect on the selection process. Before you schedule your first applicant for an interview, make sure you have drawn up a list of questions that will give you the information you need to make an informed hiring decision.

Close-Ended Questions

Close-ended questions are designed to verify specific information. They tend to be very focused, finite, and direct.

- Did you resign or were you terminated from your last position?
- What was the salary at your last position?
- Did you have responsibility for keeping track of inventory?
- What were the hours of your last job?

There are many times when close-ended questions are appropriate, especially when used to clarify facts on a resume or application during an initial screening interview. However, if you use too many close-ended questions, the interview won't progress much beyond the factual information you already know.

Open-Ended Questions

Open-ended questions are an excellent way to prompt an applicant to provide a great deal of information in a short time. An open-ended question is one to which there is no one-word answer. These questions encourage an applicant to talk while allowing the interviewer to listen and observe the applicant's communication skills.

- What are you looking for in a job?
- Why do you want to work here?
- Tell me about your last job.
- What is the greatest challenge you've ever faced?

These leading questions are designed to get an individual to open up and provide as much information as possible. It has been said, "If you can determine what a person thinks, you can predict what he or she will do." How an applicant feels or thinks about something is the best, and usually the most reliable, way of predicting future behavior.

You can most effectively use open-ended questions by using a simple three-step questioning strategy:

1. Begin by posing an open-ended question such as, "Tell me about your last position." Listen until the applicant seems to have offered all of the information possible to answer the question.
2. Ask for more detail on a specific point of the given answer. Press for details by saying, "Tell me more about [the specific point]." Or, you might ask, "Tell me more about how you accomplished this." Or, "Tell me more about your level of performance as compared to your peers."

3. Ask a *why* question. This kind of question probes the applicant's rationale or reasons. If an individual claims to have been very successful in a position, you might ask, "Why do you feel you were successful?" Or, "Why was your success level greater than your peers?" This is an excellent way to find out if what is claimed in the interview or on a resume is factual. If someone really hasn't done what they say, it is difficult to give consistent, logical, and rational reasons for why it happened.

The problem with some open-ended questions is that they can be too vague to garner any worthwhile response. Questions like, "How did you like it at your old job?" And, "What are some of the things you did there?" are not as effective as, "What did you like most about your job and why?" Or, "What did you like least about your job and why?" Even open-ended questions should be specific. If they are not, you won't get specific information you can use to evaluate the candidate. If you have had trouble evaluating job applicants in the past, it is probably because the questions you asked and the answers you received were too vague or did not delve deeply enough.

Figure 9.1 provides some sample questions.

FIGURE 9.1 • Sample Interview Questions

Close-Ended Questions

• What were your start and end dates of employment?

• What was your specific title? Duties? Responsibilities?

• What was your starting and ending pay?

• Who were your direct supervisors?

• What was your specific reason for leaving?

Open-Ended Questions

Questions about past positions:

• How would you describe your performance at your last position?

• What do you like most about your current or previous job?

FIGURE 9.1 • Sample Interview Questions (continued)

- What do you like least about your current or previous job?

- How did you gain your knowledge about this industry?

- Tell me about the kind of customer contact you have had. Describe a typical day.

- How did you get the job at your last company?

- How well did you perform against your quota in the past two or three years?

- How did your performance rank in your company?

- How did you handle customer complaints?

- What kind of reference will you get?

Questions about this job:

- What are you looking for in a job?

- What do you look for in a company that you would like to work for?

- Why should I hire you?

- Why do you want to work here?

- What training or qualifications do you have for a job like this?

- What do you think will be the most challenging aspect of this job?

- Tell me more about how you will handle this aspect.

- Why do you want to change jobs?

- Why will this job be different from others that you have held? Similar to?

- What are your income expectations from this job?

Questions about work habits:

- What have you been praised for in the past two years?

- What have you been criticized for in the past two years?

FIGURE 9.1 • Sample Interview Questions (continued)

- What does a supervisor do to get the best out of you?

- Give me an example of a work crisis you were in and how you handled it.

- What would you do if management made a decision you did not like?

- How do you handle conflict with coworkers?

- How do you keep track of what needs to be done?

- Describe a situation where you performed at an exceptionally high level.

- How do you set goals/manage your time?

Questions about personal characteristics:

- How would a friend who knows you well describe you?

- What are the reasons for your success?

- How do you establish working relationships with new people?

Questions about values:

- What is your primary interest? Money? Power? Leisure time? Why?

- How would you describe success?

- How would you describe a successful career?

- Who do you admire and why?

- What would you do if you saw another employee steal money from the register?

- What would you do if you could not master a new computer program in the time expected by your employer?

- What would you do if you made an important business decision and another employee challenged it?

- What would you do if another employee was performing her job incorrectly?

FIGURE 9.1 • Sample Interview Questions (continued)

- What would you do if a child began screaming in the middle of the store and you saw that it was upsetting the other customers?

- What would you do if a customer left behind a sloppy mess?

- Would you feel comfortable switching to another department for the day if they were short-staffed?

Questions about attitudes:

- What is the biggest challenge you've ever faced? How did you handle it?

- How long will it take you to make a contribution here?

- What do you expect from your employer?

- Describe the ideal supervisor.

- Think of a time you have seen another person show poor judgment with a customer. Describe what happened.

- Describe the most boring job you've ever had to do.

- Show me how you would greet a customer coming into the store (office).

Questions about capabilities:

- What are your strengths/weaknesses?

- How can you take advantage of your strengths? Compensate for your weaknesses?

- What job would you like to be doing in the next five years?

- What are your long-term career plans?

- What training do you have that might be of use to this company?

- Describe an experience when you were asked to do something you were not trained to do. How did you handle it?

Legal and Illegal Questions

As you conduct your interview, there are innumerable ways you can unintentionally stray into legal difficulties. Questions asked innocently during the interview can come back to haunt you and the company. Unfortunately, even friendly inquiries before the interview, asked simply to break the ice, can land you in court. An offhand question such as "Do you have family in this area?" or "Are you related to James McDaniel that I go to church with?" could be a potential cause of trouble. Keep all questions job-related.

It is important to examine all the questions you plan to ask potential employees for legal considerations. For years lawyers have counseled clients to avoid questions that relate to age, gender, race, religion, national origin, or disabilities. But even the most savvy companies make mistakes that can open the door to a civil rights or discrimination charge. As you create your list of interview questions, be sure to review Chapter 4 to refresh your memory about the legal aspects of hiring. Also refer to Figure 9.2 for examples of illegal questions.

Today's applicants are very sensitive to the type of questions that can and cannot be asked. In addition to the federal law, you must also know state and local regulations which may be specifically applicable to your business or location. Some state civil rights statutes go further than the federal law in protecting job applicants from bias on ethnic origin, gender, sexual orientation, and even smoking during off-the-job hours.

The easiest way to stay out of trouble is to look at each question on your list and ask yourself, "Is this question truly job-related?" There is no reason to use questions that probe other areas such as a person's family life or plans to start a family. The courts have consistently said that asking for information on the grounds that it might interfere with the job is not justified. If the job requires long hours, then simply ask the applicant about his or her ability to do extensive overtime work. Also, make sure the same questions are asked of both male and female applicants. This will provide you with the information you need to make an informed decision without any legal entanglements.

For Further Study

The use of effective questions is the core of a successful interview. You now have a few tips that will help you create questions that will generate answers you can use to evaluate each candidate. If you'd like to investigate the skill of questioning further, I recommend Dorothy Leeds' book, *Smart Questions* (McGraw-Hill, 1987) and Dianna Booher's book, *Communicate with Confidence!* (McGraw-Hill, 1994). There's a lot to learn about this often overlooked area of the hiring process.

FIGURE 9.2 • Illegal Questions

- Are you married or planning to get married?

- What are your plans for a family?

- How old are you?

- When did you graduate from high school?

- What was your maiden name?

- Have you had any medical problems?

- What clubs or societies not related to work do you belong to?

- Have you ever been arrested or convicted of a crime? (You can ask if the applicant was ever convicted of a felony, but you cannot probe for non-felony convictions.)

- Where were your parents born?

- Do you belong to any religious organization?

- Have you ever changed your name? (This prevents national origin discrimination against people who may have Americanized an ethnic name.)

- When you left the military, what type of discharge did you get? (You cannot discriminate against veterans who have a less than honorable discharge, but not a dishonorable discharge.)

FREQUENTLY ASKED QUESTIONS

Q. Can I combine a serial interview in a patterned interview format?

A. Yes. Combining the elements of both creates a very effective interview that not only covers consistent topics but also is in-depth and thorough.

Q. *What is the difference between serial interviews and multiple interviews?*

A. In serial interviews, information learned in one interview becomes the basis for the next interview. Areas of concern are passed to the next interviewer so he or she can ensure these areas are addressed. In multiple interviews, each interviewer asks his or her own questions without regard to what was learned in earlier interviews.

Q. *Should you schedule multiple interviews on different days?*

A. Though you want to fill the position as soon as possible, there is an advantage to scheduling interviews on different days. This gives you a second look at the individual, whose grooming, readiness and preparation may appear different.

Q. *Should I write out all my interview questions?*

A. No. It is not necessary to write them out fully. However, it may help to write out key phrases to remind yourself of the areas you need to cover.

CHAPTER 10

Conducting the Interview

MAKING THE HEART OF THE PROCESS PAY OFF.

There is no one simple procedure called "The Interview." Effective interviewing is a process that takes time—no matter what position you're trying to fill. From the person who cleans your office to the person you trust with important business decisions, all positions should be filled with care. It only takes one weak link in your employment chain to affect the strength of your entire business.

The In-Depth Interview

During an in-depth interview you ask probing, open-ended questions that dig into the qualifications, values, attitudes, and capabilities of each job candidate. This part of the interview process is the most time-consuming and should be thoughtfully planned out beforehand. (See Chapter 9 for the details on planning the schedule, timing, and type of interview.)

The in-depth interview is easily divided into four parts: (1) the introduction, (2) the body, (3) the closing summary, and (4) the evaluation.

The Introduction

The purpose of the introduction is to relax the candidate and promote open, candid communication. Begin by greeting the candidate and talking with him or her to establish a level of rapport.

Explain to the candidate what will occur during the interview:

- Give the approximate length of the interview.
- Assure the candidate that he or she can ask questions at the end of the interview.
- Explain that the focus of questioning will be on the candidate's interests, background, skills, and career objectives.

118

- Ask the candidate for permission to take notes by saying something like, "What you say is important and I want to be sure I remember it. I am going to be taking notes. Is that okay with you?" This will remove the candidate's fear that something is wrong when you jot down information.
- State the fact that a hiring decision will not be made at the end of the interview.
- If you require additional interviews in your hiring process, explain this to each candidate.
- Tell the candidate when and how you will notify him or her of your decision.

The candidate should now feel more comfortable and be ready to focus on the interview without wondering about what will happen next.

The Body

In the body of the interview, use the open-ended questions you have prepared in advance. As detailed in Chapter 9, these questions probe the candidate's past positions, qualifications for this position, work habits, personal characteristics, values, attitudes, and capabilities.

Remember not to ask about family, spouse, children, age, nationality, health, or disabilities. Some interviewers feel if the candidate volunteers information it is "fair game" to explore further—but it is not. The best way to handle the situation is to avoid commenting on the information and steer the discussion back to a work-related topic. Be aware that the candidate might volunteer information and then, if turned down, file a charge of discrimination. Even if the interviewer makes a simple comment like, "Oh that's interesting," a disgruntled candidate might claim the subject was discussed in the interview. Your best response would be, "Information like that is not considered in making a hiring decision. Let's move on to an area that is considered." (See Chapter 5 for a review of questions that can get you into legal trouble.)

With prepared questions in hand, your responsibilities during the actual interview are to (1) listen carefully to what each candidate says, (2) use any moments of silence during the interview to study the candidate, and (3) invite the candidate to ask questions and then evaluate the quality of these questions to learn more about this person.

Using active listening. When you ask open-ended questions you need to actively listen to the response. Active listening is the process of being actively involved in the conversation while saying very little, not interrupting its flow, and encouraging the individual to continue talking by using phrases like these:

- Go ahead. I'm listening.
- Tell me more about that.
- Yes, go on.
- You were saying?

You want to encourage the candidate to fully respond to your questions. If you do not use active listening, your own voice dominates the interview and you learn little about the candidate.

Overcoming the fear of silence. Many interviewers are unable to wait for a response to a question. If there is any significant pause, they fill in the silence themselves, taking the candidate off the hook. To be an effective interviewer, it is very important to become comfortable with silence. After asking tough questions, make yourself stop, focus on the candidate, and listen.

During the silence, use direct eye contact and take note of what happens. Some people are very uncomfortable with eye contact because of their level of self-confidence or problems with direct communication. They may not be able to look you in the eye, especially when asking or responding to thoughtful questions. What happens during the silence that keeps the individual on the spot will tell you much about the candidate's ability to deal openly and assertively with other people. Sometimes, it's not *what* an candidate says in response to a question, it's *how* he or she says it.

Figure 10.1 outlines the strategies discussed above.

Learning from questions asked. At the end of this part of the interview, invite the candidate to ask questions of you. Note the type and tone of questions the candidate asks because they can tell you more about the candidate than his or her responses to your questions.

A serious candidate should come to an interview prepared with a basic knowledge of the company. If you hear questions like, "What do you manufacture?" this is a sign that the candidate hasn't taken the time to research the position and match it to his or her own skills and goals.

A candidate who asks questions that show an interest in staying and growing with the company is the kind of candidate you're seeking. Take note of questions like, "How do you reward your people who are successful?" or, "What will I have to do to meet your expectations?" If the individual's interest is in security, they will ask questions about retirement, benefits and tenure such as, "What type of retirement plan do you have?" or, "How long have most people been here?" But beware of the candidate who asks questions that indicate a selfish or short-term view of employment like, "How long do I have to work before I can take a vacation?" Or, "How many sick days do I get?" Or, "What's the earliest I can leave each day?"

FIGURE 10.1 • Interview Strategies

There are a number of things you can do to improve the quality of the interview.

- **Don't talk too much.** Limit the conversation to job-related topics. A good rule-of-thumb is to have the candidate talk 80 percent of the time, which means you must be silent all but 20 percent of the time.

- **Provide short, noncommittal responses.** One of the biggest time-wasters is giving elaborate responses or comments to the candidate's answers. Focus your time on listening and asking questions.

- **Limit interruptions.** During the time you have scheduled for interviews, do not give your attention to telephone calls or other interruptions. If the interview must be conducted in a public place, like a restaurant or store, position yourself with your back to the area of greatest distraction. This will help you focus more on the candidate than your surroundings.

- **Take notes while the candidate is talking.** This is an excellent way to stay focused and record responses you want to remember and also to plan follow-up questions for later in the interview.

- **Listen carefully to responses.** Listen to each answer all the way to the end. Some interviewers miss the end of a response because they are thinking ahead to the next question.

- **Don't rush the questions.** Pause after the response to ensure the candidate has finished. Give yourself time to register a reaction and allow time to develop the next question.

Red flags. Occasionally, something comes up during the interview that indicates an issue that should be resolved before an individual is considered for employment. These red flags are your perceptions of inconsistencies or patterns that need further probing. Such comments about past employment as the following should alert you to ask for more information:

- The company had management problems.
- They favored others in promotion.
- I am not progressing as fast as I should.

- There is not enough opportunity at the company for promotion.
- The job was temporary.
- I don't really remember.

These comments, along with vague descriptions of job responsibilities or lack of a sound reason for termination, should be examined more closely. A red flag statement does not mean the person is not a good candidate, it's just a signal for further clarification either during the interview or in your reference checks.

Employee agreements. If you plan to ask the new employee to sign an employment agreement, you must mention this during the interview. The candidate must know early in the process that a signed employee agreement is a condition of employment so he or she does not feel coerced to sign it if offered the job. You wouldn't want to tell someone that has left a job and reported to work with you that signing an agreement is a condition of employment. Also, it would not be valid if signed under this condition.

Companies benefit from employment agreements in many ways. In some industries, it is common to compel employees to resolve disputes by arbitration rather than costly litigation. Restrictive covenants can also protect a company by barring former employees from starting a competing business, limiting employment with competitive firms under specific conditions, or disclosing the firm's confidential information. However, these covenants can be included in a stand-alone agreement without the necessity of an employment agreement. These agreements tend to be more preventive than punitive.

The Closing Summary

In closing, thank the candidate for his or her time and interest, and acknowledge the effort required to take time off from work, prepare, and come to a job interview. It's a good idea to compliment several strong points you've noticed about the candidate. Then remind each person of the time frame you've established for further contact. End with direct eye contact and a firm handshake.

The Evaluation

Immediately after the candidate leaves allow yourself time to write out a brief evaluation of the interview. You will not remember the details of each candidate at the end of a long day of interviewing. Too often, the last qualified person interviewed has the greatest chance of being hired simply because the interviewer remembers the most about that interview. If a written record of each interview is made while the impression is fresh, and that record is reviewed prior to making the hiring decision, you have a better chance of hiring the best candidate rather than just the one you remember the best.

Also use this evaluation time to identify areas to be checked or probed during reference checking. Writing down questions or points to verify later prevents important information from being overlooked.

If you conduct thoughtful, organized interviews that allow you to focus your full attention on the qualifications, personal characteristics, and future capabilities of each candidate, you will assure yourself and your company that you have chosen the most qualified new employee.

FIGURE 10.2 • In-Depth Interview Evaluation Form

In-Depth Interview Evaluation

Applicant: _____   Job: _____

Interviewer: _____   Date: _____

FACTOR	COMMENTS	RATING*
Background Experience		
Drive for Success		
Job Skills		
Work Behavioral Style		
Mental Ability		
Communication		
Additional Factors		
Overall		

*Ratings: (1) unsatisfactory, (2) marginal, (3) satisfactory, (4) excellent, (5) superior

Summary

To Clarify During Reference Checks

FREQUENTLY ASKED QUESTIONS

Q. *I don't have a private office to limit distractions so how can I conduct an effective interview?*

A. It is important to find an area where both you and the candidate have limited distractions. You might try a corner table at a small restaurant during off-peak hours. Try to sit so you are both facing the corner.

Q. *I am the only supervisor in my company. How can I get two interviews or a second opinion?*

A. It is valuable to have a second interview with candidates you are seriously considering. You might trade with an associate or friend who works outside your organization. You can swap interviews to provide each other with a second opinion. You can also use an outside consultant who specializes in interviewing, or conduct the second interview yourself on a different day.

Q. *What do I do when the candidate doesn't respond after I've asked a tough question?*

A. Be patient. Give the candidate time to think and formulate an answer. Don't become uncomfortable and let the silence push you into moving on and leaving the concern or problem unanswered.

Q. *If someone mentions an illness or medical problem in the interview, can I pursue it?*

A. No. Probe only to determine if the individual can perform the essential job functions.

Q. *What do I do if I ask an open-ended question and the candidate responds with an answer in an area that's off-limits, such as plans for having children?*

A. Inform the candidate that this area is not considered in the hiring process. Suggest the candidate focus the answer on an area such as [you supply the direction].

CHAPTER 11

Conducting Pre-Employment Evaluations

INVESTIGATING BEFORE YOU HIRE IS PRUDENT MANAGEMENT.

Once you have identified qualified candidates, you should *diligently* continue the interview process through pre-employment evaluations. These can be conducted in two steps: (1) background checking and (2) applicant testing. These two steps are too often ignored by small business owners, yet they can keep the small business person from going under.

Most large corporations are aware of the necessity of pre-employment evaluations, but smaller companies often perceive these checks as overkill. Not true! In smaller companies the need is even more critical. If you employ only four people and one of them turns out to be a poor choice that must be fired, you've lost 25 percent of your workforce! Organizations of all sizes have proven that using pre-employment evaluations can reduce turnover. In "Attracting the Right Employees and Keeping Them" in an issue of *Personnel Journal*, it was reported that Service-Master was able to cut its annual turnover rate from about 180 percent to 14 percent through extensive pre-employment evaluation. Imagine what you could do for your company if you could reduce your turnover by even 10 or 20 percent!

The time, effort and money lost every time you have to go through the hiring process due to employee turnover should be motive enough to make sure pre-employment evaluations are done.

Five Good Reasons for Pre-Employment Evaluations

Reason 1: Limit Liability

If a new employee is placed in a position where the company could be legally vulnerable (almost any position at all), pre-employment evaluation is an essential part of limiting liability. Certainly you have heard horror stories about companies who have not done this basic hiring homework, only to have the employee engage in a questionable act which resulted in loss or damage for which the company was liable. Diligent evaluation is critical to limiting legal liability.

Reason 2: Determine Prior Performance

Even if an employee does not do something that leaves you legally liable, poor performance will still cost you money. If you find out that a candidate performed poorly in a previous position, it's a good bet that he or she will repeat the same behavior at your company. Knowing in advance saves you the headache of having to fire an employee for poor performance.

Reason 3: Identify Potential Problems

Problems tend to recur. During pre-employment evaluations problems such as poor attendance, tardiness, substance abuse, a criminal history, and propensity toward theft or laziness can be uncovered.

Reason 4: Reduce Turnover

Pre-employment evaluations result in better hiring decisions, which automatically reduces turnover and increases productivity. Both are good for your business.

Reason 5: Increase Quality of Employees

Some applicants are better and more persuasive than others during interviews. By checking references, background, skills, and abilities you can identify the true superstars from those who say they are superstars.

Why Job Applicants Lie

As mentioned earlier, the Liars Index published by Jude M. Werra states that about 15 percent of applicants for top-level jobs falsify information. Because this index is published annually in a number of well-known publications, including *USA Today*, Werra hoped the attention drawn to the number of people falsifying academic credentials would reduce the index—but that has not been the case. Werra tells me that applicants for executive positions falsifying academic credentials remains steady at just under 15 percent each year. The question is: Why?

Maybe lying just doesn't mean what it used to. There were so many lies exposed during the 1992 presidential election campaign that *Time* magazine ran a cover shot of a person with a wide grin and sunglasses. The caption read, "Lying: everybody's doing it (honest)." The perception that everybody lies has taken the stigma away from telling "white" lies, omitting facts, fudging, or making misstatements.

Why do people lie in the first place? Job applicants lie, fudge, or make misstatements to conceal a shortcoming or problem, or to gain a perceived advantage. They might lack expertise in a particular area or experience in a specific discipline and want to "get their foot in the door." They may lie to cover up periods of unemployment, performance problems, or the fact that they left the position under less than desirable circumstances. Applicants rationalize the inaccuracies by stating that they help to "open the door" or compete with others who do the same thing.

It is important to state again that applicants and employers see resumes differently. Employers see a resume as a precise document that should be entirely factual. Job hunters, however, view a resume as a marketing tool and feel embellishments are natural and will be forgiven. Many lies are put on a resume early in a career to get a foot in the door or to give the applicant a greater chance of getting the position. Some see embellishing as the only way to compete for any job because "everybody" does it.

Background Checks

A thorough examination of all applicants' references should help sort out the qualified candidates. After you have interviewed your applicants, it's time to do a background check. Background checks normally include a person's criminal history, credit rating and driving record. They can also confirm employment, education and licensing. This kind of "undercover" work is now routine in many businesses largely due to the liability of negligent hiring and the legal maneuvering sometimes necessary to fire an unsuitable worker. An employee can sue for wrongful termination, so you need to be certain about a person before you hire them.

Recently, a fellow consultant shared a story about a candidate whose application only listed job experience with her father's company. She was hired without reference checks because it seemed futile to contact the father looking for a recommendation. After hiring, this new employee began a pattern of misconduct that ended when she took a sizable amount of money from the consultant's company. Finally, he began a background check that uncovered the truth. She had never worked for her father, had a consistent record as a problem employee, and left jobs several times under a cloud of suspicion of theft. This background work must be done *before* an employee is hired.

Much of the information you need is public record and available to anyone, but it is smart business to hire a professional who can do the job quickly, thoroughly, professionally, and legally. Security companies and private investigators stay very busy doing these routine checks for a minimal fee between $50 and $500 (depending on where you live and how much information you need). You can also find security investigators in the yellow pages under "Personnel Services" or "Employment Screening." They can also be found on the Internet, but tread here with caution. You must have a way of confirming an investigator's credentials, licensing, or capabilities. Ask them to provide references and credentials just as you ask applicants to verify performance. You need a reputable firm that will help you stay out of legal trouble. The firms listed in Appendix G can help you get started.

You do not have to worry about running afoul of privacy laws when conducting a background check if you've done your homework. Your application should clearly state your intention to conduct pre-employment evaluations and secure the applicant's approval. Most investigative firms will not begin without this signed form in their hands. You should also be careful to investigate only those circumstances that are directly related to the job. You need driving records only if driving is a part of the job. You want a consumer report even if the employee will not work with money. (Although it's always a good idea not to put someone who is heavily in debt too close to the cash register!) A consumer report provides data ranging from names of past employers and residential stability to divorces and estimated prior earnings.

The turnaround time for a full background investigation is usually less than seven working days. If you do a lot of hiring, you might want to develop a relationship or enter into a contract with a pre-employment evaluation firm in order to speed the process.

A word of caution about consumer reports. Increasingly, employers look to consumer reporting agencies to investigate the credit history of job applicants. Be aware, however, that under the Consumer Credit Reporting Reform Act (effective September 1997) employers must disclose in a separate document that consumer reporting will be used in connection with employment decisions. Failing to do so exposes the employer to possible civil and criminal procedures.

There are two types of reports: consumer reports and investigative credit reports. A consumer report is simply any written or oral communication made to the employer regarding the applicant's general creditworthiness, credit standing, personal characteristics, general reputation, or mode of living. An investigative credit report has the same information, but goes a lot further. It adds information from interviews with people who are close friends, neighbors, and associates.

According to the law, if you deny employment in whole or in part based upon information contained in a consumer report you must provide the applicant with (1) a copy of the credit report, and (2) a written description of the individual's legal rights concerning the use of credit reports. The credit reporting agency will provide you with a statement of these rights.

Credit checks can provide excellent information to assist in making an informed hiring decision; however, they must be used properly. It is in the best interest of the firm to receive competent legal advice on how to legally use credit checks. Since rules vary from state to state, be sure to get advice from someone who knows the local situation such as an employment consultant or an attorney specializing in labor and employment law.

Applicant Testing

There are hundreds of different tools for applicant testing, but most can be grouped into the four types discussed here: (1) integrity tests, (2) values evaluations, (3) behavioral style evaluations, and (4) job skills tests. (Physical exams and drug tests are other pre-employment tests, but they are conducted further along in the hiring process. See Chapter 13 for details.)

It is impossible to dictate which applicants must take which tests or instruments. As a general rule, integrity testing is used when the honesty of the applicant is critical, such as when handling money or merchandise. Values and behavioral instruments are used for positions that require independent decisions, such as sales or management, and when there is significant interaction with others. Job skills tests are used to verify demonstrable skills such as typing, electronic knowledge, or computer programming.

To determine which tests or instruments will benefit you in your hiring process, consult an employment specialist who is knowledgeable in the law, uses of pre-employment evaluation, and the position you're trying to fill. The following information will give you a working knowledge of the tests you can use in your hiring process.

Integrity Testing

The banning of polygraph ("lie-detector") tests in 1988 has spawned a growth industry of paper-and-pencil integrity tests. These tests ask applicants their attitudes about theft, uncover admissions of employee theft, and explore other work-related wrongdoings. They ask questions that seem to be routine and innocent, such as, "Have you ever taken any items from work that belong to the employer?" They also assess personality traits that are usually associated with irresponsible behavior such as, "I sometimes went against the wishes of my parents."

Though there is some disagreement on whether these tests invade privacy and incorrectly diagnose some people, many business owners swear that their use helps curtail employee theft and substance abuse, and predicts the individual's tenure and manageability.

The first paper-and-pencil integrity test was developed in the 1960s by John Reid, a polygraph examiner for the Chicago Police Department. Today *The Reid Report* is widely used. Two other popular pre-employment evaluations are *Orion Systems* and *Stanton Survey*. These tests are scientifically validated, reliable, time-tested, and produced by reputable companies. There are other reputable test publishers listed in Appendix G. If you choose a test that is not mentioned in this book, be sure to ask if the test has a validated scale of control questions that act as a built-in safeguard to determine whether the respondents are answering honestly. This is an important gauge of reliability. Before using any test, ask the publisher for a copy of studies demonstrating that the instrument meets all Equal Employment Opportunity Commission guidelines and does not discriminate. And also ask if they will defend you in court against charges of discrimination, at no charge, if you use their test within the prescribed guidelines and still end up with a suit on your hands—some will!

The tests are relatively easy to administer and can be done within thirty to forty minutes at the place of employment. The responses are usually called in to the testing firm which quickly returns a score and its related level of recommendation. The cost is usually less than twenty dollars per applicant. This is an excellent investment because it can identify applicants with the propensity for theft and/or alcohol/substance abuse, and it can predict level of manageability and probable tenure.

Values Instruments

A person's values determine the decisions he or she makes in business and personal life. Although values instruments might sound similar to integrity testing, they are quite different. Integrity tests focus in-depth on what impacts the behavior of theft, substance abuse, and response to authority. Values instruments can index or measure very important values, such as the drive for economic benefit or money motivation. In short, they can reveal what makes a person tick. They can also indicate the amount of drive a person has to move forward.

Being able to index or measure the strength of these values is especially critical when the position requires independent thought. We initially assume these are executive positions, but today almost all positions in smaller organizations require independent thought and initiative.

Value instruments are available from the sources listed in Appendix G. These firms generally give you a summary report that describes the individual. The cost of this kind of paper-and-pencil instrument tends to be under $20, although more complex computerized reports may be higher, and an in-depth test can cost up to several hundred dollars. Regardless of the cost, these tests are a bargain compared to the possible consequences of hiring one wrong person for a key position.

Behavioral Style Instruments

Behavioral style instruments look for certain qualities that are part of a person's natural makeup. For example, a behavioral style profile (sometimes incorrectly called a personality test) may uncover that the individual you felt would make a superior parts clerk does not like detail work and becomes bored easily. If this was not discovered before you hired this individual, imagine the chaos a few months later when you find your prized new employee has not been documenting the records well, has not placed the parts in the appropriate bins, and has brought total disorganization to the parts department. This problem stems not from lack of skill, but from a behavioral style that is not suited to the job.

Behavioral style profiles can be geared toward specific positions and are especially common in the evaluation of salespeople. Based on the individual's natural behavioral style, these tests can identify whether a person has a natural ability for a specific type of selling, such as sales floor or cold calling. Some instruments probe the individual's ability to work with customers. If an individual has a natural tendency to be direct, abrupt, and brash, this would not be an individual you would want talking with irate customers, no matter how talented he or she is in other areas. It is much better to hire an individual who naturally fits the job rather than one who has to struggle to adapt to the job.

Most behavioral style tests ask applicants to choose terms to describe themselves, such as *open-minded, bold, daring, loyal, faithful, charming,* or *delightful.* The applicant's choices are then scored to measure and predict behavior.

Most instruments that index or measure behavioral style can be used in the work place and may be scored on site. The cost for the paper-and-pencil versions generally is under twenty dollars, while detailed and extensive computer reports may cost up to several hundred dollars.

You might want to consider combining a values test with a behavioral style instrument to give you insight into how an applicant makes decisions and then implements them. In short, values determine what we do and behavioral style determines how we go about it. To really match an individual to a position, it is important to understand both the values and behavior required to do the job. For example, if an individual is applying for a sales position and has values which include a high drive for economic gratification, yet dislikes going into new situations or contacting new people, the individual would not be successful in a sales position which requires cold calling and generating new business.

Behavioral style instruments are available from the sources listed in Appendix G. Before you purchase these tests, you should get the advice of a trained professional in selection and use of these types of instruments.

Job Skills Testing

In a specialized and highly complex business environment, it is important to verify that a candidate can perform the tasks claimed in the interview. If a person claims to be able to operate a computer, type with certain proficiency, or perform other tasks, a job skills test is a good idea. A job skills test simply auditions an individual's ability to do what is claimed.

Job skills tests range from an impromptu audition, like asking the candidate to type a letter, to very elaborate tests created by outside organizations. The best tests are often those you make yourself based on the list of musts and preferreds created in determining your hiring criteria. If your list contains specific skills, such as typing, using a software package, or calculating certain math problems, a practical job skills test can be arranged. Select a few reasonably simple ordinary tasks which can be performed without having specific knowledge of your business, but will demonstrate the candidate's skill. Remember to keep these tests simple because the individual is under stress during the interview and will not be performing at the top level of their ability.

Before using a job skills test that you create yourself, it is important to ensure that both the test and its administration are legally sound:

- Use the same test for all individuals applying for the position.
- Make sure the test is job-related and reasonable. Don't ask an applicant to "sell me this pencil," for example, if selling that item cannot be related to the job. This can cause legal troubles and it's not a valid test of the skills you need for the position.
- Keep a record of each applicant's test in the folder of other employment information as outlined in "Store Employment Documents Carefully" in Chapter 4.
- Set acceptance standards in advance.
- Have a personnel consultant or an attorney specializing in labor and employment review your test before you administer it.

If you'd rather not go through the trouble of creating your own skill test, you can obtain packaged tests from professional testing companies. These are well-constructed and can provide standard scores that equate to levels of expertise. These tests are generally inexpensive, are easy to administer, and are readily available. Companies, such as Wonderlick Personnel Testing, Inc., of Northfield, Illinois, have an extensive battery of tests available and are happy to provide information about them.

Innovative Ideas

There are many ways you can match applicants to positions. The database and benchmark methods that follow are two ideas that show how employees can be evaluated. You should use an employment consultant to help you develop these methods.

Develop a Database

If you have enough employees in similar positions, you can create a database of traits or test scores common to strong performers. You can then use the database information to seek applicants whose personalities or behavioral styles are consistent with your company's best employees. Instruments can be used to measure candidates against the traits of the strong performers.

Creating Benchmarks

Some organizations have conducted their own research to determine the traits and behaviors of successful and unsuccessful employees. By evaluating employees, it is simple to determine what set of traits and values apply to achievers (and failures) in the company. Once the pattern is defined, you can select a series of statements that describe high-performing employees and compare all candidates to these statements. These statements might include

- can handle conflict with employee or customer,
- pays ample attention to details,
- handles pressure well, and
- is emotionally stable and predictable.

You might even ask candidates to rate themselves using a scale where "5" indicates "strongly agree" and "1" "strongly disagree."

These are just two more methods of pre-employment evaluation. When searching for the best candidates, look over all the options mentioned in this chapter and choose the ones that you believe will help you find the level A employee who will be a good match and stay for the long term.

FREQUENTLY ASKED QUESTIONS

Q. *What if I uncover that the applicant has been convicted of a felony?*

A. In itself, being convicted of a felony is not grounds for denying employment. To make an objective, realistic determination you must look beyond the conviction to the circumstances of the situation. For example, if a person was convicted of a non-violent and non-work related felony many years ago, it would have little bearing on a hiring decision. However, a recent conviction for theft would have direct bearing on hiring an applicant for a retail sales clerk position handling cash. If the applicant was less than truthful and did not admit to the conviction when asked on the application, it would be automatic grounds for denial of employment.

Q. *If I use a pre-employment evaluation instrument the way the creator instructs am I liable for its use?*

A. Yes. You are liable for any practices your organization conducts in selecting employees. However, many of the more reputable firms will assist you to ensure the tests are used within the law. If you follow their instructions many firms will bear the responsibility of defending you in court.

Q. *If an outside source conducting a background investigation provides information not related to the job, such as marital or family status, can I consider it in making an employment decision?*

A. No. Regardless of how it is obtained, prohibited information cannot be used in employment decisions.

Q. *Can I reject a person based solely on the results of a behavioral instrument?*

A. A behavioral instrument should never be used as the sole determination in a hiring decision. It is an excellent tool that provides a great deal of information that, when validated through interviews and reference checks, should provide a strong indication of the individual's ability to be successful.

CHAPTER 12

Checking References

PAST JOB PERFORMANCE IS
THE BEST INDICATION OF FUTURE PERFORMANCE.

Checking references is not just a passive, reactive means of fending off undesirables. It can be an aggressive, proactive way to find the best and most stable employees. Before making any hiring decision, check references to verify application information and interview impressions. It is a major mistake to skip this part of the hiring process.

Because reference checks give you an accurate way to predict a person's future job performance you would think everyone would diligently include them in the hiring process. Surprisingly, few do. Studies show that employers check references of only 10 to 20 percent of the people they hire and of this small group they check only one or two references. If you doubt these numbers, think of how many requests for references you have received as a former employer.

Sources of References

As explained earlier, your job application should ask for professional references. But keep in mind that even poor candidates can provide several favorable professional references, such as former co-workers. To make a thorough check, you'll need to go beyond the few carefully chosen references which most candidates provide. Knowing where your candidate previously worked, seek out those who best know the actual work conditions and job performance of the individual like:

- Former bosses or supervisors
- Other managers or supervisors
- Former teachers or professors
- Subordinates or those supervised
- Peers at previous positions

135

- Fellow members of professional associations
- Suppliers to the company the candidate worked for
- Customers of the company the candidate worked for

Number of References

It is important to check an ample number of references to verify facts, not for the health of your business, but also to keep you out of court. A court might hold that a perspective employer should know that the information from a single reference may be questionable, so the employer conducting only a cursory check of references can be held liable for negligent hiring (see Chapter 4 for more details). In-depth checking of multiple references is a vital part of your hiring process. By contacting a number of references, you can more accurately judge the reliability of information received and demonstrate reasonable care in the hiring process. If three references, rather than one, indicate a former employee was fired for stealing, the prospective employer can feel reasonably safe in denying employment.

In my workshops, I recommend the 3x3 Rule of Multiple Checking. This requires that you obtain three references from each of these three key sources.

1. Former bosses
2. Peers at key companies
3. Subordinates (if in management) or customers (if the job involves customer contact)

This provides a minimum of nine references and allows you to check beyond the candidate's hand-picked choices.

One of my clients has taken my 3x3 rule further. At the last in-depth interview, after the individual has passed the screening interview and pre-employment checks, the candidate is asked to complete an Applicant Reference Data Sheet. This sheet asks for the following information about each of the candidate's last four companies:

- Name of company and location
- Exact position and title at last position
- Four previous supervisors at each company
- Each supervisor's title and phone number
- Period of time each supervisor managed the candidate

This Applicant Reference Data Sheet provides up to sixteen references. From these, the manager can usually get an ample number of people to verify the information obtained during the hiring process.

After completing the Applicant Reference Data Sheet, the candidate signs an Information Release Statement that certifies the information furnished is accurate, complete, and is given in the pursuit of employment. This release authorizes the investigation of all statements contained in the application, made during interviews, and offered by references. A blank Information Release Statement is provided in Appendix I, and the Applicant Reference Data Sheet found in Appendix H can be adapted to fit your needs.

Contacting References

All references should be contacted before any job offer is made. Offering a job contingent upon satisfactory completion of reference checks is asking for trouble. If you uncover a problem it will be difficult to withdraw the offer without opening the door to an allegation of wrongful denial of employment. Schedule the time for reference checking right into your recruiting plan.

When you check references, avoid calling personnel or the human resources departments. They usually only know what is in the personnel file, not the actual person. Even if they know the individual, in most cases personnel will simply give you a "name, rank, and serial number." Instead, call the individual's former supervisor or the owner of the company. Usually, they will give you a more candid and useful response.

When you call, it is a good idea to avoid using the word *reference*. An excellent approach is to say, "John is being considered for a position at our organization. He suggested I contact you to verify a few facts about his background. Can I ask you a few questions?" Using this low-key approach gives you a much greater chance of receiving frank and accurate information.

"Stonewall" References

Once in a while you will encounter references attempting to stonewall or not provide any information at all. This may happen for many reasons. They may have negative information about the candidate they do not want to acknowledge. Some former employers may also be fearful of being sued by the candidate for defamation of character. Or it may just be the company's policy to release only the name, dates of employment, and job titles of former employees.

If the reference resists your efforts to gain useful information, try several of these approaches to break through:

- Explain that you cannot consider the candidate for the position without the needed information.

- Add that you would hate for this job opportunity to be missed because this necessary information is missing from the candidate's employment package.
- Explain that the candidate seems perfect for the position, but can't be considered any further without complete references.
- Assure the reference that if all the information given is factual and can be verified, the company cannot be held liable. Courts generally hold this "qualified privilege" which protects the reference. Remind the reference that facts honestly given or opinions honestly held constitute a solid defense against defamation claims.

If you still cannot get the information you need from a reference, ask the candidate to contact the reference to give expressed approval for the release of information. If this still does not break down the wall, simply ask the candidate for additional references. Ask particularly for someone who is no longer with the company or someone you can contact at home to speak with confidentially.

If you can't find someone to verify the individual's job performance in a company, it is a cause for concern. When performance is good, the candidate can always find someone who will confidentially share information. If no one will speak for the candidate, this is a red flag warning. Heed it.

Questions for References

The questions you use to interview references should be based on information from the application and interview that you want to confirm. If you noted any areas of concern during the interview, now is the time to explore them. If you need to verify the level of skill a candidate claims, this is the time to do it. The questions in Figure 12.1 offer an idea of the kinds of information that many smart employers seek to verify. Use them only as a guide, because your list of questions should be based on your experience with the candidate so far.

FIGURE 12.1 • Sample Questions for References

Questions regarding candidate/reference relationship

- How long have you known the candidate?
- What were your position(s) and responsibilities when you supervised the candidate?

FIGURE 12.1 • Sample Questions for References (continued)

Questions regarding the facts

- What were the candidate's start and end dates of employment?

- What was the candidate's specific title?

- What was the candidate's starting pay and ending pay?

- What were the candidate's exact duties and responsibilities?

- What was the candidate's specific reason for leaving?

- Was the candidate terminated or did he or she leave under less than desirable circumstances?

Questions regarding past performance

- How did the candidate perform compared to standards/expectations?

- How did the candidate perform compared to others?

- How would you rate the candidate's contribution to your company?

Questions regarding personal characteristics

- How would you rate the candidate's honesty?

- How would you describe the candidate's attitude?

- How would you describe the individual's work habits? How does this compare to other employees?

Questions regarding the recommendation

- What are the areas the candidate should improve to increase success in the future?

- Would you rehire? Why? Why not?

If in sales

- How did the individual work his or her territory?

- What did the candidate do when faced with a difficult situation, such as being below budget or having a difficult account?

Answers to questions like these should give you insight into a candidate's potential.

Evaluation of References

Like the evaluation of an interview with your candidate, you should not count on your memory to recall the details of your interview with a reference. Use the Applicant Reference Summary Sheet provided in Appendix J to record your impressions. Attach this form to your interview notes and you'll have another solid document to help you make your final decision.

The Applicant Reference Summary Sheet will help you quickly compare your top candidates. It allows you to rank the basic facts of previous employment as *poor, good,* or *excellent.* This form also gives you a place to note important information such as the reason for leaving this employment, strengths, and weaknesses, and the response to the very important question, "Would you rehire this candidate?" It also gives you space for making your own observations. You can record whether the reference's view of the candidate matches the candidate's own view of performance and work habits. You can also note any concerns that warrant further investigation.

If a reference provides no more than the dates of employment and a job title, make note of this and then consider the speaker's tone of voice—is it short and nervous, or pleasant and natural? If you feel there is a problem, be sure to pursue it further in other reference checks to uncover needed information and clarify any issue or concern before the individual is hired. Figure 12.2 highlights some red flags to be aware of when evaluating references.

FIGURE 12.2 • Reference Red Flags

Any situation that causes concern or caution is a red flag. You should not proceed to make a positive hiring decision until all concerns or red flags have been resolved. Here are several red flags and the concerns they raise:

- **No references are listed.**
  Someone must be able to verify the candidate's performance. No references may indicate a problem the candidate did not want to disclose.

FIGURE 12.2 • Reference Red Flags (continued)

- **No direct supervisors are listed as references.**
  This may indicate that the candidate may not want anyone to talk to former supervisors.

- **All previous companies are "out of business."**
  The companies may be ficticious to hide periods of unemployment or the candidate may want to prevent you from contacting former employers.

- **Everybody at previous companies has transferred or cannot be located.**
  The candidate may be fearful of what references might say.

- **Income inconsistent with responsibilities or title.**
  The candidate may have embellished or lied about responsibilities or title

- **Only home numbers are given for references.**
  The candidate may desire to limit access to people at the company for fear something may be uncovered.

- **Candidate says "Reference didn't like me."**
  This may indicate that the candidate was a problem employee.

- **Reason for termination is vague.**
  The candidate may be hiding the real reason.

- **Reference provides vague information.**
  This may indicate the reference does not want to volunteer damaging information.

- **Reference is overly complimentary.**
  This may indicate that the reference has a motive for wanting the candidate to be employed, such as avoiding future unemployment contribution rate increases.

Red flags themselves are not necessarily a problem, but indicate a need for further checking.

Checking references is one of the most valuable tools you have to reduce liability and improve your ability to make a smart staffing decision. Don't be tempted to cut short or eliminate the process because an individual looks like a great candidate. Just a few thorough phone calls can verify the information you have learned through resumes, applications, and interviews to help you find top performers based on past performance.

*F*REQUENTLY *A*SKED *Q*UESTIONS

Q. *What do I do if all the references were good but one?*

A. Try to find out why the reference was not good. The applicant may have had a personality conflict or a disagreement with the reference and should be viewed in context with the rest of the references. One reference that is not entirely positive does not automatically eliminate the applicant from consideration. You should make sure it is an isolated case, however.

Q. *If this is an applicant's first job, how do I get a reference?*

A. Even if this is the first full-time position, references are available. Teachers, coaches, advisors to school clubs, and part-time employers have had the opportunity to observe the individual and know how he or she approaches tasks, even in unpaid positions. Older applicants may have affiliations with service clubs, volunteer organizations, or their children's schools. How applicants handle nonpaying jobs and volunteer activities will indicate a great deal about how they handle paying jobs. If the applicant was self-employed, you can check with previous clients for references.

CHAPTER 13

Hiring the Best Candidate

SELECTING THE WINNER
MAY NOT BE AN OBVIOUS OR EASY DECISION.

Hiring the best candidate is the last step in the hiring process. To prepare for this moment, you have

- created a job description and list of candidate requirements,
- considered your staffing options in full-time, part-time, temporary, and outsourced personnel,
- reviewed the legal aspects of employment,
- created a legal and customized application,
- developed a recruiting plan,
- thoroughly and creatively recruited qualified applicants,
- screened those who applied,
- given pre-employment evaluation tests to a select few,
- interviewed the candidates, and
- checked references.

Like a professional recruiter, you have put much time and effort into finding the best candidates for your company. Now is not the time to rush into answering the ultimate question, "Who do I want working for my company?" The answer to this question must continue to be an objective one based on impartial evaluations of all the facts you've gathered on the top candidates. You have to be careful not to be awed by the "halo effect." Even if you feel a candidate is head and shoulders above the others, take time to evaluate the candidate objectively before making the decision. An objective last look will either support your initial impression of the candidate, or help you see things that weren't apparent before. The steps outlined in this chapter will show you how to choose and hire in the same careful manner you have used to find the best in the field.

Get Organized

Clear everything else off your desk and get organized. Review the job description, candidate musts and preferreds, and recruiting plan for this particular job. Place before you the employment folders of each candidate still in contention for the position. Each folder should contain

- employment application/resume.
- all screening and interview paperwork.
- the reference summary sheet (Appendix J).
- the results of all pre-employment evaluations (background checks, integrity tests, values evaluations, skill tests, and candidate behavioral style instruments).

Compile the results of all these forms on one simple Hiring Check Sheet (found in Appendix K) to easily and objectively compare candidates. The completed sheet in Figure 13.1 will give you an idea of how the information can be summarized for a candidate applying for the job of sales clerk.

FIGURE 13.1 • Hiring Check Sheet

CANDIDATE:

Name ___Bill Jones___ Date Applied ___5/19/98___

Position ___sales clerk___ Location ___downtown___

Initial Screening: Date ___5/20/98___

resume? ___✔___ yes _____ no

phone contact? ___✔___ yes ___ no

application complete? ___✔___ yes _____ no

Screening Interview: Date ___5/21/98___

Interviewer: ___Todd Joye___

___✔___ phone ___ in-person

Recommendation or notes: ___very good candidate; strong retail background; high drive for success___

FIGURE 13.1 • Hiring Check Sheet (continued)

In-Depth Interview: Date ___5/26/98___

Interviewer: _____Clyde Costello_____

Recommendation or notes: _excellent candidate looking for_
position with greater income opportunity; can grow with us

Pre-Employment Evaluations:

References:

Checked by: _Clyde Costello_____

Notes: _reliable, good sales record, high integrity_____

_____

Background check:

Areas investigated:

_____credit report — excellent_____

_____driving record — no violation in 5 yrs._____

_____education — BA in history, State University_____

Notes:_____

_____

Tests/Instruments:

Name of Test	Results
Station Survey	recommended level

Hired:

Date Offered: ___5/28/98_____ Date Started ___6/15/98___

Location: ___downtown_____ Salary $25,000 + commission

Weighing Your Needs and Rating the Candidates

Not all factors contained in candidate's folders are of equal value. Remember, you have your must list and your preferred list so that you can easily separate what is vital from what is not so essential. In this final step of the hiring process, it is time to objectively weigh each job requirement and each candidate in view of what is most important to you.

Weighing Your Needs

Looking back at your complete job description, candidate requirement list, and the folders for each candidate, select the factors you feel are the most important in aiding your hiring decision. Let's say that for the job of sales clerk you choose (1) written and verbal communication ability, (2) track record of past performance success, (3) behavioral factors such as respect for authority and a positive attitude, (4) values of honesty and determination, and (5) experience in sales.

Now assign a weight, in percentage, to each factor based on importance, so that the total value of all factors is 100 percent. If, for example, you feel that a good track record and values are most important, you may assign each a value of 30 percent, giving communication skills 20 percent, and experience and behavioral factors 10 percent each. Or, you might feel they are all equally important and weigh each 20 percent. You can weigh factors however you choose, as long as the total equals 100 percent. Then record these figures on your Final Evaluation Form (in Appendix L) under the heading "Weight."

Rating Your Candidates

Once the value of your needs has been weighed, rate how each candidate meets the needs. Some employers use a five-level rating scale and others use a three-level scale. Either one, shown in Figure 13.2, will give you satisfactory results.

FIGURE 13.2 • Rating Scales

Five-level Scale:
5: outstanding   4: excellent   3: satisfactory   2: marginal
1: unsatisfactory

Three-level Scale:
3: excellent   2: good   1: poor

Now give each job factor listed on the Final Evaluation Form a rating. A five-level rating system has been used in Figure 13.3.

When you have entered your rating of the candidate, multiply this by the weight to determine the candidate's score for each factor. In the example, the candidate for the sales clerk position earned a score of 150 for track record. The weight of 30 percent was multiplied by the rating of 5 to equal 150. All the factor scores are added to determine the final total score. The final score for this candidate is 420. I now have a very objective number with which to compare this candidate to the others.

Sometimes you may use the individual factor scores, rather than the final total score, to make your decision, especially if the total scores are very close. For example, if one candidate has a final score of 380 and another 370, you might decide to look more closely at which one better meets the needs of the factors you've weighed most heavily. You might also go back to your notes from reference checks and interviews. These things, combined with your scores, can be the deciding factors.

Even if you have only one qualified candidate at this point in the hiring process, you should still use this final evaluation technique. The scores the candidate receives will tell you if the individual can truly be successful.

FIGURE 13.3 • Final Evaluation Form

Candidate Name ___Bill Jones___

Factor	Weight		Rating		Final Points
values	30	×	5	=	150
track record	30	×	5	=	150
communication skills	20	×	3	=	60
behavioral factors	20	×	3	=	60
		×		=	
Total	100				420

Timing

The final candidate evaluation does take some time and effort—like all things worth doing. The timing involved in this final phase can be critical to landing the best future employee, so keep time in mind when scheduling these evaluations.

Of course, the best candidates may be interviewing at a number of companies, and you don't want to lose someone in which you have invested so much. While this is a valid concern, some employers rush to make an ill-conceived job offer with conditions still undetermined. This can lead to problems because the candidate's perception of the offer can be different from yours. Disappointment or disagreements can be a bad start for the new employee—exactly what you tried to avoid by using a smart staffing approach. If you have followed the smart staffing steps this far, it is important to take the time to finish the process before making an offer.

On the other hand, some employers take too long to make a decision and lose the best candidate for the job. The candidate may accept a job elsewhere, or simply lose interest and enthusiasm because the company has kept the individual hanging on for so long.

Look back to your recruiting plan developed in Chapter 6. Here you have stated the time line for filling this position. You have given yourself a certain block of time to go through each stage of the hiring process. Use this guideline to remind yourself of how long you have to finish the job. If you've gotten off track, now is the time to get back on. Set a reasonable time limit to evaluate your top candidates, choose the best one, and make an offer. Let the candidates know exactly when they can expect to hear from you.

Final Testing

In certain employment situations, the candidate you choose will need to take a physical exam and/or a drug test. When this is the case, these tests must be scheduled either before the final job offer is extended or after with the understanding that the offer is contingent on the results of these tests. The timing is up to you based on your schedule, the candidate's schedule and mutual convenience.

Physical Examinations

Requiring an employee to take a physical examination after making a conditional offer of employment has been a common practice for quite a long time, especially for positions that require the employee to perform some kind of physical activity. Not only is it beneficial to check the individual's health, it is a good idea to document the person's physical condition prior to beginning employment. This may be important later if an injury or a health-related problem is reported after the employee is hired.

If you require your prospective employee to have a physical examination, it is important to use a physician who is familiar with the type of job the potential employee will be doing, especially if the job is physically demanding and requires the employee to do things like lift heavy weights or stand for long periods of time.

Drug Testing

If drug testing is a requirement for employment, it is important to tell the applicant at the beginning of the hiring process that your company is drug free. This is done by placing signs in the employment area, through documentation given to each applicant, and by verbally mentioning it in the first interview. While the overall drug-free policy should apply to everyone in the company, the drug testing policy may apply only to some employees based on their job duties. If this is the case, your testing policy should clearly identify the positions included.

If your place of business is drug and alcohol free, candidates must know this well before this final phase of the hiring process. As a practical matter, informing applicants early in the hiring process sorts out any that might have difficulty passing a drug or alcohol screen.

The actual drug test is usually given after the prospect signs a consent form and is offered conditional employment. In short, the test is given after an offer of employment but prior to starting work.

Legally, there are some instances where drug tests cannot be given and others where drug tests are a must (such as commercial drivers). The laws are complex and ever changing, so it pays to seek knowledgeable assistance before setting up drug and alcohol screening programs. The Center for Substance Abuse Prevention Help Line (800-843-4971) is a government-funded program which provides a great deal of high-quality free information. Be sure to ask about specific requirements because many state and local laws may prohibit items the national statutes allow.

Drug and alcohol tests are given to decrease the chance of hiring someone who is currently using or abusing drugs or alcohol. Candidates are employed only after a negative drug test. If a candidate tests positive, the individual is usually denied employment. Some employers will allow the candidate to be re-tested immediately or to re-apply after a period of time, but that is a personal decision that should be made with the advice of a knowledgeable professional.

Some individuals feel that mandatory drug or alcohol testing violates the Fourth Amendment which addresses privacy issues. But the courts have generally found that testing of applicants is not unlawful if the employer conducts the testing in a fair and unobtrusive manner.

Written Employment Offer

Your offer of employment should be made in writing. If conditions and agreements are not clarified and written down when the candidate accepts the position, there may be significant differences of opinion about the meaning of what was communicated verbally. Even the best memory is not as good as a written offer.

Once you have selected the best candidate, create a clear, concise, and attractive offer. If the offer is for an entry-level position or one that consists of only salary and standard company benefits, don't assume your new employee knows what is standard—write it all down in great detail. (See Figure 13.4 for a sample offer of employment letter.)

Back in your recruiting plan you determined a salary range and possibly financial incentives, like bonuses and commissions. These terms were written with an objective eye on what your company can afford and what the position warrants. Don't change them now because you are emotionally invested in getting a particular candidate. Your recruiting plan contains the terms you can offer—now put them in a written offer of employment. (In the recruiting plan you also stated if the terms are negotiable and if you plan to offer any incentives, like relocation costs or signing bonus to lure a hesitant candidate.)

Compose your written offer of employment before extending the offer because it will help clarify exactly what you're offering. Begin your letter in an upbeat tone offering congratulations to the candidate for being selected and expressing hope that the individual will accept the position and join the company. Then include key information such as:

- Job title, location, the person to report to, the start date, and the duties and responsibilities
- Total compensation (including salary and incentives)
- Review dates (if any)
- Any special considerations offered such as moving expenses, signing bonus, considerations of future promotions, or performance incentives
- Information required by employment laws such as proof of citizenship or proof of earnings
- Plan to have the new employee sign an employment contract (containing a noncompete clause, for example, as explained in Chapter 9)
- Any contingency such as the results of a physical or final check of references

FIGURE 13.4 • Letter Offering Employment

October 2, 1998

Dear Ms. Jones,

I am pleased to confirm the verbal offer of employment at XYZ Company as a sales clerk. I am very impressed with your credentials and experience. I am hoping you will join our company. Your starting date will be November 10, 1998. You will be reporting to Ms. Johnson, the store manager.

As a sales clerk you will be responsible to greet and sell customers, take and input customers' payments, handle incoming phone calls, assist in merchandising sales floor, make outgoing telemarketing calls, complete and file paperwork, and work the hours assigned from 9:30 AM to 7:30 PM, Monday through Saturday.

Your compensation for the position will begin at $7.00 per hour with overtime of 0–5 hours per week.

Please signify your acceptance of this offer by signing and returning it to Ms. Johnson by October 15, 1998. We are looking forward to your positive acceptance of this offer and to your joining our company.

Sincerely,

Tracy Smith

Extend the Offer

When the offer of employment is written down, it is time to extend the offer. You can do this in person, on the phone, or in writing. Because verbal offers allow you to communicate your excitement and measure the candidate's reactions, they are preferred.

If you are worried that the candidate may not accept your offer, use some timing strategy. Make your offer on a Friday. This gives the candidate an opportunity to consider the offer with family and friends over the weekend away from the current job. Being away from co-workers and projects that will be left undone tends to increase the chances of the individual accepting the position.

If you offer the job by phone, use your offer of employment letter to convey the terms. This will help the candidate get a clear and accurate picture of what you're offering.

End your conversation in an upbeat manner and suggest that the candidate give the offer careful consideration. Be sure to ask the candidate how long he or she thinks it will take to make a decision. You don't want to apply pressure, but a reasonable deadline is helpful in getting a positive response.

If the offer is made verbally, be sure to immediately follow up the conversation by sending the written offer of employment. It is important to get the offer letter in the person's hands quickly because it will give the individual more confidence to accept. The written offer of employment is tangible proof of your desire to hire.

Counteroffers

If you're offering the position to a much-sought-after or hard-to-find candidate, this is a good time to consider the subject of counteroffers. It is best for you if the candidate accepts your position before telling the current employer. As an executive recruiter, I always said, "Now is a very critical time. You wouldn't want your employer to know you are considering another position because if you decided not to take it, they might question your loyalty and desire to remain in your current job."

As soon as the offer is accepted, it is good to warn the candidate that it is common practice for companies to try to keep employees for the short term with counteroffers of increased wages, benefits, bonuses, perks, etc. Help the candidate understand that counteroffers are no more than short-term strategies offered under duress. Whatever it was that made the candidate seek other employment will not change in the long run. While you don't want to react too negatively against the current employer, you want to prepare the candidate for the possibility of a counteroffer.

If the candidate comes back to you with the news of a counteroffer, don't get into a bidding war. It may be a natural reaction to try to keep this top candidate and not lose the time and effort you have invested, but do not allow your objective judgment to be overruled by emotion. Many employers who "won" the bidding war find that they now have an employee who is paid more than he or she is worth or more than the company can afford. This bidding war can also sour an employer-employee relationship. In these cases, "winning" is not good for business.

Offer Declined

Unfortunately, you always have to be prepared for a no response. Candidates do turn down positions. If this happens, it is important to move forward immediately and not get stalled by your disappointment. If your first choice for the position turns you down, move to your second choice candidate. If you have followed the steps of smart staffing up to this point, you have backup candidates who also meet all the must requirements. You should not have to start the process all over.

Notifying Other Candidates

It is important to notify those not selected for the position in a professional and timely manner. Those who were eliminated from consideration early in the process should have been notified at that time (see letter of rejection in Chapter 8). The ones still being considered at the end of the process are ones you have probably met several times and need to make contact with one last time. It is the considerate thing to do, of course, but it is also self-serving. These people know many other people in the industry and local area, and they also may become customers at some time. If you do not quickly and professionally inform the candidates who are not selected, it damages your company's image and may cause difficulty hiring others down the line. Notify those who do not get the position in writing. Even if you tell them by telephone, the formal step of writing them to conclude their candidacy is important.

Compose your letter carefully. A good rejection letter should communicate that the person was not selected, but leave self-esteem intact. It should also leave the individual with a professional impression of the company. The letter should also express appreciation for the time they spent interviewing and for their interest in the company. Use the sample letter of rejection in Chapter 8 (Figure 8.5) as your guide.

If you expect more openings for the same type of position in the future, you may want to tell your top candidates about this possibility. Explain that they were not selected for this position, but will be considered for future openings. Be sure to be truthful and accurate about potential openings so you don't create false

FIGURE 13.5 • Sample "Bank" Letter

October 4, 1998

Dear Mr. Taylor,

Thank you for your interest and the time you have invested in exploring our company. Your background and credentials are impressive; however, currently we do not have the ability to offer you a position. I feel you would make an excellent addition to our staff in the future. We will keep your information in our active files for a period of one year. If a position becomes available, we will contact you to renew our discussions.

Thank you again for your interest in our company. I hope we can be of assistance to each other in the future.

Sincerely,

Tracy Smith

expectations. This type of letter, as shown in Figure 13.5, keeps possible future candidates "in the bank."

When rejected, some candidates ask why they were not selected. While you may have developed an affinity for some of the individuals and want to help them, disclosing too much is a mistake. Giving out too much information about perceived weaknesses is bound to cause hard feelings and the candidate may file a complaint or pursue legal action. Simply bow out with a noncommittal statement like, "All candidates were given full consideration based on very objective criteria, and another candidate more closely matched our needs."

Through the smart staffing process you can now feel confident that you have the best possible candidate working for your company. But don't sit back and rest now—in front of you lies the job of keeping this employee.

Frequently Asked Questions

Q. *Is it a good idea for more than one person to evaluate a candidate?*

A. It is an excellent idea to get input from all who will supervise or work closely with the candidate.

Q. *We have two significantly different scores on the same candidate. What should we do?*

A. Compare evaluations and examine the factors that were rated differently and determine why. Many times one person may have discovered something in an interview that is important for all to know.

Q. *If we have two good candidates and the one who scored lower on our evaluation form is available for a much lower salary, should we save money by taking the one with the lower score?*

A. That would depend on whether the candidate with the lower salary requirement can do an excellent job in the position. You don't want to compromise performance for a few dollars and you don't want to overpay for competence.

Q. *How detailed does a noncompete agreement or employment contract have to be?*

A. To be enforceable, the agreement should be drafted by an attorney. It will be enforced only if reasonably limited in time and geographic area and only to the extent necessary to protect the employer from unfair competition that stems from the employee's use or disclosure of trade secrets or confidential customer lists, or if the employee's services are unique or extraordinary.

Q. *If the position has a very high earning potential, how can I communicate that to a person?*

A. Offer a minimum guarantee of earnings over 6 months, 12 months, or 18 months so the individual sees the potential of the job. If the individual performs poorly or is terminated for cause prior to the agreed date, the company is absolved of its responsibility to make up for the earnings shortfall. This keeps the company from having to pay a guarantee to an individual who is not performing well.

Q. *Should you tell a candidate the reason he or she was not selected for the position?*

A. No. Experience has shown that there is very little you can tell a candidate that will not cause problems. The person can become angry, disagree with your perception, or begin trying to convince you that he or she should have been hired. It is best to leave the individual's ego intact and close the issue.

Q. *Can I institute a drug testing policy for new employees only?*

A. No. For drug testing to be a requirement for employment, it must meet specific guidelines and be part of an overall program to create a drug-free environment. It must be unbiased and nondiscriminatory to be allowed. Testing only those applying for work would violate the nondiscriminatory principle.

Keep and Reward Top Employees

CHAPTER 14

Implementing Strategies
to Keep Your New Employees

THE HIRING PROCESS CONTINUES
AFTER THE FINAL DECISION IS MADE.

John Case reported a startling discovery in the *Inc.* magazine article, "Best Small Companies to Work for in America." He stated

> We've made our editorial living for the past thirteen years finding exemplary companies and teasing out their secrets. We've reported on clever innovators, on marketing geniuses, on the financial wizards. We've written about imaginative ways entrepreneurs solve common problems on all these fronts. The one common denominator for their success was their retention of good people and the creation of a workplace that allowed that.

That's how important retention is to your company.

Even larger companies, such as General Electric, IBM, and PepsiCo are borrowing from the script the best small companies have been following for years. They are learning what makes employees feel good about their jobs and their companies. The result is not only reduced employee turnover, but also greater commitment to the company, to the work they are doing, and to themselves.

Turnover is a problem in all businesses and one that is on the rise. *What America's Small Companies Pay Their Sales Forces and How They Make It Pay Off* found the turnover rate of salespeople in companies under $5 million in sales in 1990 was 4.8 percent. By 1992 it had jumped to 20.3 percent, in 1994 it was 21.4 percent, and 1996 leveled out at 20.4 percent. At this rate, a company has an entirely new sales force every five years. With this in mind, is it any wonder that we can't keep our customers? (These numbers are illustrative of what's going on in industry, but keep in mind that the numbers vary from business to business—from 3.4 percent in auto repair services to 50 percent in construction.)

While the rate may vary by position and industry, there is definitely a greater tendency for employees to be mobile and not "married" to the company. The recent downswing and re-engineering has had an effect on employee attitudes. Many applicants for your open position may have been involved in corporate restructuring and lost their positions or know a friend or relative who has lost a job. The result of this drive for leaner operations and lower cost has left employees skeptical about management's real concern for them and their commitment to employees' long-term welfare. Many feel work is an exchange of services for a fee rather than a commitment to a vision, a dream, and long-term employment.

It would be naive to believe an organization could create an atmosphere where every employee was totally committed to its vision and dream of success. There will always be employees who have a "day worker" mentality providing services today only for today's paycheck. But for the organization to be successful, especially those in highly competitive, fast-moving environments, you must have a strong group of loyal, dedicated workers. According to Frederick Reichheld, the author of *The Loyalty Effect*, "You can't get customer loyalty if you don't have employee loyalty." To be successful, it is critical to have a happy, loyal and stable workforce.

Recognizing the Seven Myths of Retention

There are lots of valid reasons why employers lose good employees. But when you ask these employers to talk about their plans for keeping level A employees in the future, they often respond with excuses and false notions that contribute to their employee retention problems. This section discusses the seven most common myths affecting retention. Take a good look at each one and be sure to never use them as excuses.

Myth 1: Losing an Employee Doesn't Really Hurt the Company

The truth is, employee turnover has a significant effect on the productivity of those who remain. When someone leaves, the remaining employees often have internal struggles and questions like, "Why did that person leave?" "What caused the problem?" and "How did management handle the situation?" These questions are not prompted by curiosity alone. Employees begin to empathize and put themselves into the departed employee's position. The departure of an employee can sap the enthusiasm and productivity of a group as they internalize their questions and concerns. In organizations that have gone through downsizing, this reduction in enthusiasm has become so prevalent that it has been called "the survivor's syndrome." Those remaining go through many of the same questions as survivors of major catastrophic events such as "Why them and not me?" It is easy to see that losing people, especially good ones, really does hurt the whole company.

Myth 2: We Don't Really Know Why People Leave or Stay

Some companies approach turnover with a "don't ask, don't tell" mentality. If they don't ask what makes people unhappy and causes them to leave, they don't have to deal with the answers. They may be afraid of opening Pandora's box. They worry that if they start examining the real feelings of employees they may not be able to handle what they hear. They fear that the reasons people are leaving might be embarrassing or offend management. They realize that once you find out why, you are obligated to do something about it. Many times organizations want to stop turnover but are not willing to pay the price of changing behavior and policies.

As long as the company and its management ignore a turnover problem, they will not be able to reduce it or its negative effect on the organization and its customers. The only way to really reduce turnover is to truly understand why people leave. Reading a statistical survey of a group of companies, no matter how similar to yours, will not tell you why your people leave. The only way to know is to conduct an investigation in your own organization to determine the real reasons people leave. (See Chapter 20 for information on exit interviews.) If you make the effort, you can find out why people leave or stay.

Myth 3: We Can't Afford Higher Pay so There Is No Way We Can Keep Top Employees

Some organizations may feel they are severely limited by what they can afford to pay. While these constraints on wages appear very real and significantly affect the bottom line, the question which needs to be asked is not, "What does it cost to have the employee at work?" but "What does it cost to not have the employee at work?" Examples of average pay levels or wages are available, but you can't just look at your industry to see if your wages are competitive. Many individuals earning minimum wage will jump at the first opportunity to increase their income, regardless of the kind of job. If employees are not able to meet their basic financial needs, they will change jobs, no matter how much they like the company or their coworkers.

While it may be a difficult decision to rationalize paying a higher wage, it has to be seen not as an increased cost, but as a decrease in turnover and loss of customers that affects the company's bottom line, and even survival. You'll find that you can't afford to not keep top employees.

Myth 4: My Employees Won't Leave Because They Know We Have Their Best Interests at Heart

You do have a better chance of keeping your employees if they trust that you care about them, but do your employees have trust in you? A recent survey of 1003 adults by Pew Research Center of People and the Press indicates that only 51 percent of employees say they have "a lot" of trust in their boss or supervisor. This gives you about a 50–50 chance that trust will be a factor in stopping your employees from leaving.

Don't mistake respect or fear for trust. If employees are respectful and not openly belligerent, some assume it is trust. The absence of negative comments may be a sign of a lack of confidence and trust to be able to express negative opinions without retribution.

Organizations, especially small ones, take on characteristics similar to a family when it comes to this issue of trust. There may be an environment where people openly share their feelings, concerns, and worries, or one where no one confides in anyone else. In organizations where people cannot share their feelings and concerns, upper management may be deceived into thinking everything is great. Only with the resignation of a key employee or an increase in turnover do they recognize a significant problem.

Unless there is an open relationship of trust, it is almost impossible to convince the employees that the company has their best interests at heart. If you want high levels of commitment to your company, the employees have to trust you.

Myth 5: You Just Have to Live with Turnover

A company can never eliminate all turnover. Some turnover, such as retirement and separation for medical reasons, is inevitable. But the cost of turnover is like any other business expense—if allowed to run rampant, it can bankrupt your organization.

Naturally, some industries and situations are prone to greater turnover than others. But that is not a reason to stop trying to keep your employees on board. An attitude of complacency or futility will doom the organization to repeat its mistakes. Bruce Upbin, in his *Forbes* article "Happy Drivers, Happy Customers," reports that in an industry where 100 percent turnover is typical, Knight Transportation, a Phoenix-based company, has a 50 percent turnover rate. Knight's drivers also reach their destination at the promised hour 98 percent of the time. It is not surprising to learn that Knight is the fastest growing and most profitable publicly traded trucking company in America. Over the last five years revenue has grown 43 percent and earnings have grown at a rate of 61 percent annually.

This case proves that regardless of your industry or situation, you can reduce turnover and improve employee satisfaction. Investing in these two areas produces happier customers and greater profits. You don't have to live with rampant turnover.

Myth 6: People Leave Because the Work Is Naturally Boring and Repetitive

The sales managers who have the greatest success in getting salespeople to make cold calls (a very important, but repetitive function in some sales jobs) are the ones who make it fun, exciting, and even rewarding. While you cannot change the nature of some jobs, you can change things that affect it. For example, you can increase the recognition and excitement factors, and even create challenge in accomplishing targets. Employees will do a great deal of repetitive and boring tasks for a reward and recognition. Something as simple as having pizza brought in after work to recognize and reward accomplishments does a lot for motivation and morale.

The first step in making a boring and repetitive job better is your refusal to accept that the job has to be boring. Examples abound of managers who have examined a job and added tasks to make it more enriching to the employee. If you want to keep your employees, don't let their work get too boring or repetitive.

Myth 7: People Can Be Easily and Inexpensively Replaced

People can be replaced, but not easily or inexpensively. With the increasing complexity of jobs and the decreasing labor pool, positions are staying open longer. The higher or more specialized the position, the longer the position is likely to remain open. Even if the position is filled quickly, a significant amount of effort, time, and company resources are required to identify and hire a top employee. Once the person is on board, the employee still has to become acclimated to the organization and "get up to speed" in the position. Clients tell us that even when an employee fills a position almost immediately after it is vacated, it takes about six months to learn the routines, get to know the people, and become fully productive. Even after the departing employee is replaced, reduced productivity and lost customers or sales opportunities can be costly. It is critical to keep high-performing employees—they cannot be easily or inexpensively replaced.

Welcoming Your New Hires

All the effort invested in identifying and hiring top employees will be wasted if they are not treated properly from the moment the offer of employment is extended. We have all heard, "You never get a second chance to make a good first impression." This is especially true with new employees. The minute they accept a job offer, they begin to assess or evaluate their decision. They determine if this is the place they want to work and spend their career.

Don't make the mistake of letting your new employees be in limbo between the old job and the new without personal contact. And then don't let them report to work on a day when you are too busy to take the time to properly welcome and orient them. As you read through the rest of this chapter, take note of the ways you can quickly and effectively assimilate new employees into your organization, make them feel welcome and appreciated, orient them, and teach them the knowledge and skills to be productive.

Keep Up the Excitement

Once the offer has been accepted and all other candidates notified, your job is not over. Keep in touch with the new employee to keep the connection and build a relationship. This connection is critical during the transition period.

Immediately after acceptance of the offer, new employees probably experience the greatest level of positive excitement. But just as when purchasing a new car, soon after the initial excitement wears off, "buyer's remorse" sets in. This has caused many people to regret a major decision. The same thing can happen to your job offer.

To keep this phenomenon from occurring, stay in touch and keep reinforcing the benefits of accepting the offer and working for your company. It is critical to phone and drop notes to keep the new employee pumped up, especially if the individual has yet to tell the current employer or if it will be several weeks before the new job starts. It might be a good idea to meet for lunch, or invite the new hire to come in and meet other employees. If you have company information or benefit packages, give them to the individual as tangible proof of the new position. Keeping in touch will allow you to keep the individual excited, spot problems, and eliminate "candidate's remorse."

We all know a very small thing can be the difference between success and failure. This is never more true than when extending the offer. One mistake or mishandling can erase hours of work and eliminate the possibility of keeping a top candidate. The job of hiring isn't completed until the person is on board and acclimated to the company.

Get Off to a Good Start

It's unrealistic to expect your new employee to report to work and be instantly productive. You first must invest time to orient and train a new hire if you want that individual to become a long-term employee.

A business owner once related this story. On separate occasions two employees in the same store quit after reporting to work. The owner of the business became concerned. The store manager said he couldn't understand why this happened, but he felt it was just a coincidence and certainly not the fault of anyone in the store.

Another person was hired and sent to the store to work. After lunch on the employee's first day, the store manager called the owner to report that the third new employee had not returned from lunch. The owner of the company, now very disturbed, went to the store and demanded to know what happened. The store manager explained he welcomed the employee to the store and put him to work. The owner asked, "What did you have him doing?" And the store manager replied, "We had some work in the back and we had him cleaning up several appliances." After more questions, the owner realized the store manager had never referred to the employee by name. When she asked the manager the employee's name, he admitted he could not recall it.

Not only did the new employee not receive proper orientation, he was not even made to feel welcome. Because the manager had not taken the time to make him feel at ease, build a relationship, or even learn his name, it became obvious why the store had lost three employees.

The most successful organizations have a planned, systematic approach for integrating newly hired employees into their company. They make employees feel comfortable, help them to develop their skills and knowledge, and help them understand their job and what's expected of them.

Acclimation Plan

Anything important should be planned out and done well, and getting a new employee off to a good start is no exception. Before the individual reports to work, you should review all the information gleaned during the employment process and use it to develop an acclimation plan. Look over the employee's strengths, weaknesses, areas of concern, motivational factors, and how to manage this person. Most of this information can be obtained from the pre-employment evaluation instruments, as well as your interview and reference notes. If an employee has had a problem in any particular area in the past, you can plan how to help the employee overcome the difficulty in the new position. For example, if your sales clerk is weak at merchandising the sales floor, you can assign the individual to work with a person who is strong in that area.

Developing an acclimation plan for new employees is a wise investment of time and energy because it not only reduces the potential for turnover, it increases the probability the individual will be productive.

The First Day

The first few hours and days set the stage for the employee's attitude toward the job and the company. On the first day the new employee might be anxious or apprehensive, as well as excited with high expectations. If you can help reduce the fear, calm the anxiety, and keep the excitement and expectation levels high, it will go a long way to giving the employee a good start.

Initially your objective is to ease the employee and demonstrate your pride and commitment to the company. You should again review the notes from interviews and pre-employment tools to get to know the employee as a person. Take the time to truly communicate to the new employee and build a bridge of understanding that will last through the entire period of employment. Avoid the most common mistake of orientation and training—having employees, or even the outgoing employee, do this job. These people are unlikely to convey enthusiasm for the company or the seriousness of the job as well as you or the hiring manager. As a result, many new hires do not meet the owner's expectations and soon go through the revolving door of employee turnover. Take the time to give this important piece of the hiring process your personal attention, at the very least on the first day.

Acclimation

Provide your new employee with a tour of the department, plant, or company. Introduce the individual to coworkers. Explain the duties of each person so the employee can understand how each fits into the organization. Explain the facility and show the restrooms, break areas, and where everything is located.

Policies

Once your new employee has a good understanding of the physical location and the other people in the organization, it is time to introduce other general information. Explain all the policies that will affect the employee including, pay, benefits, sick days, overtime, etc. Many times employees are given an employee handbook and told to read it, but that's not enough. If you do have an employee handbook, it is very important that a knowledgeable person go over the manual with the new hire and answer questions when work actually begins.

Unwritten Rules

Many things are never written down, but the employee still must know them in order to feel comfortable. Employees should be told the unwritten rules right from the start. These may be simple things like when to take breaks or where to go for lunch. The new employee will also need to know basic information about daily operations such as how to handle time cards, keys, telephone systems, office equipment, mail, supplies, deliveries, and even normal housekeeping chores. Make a list of these things and go over it with your new employee, leaving the door open for questions in case you've forgotten anything.

Prepared Work Area

Be sure to have the new employee's work area ready with any necessary supplies, tools, or equipment. Nothing makes new employees feel more at home than to have a spot prepared and waiting for them.

The Job Details

Explain the levels of supervision in the organization and the schedule of activities for the first day, especially if training is involved. Take time to sit down and review what is expected using the job requirements, candidate requirements, and level of expectation information you developed for your job description (see Chapter 2).

The first day is busy and mentally tiring for a new hire. Your personal attention will give a positive picture of the entire company.

Orientation

Before you set up a new employee orientation program, you must understand that orientation and training are not the same thing—each has a different purpose. Orientation is the process of communicating to a new employee the duties of the job and how to accomplish them. Training is the process of building the specific skills necessary to carry out the job duties explained during the orientation.

All companies, even ones with only a few employees, can take a lesson from the Disney Organization when it comes to orientation. On the first day of work, all Disney employees attend an orientation called "Traditions." During this day they learn about the history, culture, and management style of the company, and how all the different parts of the organization relate to each other. Every employee (or cast member, as they are called) goes through the same orientation, whether they portray a cartoon character or are an executive. The theory behind "Traditions" is simple: the more time and effort invested in planning for successful workers, the less time spent later correcting problems.

While your company may not have the time or resources to create an elaborate orientation program such as "Traditions," it would be wise to invest the time to develop an effective orientation program for all new employees.

How Long Should the Orientation Be?

An effective orientation should last as long as necessary to ensure the new employee feels comfortable and understands the behavior and work ethic needed to become successful. It may take an hour, a day, or a week. The key to determining the length: Do it until you're done.

What Should Be Included in an Employee Orientation?

An employee orientation program should include everything an employee needs to know to develop a comfort level with the company and be a productive employee. While everything may not be covered in the first few hours, there must be a planned methodical process to ensure the employee understands what to do and what is expected. Figure 14.1 lists areas generally covered during employee orientation.

On-the-Job Training (OJT)

Structured on-the-job training is an effective way to provide new employee training when classroom training is not feasible. Unlike informal, watch-and-learn training often used in small businesses, structured OJT has an advantage because it is defined and measurable, and it has a beginning and end. More importantly, it is easier to schedule, manage, and accomplish.

Structured OJT is designed in advance and uses a planned methodical approach. This approach includes:

- Breaking the job into small bite-sized pieces or tasks
- Determining the skills needed to do these tasks
- Defining the minimum performance level
- Setting a time for reaching a certain level or learning the skill or knowledge

This method helps you determine if the new employee is progressing at an appropriate rate so you can spot and fix problems early. Figure 14.2 shows a structured OJT plan for one area of a sales position.

Methods of Instruction

To set up a structured OJT program for your company, begin by determining the methods you will use to teach these duties. Most common methods of instruction include:

- Demonstration
- Lecture

FIGURE 14.1 • Orientation Guide

Each employee's orientation should be tailored to the individual's skill, experience, and position. When developing an orientation you should consider covering:

- *History.* Give a perspective of the industry and company.

- *Company organization.* Explain the parts of the organization and their function.

- *Organizational relationship.* Describe how positions, departments, and management relate to each other and how the new employee fits in.

- *Employee philosophy.* Explain how employees are treated and how they are expected to treat others.

- *Customer philosophy.* Explain your company's philosophy about customers.

- *Product/Services.* Describe products or services offered, and the geographic area covered.

- *Tour of location.* Include information on break areas, restrooms, and where food and beverages are permitted. Explain the smoking policy.

- *Employee's position.* Define responsibilities, duties, essential job functions, and expected level of performance.

- *Dress code.* Explain both written and unwritten rules for dress and appearance.

- *Work time.* Review starting, quitting, break and lunch time procedures, as well as how employees check in and out and keep time.

- *Store or office procedures.* Explain the specific ones the individual must know, such as security and safety.

- *Assistance from management.*

- *Assistance by peers.* Explain any peer assistance program you have (if any) and how it works.

- *Employee's questions.* Uncover any questions the new employee may have.

- Personal coaching
- Written instruction (product manuals, procedure manuals, instruction guides, etc.)
- Prepackaged training programs
- Audio and video tapes and CDs
- Interactive computer programs (This will be a very popular method of job training in the near future.)
- Outside consultants (These are most useful if you have several employees with a similar need, like sales clerks who all need to learn better sales skills.)

Conducting a Training Session

A training session should take a building block approach to build skills one on top of the other in small steps. Depending on the skills, you may need only one session or you may need several. The following format has been very effective in training new employees.

Introduction to the training session. Explain to the employee why this training is important and how the individual will benefit from it. Then map out the details. Explain the objective, what will be covered, what the employee is expected to learn, and how long the session will last.

The body of a training session. The session should follow a clear six-step process:

1. Explain in detail how the task is performed.
2. Show the correct way to perform the task.
3. Let the employee practice the skill.
4. Watch as the employee practices.
5. Critique the performance.
6. Reinforce the importance of this skill and the benefits to the employee.

Evaluation of a training session. After a group of tasks has been satisfactorily learned and the individual responsible for training has checked to see the new employee meets the expected level of performance, the trainer can sign off to attest that it has been accomplished. It is a good idea for the trainee to sign that he has been trained and can perform the tasks listed at the expected level. This acknowledges that the trainee feels he or she has been fully and satisfactorily trained and is now responsible to perform the skill or task. If the trainee does not feel competent in the task or skill, the individual should be encouraged not to

FIGURE 14.2 • Structured On-The-Job Training—Sales

Structured On-The-Job Training

Area: INDUSTRY

Task	Standard	Resource	Completed ___/___
Learn the history of the computer industry.	Interview the two most knowledgeable people in your company. Be able to describe the major events that have created today's business climate.	- Employee - Coach	

Task	Standard	Resource	Completed ___/___
Learn trends and changes that are likely to affect you and the company in the next several years.	Interview the two most knowledgeable people in your company on trends. Be able to describe the trends that affect the customer, company, and you in the next several years.	- Current trade periodicals - Employees - Coach	

Task	Standard	Resource	Completed ___/___
Visit Web sites of major vendors and review future information on future products/trends.	Be able to describe the view of the future of the top three vendors.	- Web sites	

I have been satisfactorily trained on all the items listed above and can meet company performance expectations.

Signature _____ Date _____

sign. My experience with clients indicates that the employees are relieved when they can ask for additional assistance before signing if they do not feel competent.

If you take the time to figure out what the employee needs to know, what methods of instruction will best meet those needs, and then offer an organized and methodical training session, you will have higher skilled employees who are more competent and will stay with your company longer.

Mentors

Although you should be personally involved in orientation and training, many times having another employee act as a mentor is very helpful to the new hire. These experienced employees are usually more available to devote their time than you or the hiring manager. The new employee may also feel more comfortable asking questions of another employee and will generally receive more candid answers to certain questions. In addition to formal policies and procedures, the mentor is in the best position to explain the unwritten rules and how things are really done.

Because the role of mentor is an important one, it is essential that you choose someone carefully. Attitude, level of expectation, loyalty, and commitment are more important than tenure or even skill. As a matter of fact, a mentor does not even have to be in the same position as the new employee.

To be beneficial and productive, this relationship will require time and effort from the mentor, who should be rewarded for this extra duty. Sometimes simply recognizing the mentor for their efforts may be enough motivation during the development of the new employee. Providing a cash bonus for the mentor when the new employee reaches a specific level of performance or tenure is another way to reward effort. A mentor program can also be a way to develop a management candidate for a future position.

Performance Appraisal

It is important to give your new hire feedback on performance. The initial performance appraisal is designed to ensure that individuals can do their jobs and reach the expected levels of productivity in the required time period. Many companies call this a probationary period. I suggest you avoid *probationary* because it has a negative connotation and even suggests guaranteed permanent employment if successfully completed. Regardless of what it is called, it is essential to evaluate your new employee during the initial performance period.

The employee should be able to expect performance feedback at specific periods. Depending on the job level, a formal performance appraisal could be done in as soon as a month or as long as a year. But keep in mind that habits are formed from the moment the new employee begins to work. The longer the bad habit or negative behavior continues, the tougher it is to change. For this reason, you should give routine feedback as the job is being performed. Most jobs offer opportunities for an informal appraisal of the individual's progress and performance on a weekly basis.

The performance feedback must be detailed and current if you want your employees to grow at the fastest rate and perform at the highest level of their ability. Figure 14.3 lists areas to focus on when providing feedback. Usually, an employee who is new and inexperienced in a position needs the most immediate and frequent performance feedback.

For example, if a sales clerk was hired with little experience the manager might spend time each day giving the employee feedback, answering questions, and coaching. After a week, the frequency might become every other day, then later, twice a week. By the end of the first month, performance feedback might

FIGURE 14.3 • Performance Appraisal Guide

Each time you meet with your new employee to provide feedback on performance, consider these areas of discussion. They will give both of you a good idea of what's going on.

- Examine performance, exploring both your perception and the employee's.

- Note areas of strength, look for trends, and emphasize positive traits.

- Note areas needing improvement, such as skill deficiency, problems, and future opportunities

- Assess performance level in relation to expectations.

- Set new goals, objectives, or targets.

- Get commitment to change or improve weaknesses and continue positive effort.

only be given weekly until a 90-day initial performance period is completed and the employee's performance is formally appraised.

Of course, the frequency or schedule will vary depending on the individual's progress and need for assistance to reach the expected level of performance as defined in the job description. Even after this level has been reached, the employee will require regular feedback, coaching, and goal setting sessions. It is a mistake to put an employee on automatic pilot after the employee has been trained. If you want an A level employee, you'll need to conduct regular performance appraisals and provide feedback to spot problems, address performance deficiencies, and help the employee reach his or her performance potential.

Conducting routine performance appraisals can keep you in tune with the employee and help to discover problems that might be brewing before they boil over.

FREQUENTLY ASKED QUESTIONS

Q. *How can I conduct orientation in a small organization when I need all my employees to do their jobs during normal work hours?*

A. Orientation in small organizations is generally scheduled for off-peak hours when key people are less busy or it can be scheduled outside normal work hours. You or your managers should do whatever is required to devote your full attention to the new employee.

Q. *What if we don't have a written set of procedures? How can we give an orientation?*

A. Even informal organizations need a written set of procedures. One approach is to identify the task or information that must be explained and write it out as it is being explained to the new employee. At a minimum, the new employee will have the written information to refer back to, and the information can be the beginning of written procedures for the next orientation.

Q. *What is the difference between orientation and training?*

A. Orientation is designed to develop the employee's feeling of belonging and comfort level. Training is designed to develop skills and knowledge. If not enough effort is invested in orientation, the time and resources in training will be lost.

Q. *We have only a few people in the same position and they do things differently. How can we train an individual?*

A. Identify the person who is best at each task or activity and have them orient and train the new employee. This helps the new employee model the best behavior for each task.

Q. *I just can't pay the same wages some high-tech or union employers can afford. What can I do?*

A. Pay is only one factor determining if an employee stays with a company. If it is not economical to meet the pay rates of other employers, you must find what else motivates people to stay and ensure the company provides that. Factors that I've uncovered in organizational surveys include flexible benefits, work that people find enjoyable and challenging, the ability to make a contribution, and your flexibility in working with them in difficult personal situations. These are some areas that can help you make up for a pay differential.

Q. *How much turnover is too much?*

A. Industry averages can give you an idea if you're under or over the norm in turnovers. But these averages may not give you a clear picture of what is acceptable. The real determination of what turnover level is acceptable is how much damage your company is willing to accept compared to the cost of keeping the employee.

CHAPTER 15

Communicating with Your Employees

THE LIFEBLOOD OF A BUSINESS RELATIONSHIP
IS COMMUNICATION.

Communication is the lifeblood of any relationship. Given this fact, is it any wonder that in companies where there is unexpected downsizing or re-engineering there appears to be no valuable relationship or communication between employees and management? In high-performing, stable organizations, vital information moves up and down among levels freely, candidly, and honestly. Employees are trusted with information, even sensitive financial information, and are included in the decision-making process. Well-informed employees are not only productive employees, but are involved, committed, and stay longer with the organization.

Over the years numerous studies have shown that employees place a high value on being kept informed about their job, their performance, and how the company is doing. An organization's inability to retain top employees can in large part be traced directly to the lack of positive, open communication that would provide the employees with the information they need. This weakness is not always intentional. You may not even be aware that your employees are in the dark because they do not send bulletins or carry signs that say they are dissatisfied and considering leaving. It is up to you to perceive subtle hints, identify problems, and more importantly, create an atmosphere of open and candid communication. This will promote the solution to problems before they reach a critical level and cause an employee to consider leaving.

Some business owners are so caught up in their entrepreneurial venture that they don't consider or value the insight of their employees. Owners often have an "I know what's best" attitude because they knew enough to start the company. But their actions and attitudes can leave employees isolated and unaware of what is really occurring in the organization. These owners don't realize that the growth of their company may require input from the entire organization.

176

Regardless of your company's size, you must be in touch with the employees and communicate with them candidly and frequently. It sounds easy to do but, unfortunately, it does not occur often enough. Companies of 25, 100, or even 250 employees may have more difficulty communicating than a larger business with 500 employees. Many times smaller organizations employ relatives or friends of top management people, so there is resistance to share information for fear of offending someone. But a company's small size is not a guarantee that top management will be in tune with employees and what they know.

This chapter explores ways to create an atmosphere of open candid communication. Both informal and formal approaches will be examined and ideas to improve communication will be shared. Figure 15.3 at the end of this chapter offers tips on improving communication.

Informal Communication

Improving informal communication is an easy and effective way to foster openness and trust in your company. Try some of the following ideas and add some of your own. You'll be surprised at the difference simple informal actions can make.

Increase Face-to-Face Communication

Most communication occurs informally while working together on projects, chatting in the lunchroom, or driving to a customer's office. These are valuable times for you to stay in touch with employees. During these face-to-face encounters, spend time chatting about social activities, sports, or hobbies, or focus on routine tasks or the accomplishment of a specific work project.

To get the most out of this time, ask employees questions that focus on their views. Ask how they feel about the job, what they would like to do in the future, and how happy they are with the company. Informal face-to-face communication can be extremely beneficial in learning not only what motivates the employee, but in discovering potential problems that could affect the performance of the organization and the employee's tenure.

Avoid Abuse of Impersonal Electronic Communication

Technology has greatly increased our ability to move information, but it has not encouraged the growth of interpersonal communications skills. E-mail and voice mail make it too easy to move information back and forth without any real person-to-person contact. This can upset your plans to improve communication in your company and retain employees because they feel connected. Why not do something to change this? It is not too drastic to restrict the use of e-mail between employees and managers in the same location for certain types of communication. While e-mail is good for the simple exchange of information and for keeping in touch over long distances, it does not foster the spirit of community necessary in small businesses. Reducing the abuse of electronic communication will immediately increase face-to-face communication. Make sure your employees and managers know each other—and you—as real people.

Avoid the "Inner Circle" Syndrome

Within all organizations, smaller groups or subgroups form. This is unavoidable. But as an owner or manager you can make sure that one of those subgroups is not an inner circle of people who have more of your attention than others. If the inner circle group is privy to inside information or gets perks others don't, it is detrimental to the whole company because as the select group attains higher status the outsiders slide lower on the company scale. This automatically lessens their commitment to their work and their motivation to be productive. The inner circle syndrome can be avoided by treating everyone equitably and ensuring that friends and relatives don't receive privileges or perks not available to others in the same position.

Learn to Listen

Communication, by definition, must be a two-way exchange. If a message is sent out but not received, there is no communication. You, as an owner or manager, have to take special care to make sure that when your employees have a message to send out, that you're ready, willing, and available to receive it.

The act of listening is easily overlooked when you get caught up in day-to-day activities and spend your communication time talking to employees. But this is only half the equation. After all, you already know what *you* have to say; your goal is to listen to what your *employees* have to say back. You'll find that simply listening to an employee can make him or her feel much more important. When you ask an employee, "How are you today?" or "What do you think?" listen to the answer.

Formal Communication

Companies have tried many approaches and spent a great deal of resources to create formal communication programs with employees. They provide company newsletters, video conferences, question-and-answer sessions, and other forms of media to keep employees informed and energized. As you read about the following formal communication programs, consider how you can use or adapt them to keep the lines of communication open between you and your employees.

Executive Interviews

An executive interview program provides a scheduled opportunity for you to ask questions and collect information while assuring employees that they have the opportunity to express their feelings and concerns on a regular basis. When employees know that a specific amount of time has been set aside by the business owner or manager to address their concerns, it can be very empowering and make employees feel important and valuable.

Executive interviews are usually conducted periodically, such as once a year, with every employee in the organization. The interviews are not designed to allow employees to circumvent the chain of command, but only to ensure an open flow of communication.

Employees should know in advance that the executive interview is totally confidential. They should also know that the interview does not guarantee that every concern raised will be resolved or every request honored. But they can be assured that you will give your attention to them and respond to their concerns. (It is often best not to provide an instant response, but to take the time to research the situation and get all the facts first.)

The executive interview is normally scheduled well in advance so the employee has time to prepare. It is generally held in a location where the conversation will not be overheard. They are often held outside the work place to encourage employees to speak more freely. Plan 30 to 45 minutes for an executive interview. Figure 15.1 provides a look at the format of an executive interview.

Company Newsletters

Some companies spend a great deal of time creating a company newsletter. It may be a four-color work of art that is written by a professional writer and wins design awards, or it can be a periodic personal message from the owner or manager to the employees. Your newsletter can be traditional or creative, monthly or seasonal, personal or corporate—but it must communicate information that people feel is important. If you are simply putting out dry information such as birthdays and anniversaries, or information they already know, you are not really communicating.

Barr-Nunn Transportation of Granger, Iowa, publishes a monthly newspaper called *The Manifest* that features messages on the company's mission and values, safety tips, articles about new employees, and coverage of company policies. The purpose is to show that someone back at the home office is concerned about their

FIGURE 15.1 • Executive Interview Format

- Thank the employee for his or her contribution to the company and reaffirm that the individual is critical to the company's future success.

- Explain that job satisfaction is important and that the company does not want an employee to have any unaddressed concern or problem.

- Explain that the executive interview is not a performance appraisal session. (See Chapter 14 for more info on performance appraisals.)

- Take the lead in the conversation and ask questions to get the employee to speak freely.

- Discuss the employee's satisfaction with the company, the job, management, and the work environment.

- Ask about relationships with coworkers.

- Probe to determine if the employee's manager is supportive.

- Create specific questions to address any suspected areas of concern.

- Allow plenty of time for the employee to express his or her concerns.

- Clarify any information that requires follow-up and action.

- Express appreciation for the employee's time and attention.

- Follow up on any issues or concerns.

- Relay any information (with the employee's approval) to the employee's supervisor.

- Communicate the results of any actions to the employee to show commitment.

welfare. They've also gotten creative and taken the newsletter concept a step further. Each month they provide their drivers with cassette tapes of industry news, interviews, and company information. They credit this as one of the major factors in dropping their turnover from 55 percent to 35 percent last year.

Think seriously about putting together this kind of formalized communication. There are plenty of freelance copywriters who can get you started. (Check online using the search term "freelance writers looking for employment.")

Attitude Surveys

Attitudes determine actions. If employees feel underpaid, they may respond by leaving for a position with a higher salary. If they feel unappreciated, they may look for an environment where they will be appreciated. Here again, communication is the key to heading off these kinds of problems and retaining your employees.

An excellent tool to accurately assess the attitudes of employees and identify potential problems is an attitude survey. An attitude survey can be given to the entire organization or only selected groups. Either way, its purpose is to provide a confidential method to obtain information, measure satisfaction, and listen to employees' concerns. A schedule of periodic surveys helps monitor changes in levels of satisfaction and identify concerns in key areas. It also helps examine trends, probe problem areas, confirm suspicions, and quantify attitudes that concern management.

The type of information available from attitude surveys is diverse. The areas typically addressed are feelings about the company, job, boss, and/or upper management. Other areas examined are goal clarity, planning, measurement, accountability, recognition, communications, human relations, management effectiveness, business effectiveness, and perceptions of the company and the industry. Attitudes concerning specific areas such as customer service, products, and specific departments or operations may also be examined.

Attitude surveys vary in complexity from a few simple questions (like the ones in Figure 15.2), to a long-term, in-depth study. You may conduct your own survey, but to be legally protected and ensure confidentiality and objectivity, most businesses contract an outside party to design the survey. The outside party can also administer the survey, tabulate the input and analyze the results, develop recommendations, and suggest an action plan to respond to concerns.

My experience in conducting attitude surveys for my clients has shown me that they can spot problems and suggest ways to improve. The key to their successful use is confidentiality. The employees must know that their responses will be kept confidential so they candidly express their true feelings. These are the feelings that motivate their actions.

Some companies distribute short surveys in pay envelopes and other employee communications. Others prefer a more detailed, long-term approach by having an organized, formal survey administered periodically. The timing and for-

FIGURE 15.2 • Sample Attitude Survey Questions

You can instruct your employees to answer *strongly agree, agree, disagree,* or *strongly disagree* to the following types of questions.

- My manager communicates openly with me.

- Our organization has a fair promotion policy.

- I am paid well in comparison to other companies.

- Promotion here is based on ability.

- Measurement of my personal performance is fair and accurate.

- I am recognized for good performance.

- There are enough contests, promotions, and awards to keep me motivated to do an excellent job.

- I am comfortable telling my manager what is going on, even if it is bad.

- I have a clear understanding of our company's policies and guidelines.

- I do not frequently think of quitting this job.

mat of your survey is not as important as the information you gather. Make sure the survey will give you answers that pinpoint both strong and weak areas and help you plan changes to improve employee retainment.

FIGURE 15.3 • Communication Tips

- Be sure you realize and understand cultural differences and how they affect communication.

- Don't use jargon and phrases with vague meanings. Be clear in what you say.

- Share the company's bad times as well as the good times with employees.

- Be open about the financial performance of the organization.

- Don't "shoot the messenger" who brings bad news unless you don't want any more messages.

- Check frequently to see if employees are getting the information they need and want.

- Make sure when you communicate with employees that you listen as well as talk.

- Be open to new mediums of communication such as newsletters, video reports, audio cassettes or regular e-mail updates.

- Hang charts and posters to keep people informed (even handwritten notices are good).

- Write letters of praise to employees about specific contributions. Occasionally mail these to their homes.

- Acknowledge special occasions in the employee's life such as a child's graduation or birthday.

- Seek out and talk to employees with whom you wouldn't normally.

- Spend more time with employees during stressful times, such as major projects and budget reductions.

- Ask yourself each day if you have taken the time to listen to and understand employees' needs and concerns.

FREQUENTLY ASKED QUESTIONS

Q. *Does an executive interview have to be very formal?*

A. No. The executive interview can be quite informal if it covers all the key points. Some owners/managers simply tell employees that they would like to find out how they feel about a few things and ask them to lunch. During this session they cover all the points normally covered in a formal executive interview.

Q. *What do you do if you find out in an executive interview or an employee attitude survey that employees are concerned about an issue that cannot be resolved to their satisfaction?*

A. Be honest. Let the employee know the specifics of the situation and communicate that it would be remedied if possible. Explain the restrictions, such as cost or laws that prohibit possible resolution. Candor works wonders in building relationships.

Q. *Can I create questions and conduct my own employee attitude survey?*

A. Yes. But keep in mind that for it to be effective, you must ask the right questions, tabulate the responses, and analyze the results. Also, the employees must believe that their confidentiality will be protected. To do these things effectively, it's best to hire an outside service to help you.

CHAPTER 16

Making Employees Feel Good about Themselves and Your Company

HAPPY EMPLOYEES ARE PRODUCTIVE EMPLOYEES.

A successful business requires many things, such as satisfied customers, innovation, and the ability to produce a salable good or service. Now add to that list employees with a healthy sense of self-esteem and a clear picture of their career goals. What candidates see and hear about the company during the application process helps them decide whether or not to work for a company. But what happens after the employees begin to work determines their happiness, fulfillment, and retention. Although the effects of pay and financial incentives on retention are strong (as discussed in Chapter 18), don't count on higher salaries, better benefits, or perks to keep people in an environment where they feel unhappy or stuck. Focus your initial retention efforts on building employee self-esteem and using career counseling to keep your employees motivated, productive, and on track.

Boost Self-Esteem

Self-esteem is a feeling of confidence and satisfaction, and the perception of value, worth, capability, and intelligence, by which one measures oneself. Changes in self-esteem can result from the way a person is treated and may directly affect the length of time an employee stays with a company.

The role of self-esteem has been vastly underestimated in the retention of personnel. While each individual enters your employ with a given level of esteem, what you do either builds up or breaks down this level. If you ignore this reality, the results can be disastrous.

There are several very easy things you can do in your position of authority to boost the self-esteem of your employees while increasing their job satisfaction.

185

Show Genuine Concern

Genuine concern for each employee as a person is essential to help an individual develop a sense of esteem in the workplace. Employees must be treated with respect and dignity. Care must be taken to avoid things that demean an employee and promote things that build up the employee's esteem. For example, you might try to eliminate any differentiation between management and employees by not assigning parking places based on rank or having an executive washroom.

These are the little things which allow everyone to feel valued. There is nothing wrong with providing employee perks and benefits for performance and tenure. However, creating a feeling that owners and upper management are more valuable puts barriers between employees and management. It reduces candid and open communication and decreases the employees' perception of their worth.

Set High Expectations

Many employees do not fully comprehend their capabilities. You have to lead them to see their own potential or it will never be realized. Take time to share your vision of the employee's worth and value to the organization. The greatest gift you can give an employee is to see greater potential than the employee sees and share it with that person.

Simple things, such as providing challenging assignments, not jumping in and taking over at the first sign of trouble, and sticking with the employee through difficulties, will communicate a high level of expectation. Figure 16.1 explores some more ways to communicate expectations.

Provide Helpful Performance Feedback

Just setting high expectations is not enough. It is critical that you take the time to provide feedback on performance so employees know how they are doing. This is not the same as a performance appraisal described in Chapter 14. Performance feedback provides informal observations on a regular basis.

To reinforce the employee's self-esteem, feedback must be accurate and candid without being judgmental. The focus of your feedback should be on the employee's performance—not the employee.

Don't focus on the individual by saying: "You didn't get the job done because you just didn't try hard enough." Instead, focus on the task and say: "If more had been done in this area, it would have been more successful." Don't say, "You're not trying hard enough." Instead say, "This task requires more effort and time." Don't say, "You are careless." Instead say, "To perform this task, you will have to pay more attention to your work." Don't say, "You messed that up." Instead say, "Because of your action, there is a problem with the. . . ."

FIGURE 16.1 • Communicating High Expectations

- Assign difficult work projects and set challenging goals.

- Provide detailed and accurate feedback on job performance.

- Listen to employees and allow time for them to express ideas and suggestions.

- Assign additional tasks and workload.

- Provide moderate praise for successful effort to show success was expected.

- Display confidence by allowing the employee to work through difficult situations.

- Assign tasks that require skill and judgment.

Employees rarely achieve more than their managers believe possible. Expectations are not only a measurement of performance, they are the motivation and fuel to perform.

Reward Performance and Tenure

There are many different rewards employees can be offered to recognize their contributions and tenure. Expand your thinking and look for things people really value:

- Some organizations give the employee additional or incremental vacation based on their years of service.
- Some recognize each employee's anniversary with the company with a special announcement and celebration.
- If employees are given a company car, some upgrade the quality of the vehicle after milestone anniversaries.
- Most organizations provide service pins, charms, or rings to recognize tenure.
- Logo merchandise, such as T-shirts, sweaters, jackets, and even belt buckles can be offered as rewards for contribution and tenure.

Simple, but genuine, rewards make a clear statement of your appreciation and recognition of an employee's efforts and loyalty.

Take Stock

It really isn't difficult to boost your employees' self-esteem levels, but it does take a conscious effort. It won't happen unless you make it happen. Every once in a while, check your esteem-boosting actions by asking yourself the following questions:

- Do I show genuine concern for my employees?
- Do I treat long-time employees or management better than new hires?
- Do I allow tenured employees to treat new hires poorly?
- Do I provide challenging assignments?
- Do I jump in and take over at the first sign of trouble?
- Do I stick with my employees even if they are having difficulty?
- Do I give informal consistent performance feedback?
- Do I focus criticism on the job performance and not on the employee?
- Do I recognize and rewards contributions and tenure?

The answers to these questions give you insight into your employees' feelings about working for your company. You also get a good idea why your employees tend to stay or leave.

Career Counseling

Many companies, large and small, have had the experience of being "blind-sided" by a valuable employee who abruptly decides to move to another company or career. By the time the manager learns of the decision, it is usually too late to stop the employee from leaving. Plans have been created and commitments have been made.

Employees' career plans, problems, and frustrations don't arise abruptly. However, if they surprise you, then there has been a lack of candid, in-depth conversation with your employees to discover their real career goals and desires. You need to have a planned realistic approach that includes career counseling to help employees identify and satisfy their desires within the company.

Career counseling can identify clearly defined paths of advancement and promotion for the employee within the company. Some managers mistakenly feel it is the employees' responsibility to communicate their career desires. But they are wrong. Employees have the responsibility for satisfying their own desires and career needs. Keeping the organization staffed with capable, talented people willing to be top performers is your responsibility.

Regular career counseling has been part of the culture of some large corporations for years. The Kansas City–based Hallmark Corporation works hard to identify its high-potential employees early to ensure they are challenged and kept interested. It is a major part of their culture for senior managers to identify these employees, take them under their wings, and nurture them. According to Dave Pylipow, Director of Employee Relations, once they identify high potential, they begin to figure out how to keep them "plugged in." He says, "Most folks just crave the opportunity to show you what they can do and respond well when they know they're being recognized."

Small companies also need a systematic career counseling system. The numerous demands on managers of small companies can cause them to overlook the need to listen and deal with this all-important issue. It doesn't have to be difficult, complex, or even time-consuming to create and implement a career counseling program. Staying in tune with your employees' desires and allowing them the opportunity to feel they are heard takes just a bit of your time and attention.

Scheduling Career Counseling

The first step in career counseling is to determine who will be involved. One approach is to identify the high-potential employees that your company would have significant difficulty operating without. This allows your time and energy to be focused on these critical human assets. In some companies, due to size or unique situation, all employees might be involved.

The next step is to determine how frequently career counseling should occur. Having these sessions every several months can become repetitive and time consuming, unless you are dealing with a new employee or one in transition. Anything less than once a year would probably not be frequent enough. Most organizations choose to conduct career counseling sessions annually for high-potential employees, and less frequently, such as every two to three years, for other employees.

Employee Preparation

Encourage your employees to prepare in advance for career counseling sessions. Tell them that they will be meeting with you to reflect on their goals, career objectives, and job satisfaction. Two to four weeks' advance notice is sufficient.

Instruct your employees (usually in writing) how to prepare. Ask them to examine their careers by brainstorming. Suggest they take time and use unrestricted, free-form style thinking to examine their feelings in four categories: (1) likes, (2) dislikes, (3) wants, and (4) goals. Suggest that they record all information without questioning or qualifying it. This free-form, noncritical style is designed to simply get ideas onto paper. The employee should do this several times, simply jotting down feelings, ideas, and desires.

Then instruct your employees to rate each statement in order of importance. Simply use "1" as very important, "2" as important, and "3" as somewhat important.

Now that these feelings have been translated into statements on paper, the employee can begin creating an ideal job description. Link the "1's" together to describe an ideal job. This will begin painting a picture of what the employee really wants in a career.

After employees have completed this career-goal exercise, ask them to write down what they feel and think about their present job and future plans each day for two weeks. This will serve as a reality check. Suggest that they take a few minutes each day, usually at the same time, to write what they like and dislike about work. At the end of the period ask employees to review their journals, make observations, and compare reality to their ideals.

Your Preparation

It is essential that you be well-prepared for a career counseling session. In advance consider your goals, your employee's performance record, the questions you'll ask, and scheduling.

Three goals. To begin, clearly understand the three goals of each session:

1. Assess your employee's strengths, weaknesses, and career goals.
2. Identify what must be done or learned for the employee to be ready for the next position.
3. Develop an action plan to ensure that the employee is ready for promotion when an opportunity becomes available.

Get to know your employee. Next, examine the employee's records and performance appraisals. Take note of the following:

- Strengths and weaknesses
- Assigned tasks and results
- Commitment and desire to learn and develop
- Willingness and ability to sacrifice, work, and travel
- Anything that will significantly affect the employee's ability to be successful in a future position

When you have a clear and objective picture of the employee, take time to talk with others who know the employee well and have had the opportunity to observe the individual in day-to-day situations. Compare the feedback you receive from others to your own observations.

Create counseling questions. You want to be prepared to ask questions that will help your employee to think carefully about career goals, skills, commitment, and effort. You want to ask more than the obvious questions such as, "When do you want to be promoted?" The natural response to that question will be, "yesterday." By asking more meaningful questions, such as "Are you willing to invest time and endure the travel to be a manager?" you can help your employees to think and question what they really want and are willing to commit to achieving. Plan in advance what you want each employee to consider. Sample questions are offered in the next section.

Set a date. Set up a schedule of counseling meetings and confirm the time and place of each meeting. Be sure the location will allow open and candid conversation with little distraction. It is a good idea to go to a neutral area such as a conference room or a quiet restaurant where you can have a cup of coffee and a focused conversation.

Conducting a Career Counseling Session

Begin the session by stating that your objective is to help increase the employee's success. Explain that you are committed to the success of each employee and that you will ensure the individual's career goals are met when the time is right.

Restate your commitment to long-term growth at a rate the employee can sustain and enjoy. Explain that you will help the employee move at his or her own pace.

Ask the employee where he or she is in the development process. Probe to determine career goals, future plans, likes and dislikes. You might ask questions such as:

- What is your long-term career goal?
- What do you want to be doing three to five years from now?
- What is the most exciting part of the job you would like to have?
- What is the least exciting part?

Probe the employee's perception of the new positions desired. Make sure the employee has a complete understanding of the responsibilities, duties, and expected level of performance of the position. Explore the steps that must be taken and the effort needed for the employee to get to the desired position. You might ask:

- What are the skills, knowledge, and attitudes you will need to be successful in this position?
- What are the steps you must take to get what you want?

- What do you believe is an achievable time frame for these steps?
- What is the investment in time and effort you feel it will take to accomplish this?

Determine the employee's level of self-awareness by assessing commitment and readiness to assume the position. You might ask:

- What specific new skills do you think you need to develop?
- What experiences do you think you must have?
- Are you committed to making the investment necessary to attain this position?
- Will this investment affect you personally?

Examine your employee's timeline. Look at specific periods such as now, three months from now, and six months or a year from now. Ask the employee to make an assessment of the probability of success if promoted at each period. This can add realism to the conversation. You might ask:

- How will you know when you are ready for the next step?
- How realistic is the timing you propose?

Help the employees develop an action plan to prepare for the next level. Be sure to set a timetable or a deadline for the action and a method of measurement to determine when it has been completed. Identify the resources, materials, or people to assist the employee. It is very important the employee commit to an action plan that will be followed up periodically.

Close the career counseling session with a commitment to support these efforts. Let your employee know it is really up to each individual to determine when it is time to move.

Post-Session Follow-Up

There is real power in putting agreements into writing because once something goes into writing it begins to become reality. Take the time to communicate in writing your appreciation for each employee's involvement and commitment to career counseling. Express confidence that if they apply themselves, they can grow and realize their career objectives.

If an individual's career objectives are still not realistic, explain the need to examine these desires further and plan to meet again. Set a follow-up meeting to see how the individual is progressing in completing the stated goals. This is not the same as the career counseling session. It is held one to three months later to answer questions and gauge the individual's commitment and actions.

Employee-Driven Growth

It is important for employees to understand that they can move forward in your company. This may mean upward movement where employees look forward to promotions. Or, as in many small businesses, it may mean increasing their level of contribution in the same position, knowing that as their value to the company increases, profits will increase, as will their compensation. Their commitment to developing themselves and taking advantage of opportunities available in the company determines progress. By focusing employees' attention on development rather than promotion, employees can develop their own capabilities and increase their sense of career fulfillment.

The bottom line is simple—employee satisfaction equals long-term retention. Employees who feel valued and who believe there is room for personal and professional growth and development within the company stay with the company. This reduction in turnover is invaluable to the success of your business.

*F*REQUENTLY *A*SKED *Q*UESTIONS

Q. *How important is the manager's level of expectation?*

A. The level of expectation of the manager is one of the most significant factors in the performance of the employee. Experience has shown that managers who have high levels of expectation for themselves and their employees consistently produce better results than managers who expect little.

Q. *What happens if goals are too challenging and set too high?*

A. A goal is only motivational if an individual believes it is attainable. When employees believe there is no realistic chance to achieve a goal, it no longer becomes a motivating factor and can even become a de-motivator.

Q. *What can I do when I can no longer demonstrate belief in the employee?*

A. Rarely does an employee perform well after the manager has lost confidence. If you no longer have confidence in the employee's ability to perform, it is time to take action. It is better to acknowledge reality and make plans to replace the individual accordingly.

Q. *What do you do if you have a long-term employee who does not have the desire to change to another position?*

A. While the employee may answer the same way each time, he or she should be given the courtesy of being able to discuss career plans. This discussion may simply be a short meeting to express appreciation for contributions and ask if any career goals and desires have changed.

Q. *What do I do if employees create plans to develop themselves for a promotion but fail to follow through and develop the skill?*

A. Career development is the employee's responsibility. If the employee fails to carry out this responsibility, the manager should be candid and inform the employee not to expect the promotion.

Q. *If a person needs to develop skills to assume the next position, why shouldn't I just go ahead and promote the employee and let the skills develop while in the position?*

A. You'll find that individuals are more motivated to develop skills and knowledge before assuming the responsibility. Also, with the skills in hand, the initial performance will be much higher. Plus, you can benefit from having the opportunity to identify any difficulties the individual may have while developing new skills, and avoid promoting the employee too soon.

CHAPTER 17

Providing Job Enrichment Opportunities

CHANGE THE JOB BEFORE THE EMPLOYEE CHANGES JOBS.

Employees today expect more than a job and a paycheck. They expect meaningful, fulfilling, challenging work. If you do not enrich jobs so they are perceived as valuable and worthwhile, you will continually have a problem getting employees to do their work. You will also experience higher than normal turnover and less success.

By their very nature, small organizations have an incredible opportunity to create enriched jobs that provide excitement, interest, and satisfaction. In smaller companies, there are a wide variety of tasks to be done. Diversity in job duties tends to keep employees more interested. From a job enrichment standpoint, you want to hear your employees say, "No two days are ever the same," or "I'm always doing something different."

What Is Job Enrichment?

Job enrichment is a deliberate process designed to capitalize on the employee's ability and personal skills to allow the individual to focus on something beyond a narrow job description.

Job enrichment is not a singular project or one-time effort of improvement, but a continuous process that allows for employee participation in a wide variety of areas. Job enrichment makes the job more valuable to the employee, and the employee more valuable to you.

Steps of Job Enrichment

There are specific steps to accomplishing job enrichment. As you plan your employee retention strategy, consider the following methods.

195

Create the Proper Environment

Performance is critical in all businesses. However, a climate or environment must be created so that the greatest short-term performance of an individual is not the ultimate goal. Jobs that allow time for creativity give employees the opportunity to look up from their workstation, see what is going on, and find ways to improve. For example, if a store is staffed at a level where a sales clerk can take the time to observe its operation rather than continuously being at the cash register, the individual will see what other employees are doing and build on their performances.

Design the Job for Maximum Use of Skills

Don't restrict your employees' skills and motivation by hemming them in with limited responsibility. When they prove they have the desire and ability to handle additional responsibility, enlarge their positions to incorporate other areas. This can be done within the department by assigning additional work such as training new employees or assuming some of the manager's tasks. Outside the department, an employee can work with other groups, such as those in shipping or purchasing, as a liaison.

Provide Proper Equipment and Systems

Providing the most up-to-date tools such as new computer software, information, or systems will help enrich the position and keep the employee interested. It is frustrating for an employee to try to produce top-notch work with antiquated equipment. Give your employees what they need to do the job right. For example, a state-of-the-art point of sale system will help make the job of handling customer purchases much easier for salespeople.

Provide Continuous Learning and Growth Opportunities

By providing information and training employees need for current positions and future development, you will prepare them for promotions or lateral opportunities in the future. Organizations that continue to learn will grow rather than stagnate. They may not always gain short-term profits or revenues, but expanding employee capabilities will lead to capital growth in the future. For example, setting up a lending library of audio or video tapes and books provides the opportunity for employees to continuously build skills and knowledge that will be useful in the future.

Create Alternate Career Paths

As the workplace becomes more complex, and the value of specialized and technical employees increases, successful companies are designing career ladders to reward those in professional or non-management paths. Not everyone desires or has the ability to be a manager. Still, you can offer opportunity for growth and development on alternate or parallel career ladders. For example, rather than having all your sales reps believe the only way to move forward is to become sales manager, create a specialist position that focuses on a specific product or customer type. In this way, individuals highly qualified and skilled in specific areas of the business can continue to use their expertise, move forward (not necessarily up) and be of the most value to the company.

Certify Skills

In addition to developing a parallel career ladder based on expertise, some companies, especially manufacturing or high-tech organizations, reward the development of specific skills. They provide a certification program to verify that an individual has attained the new skill. For example, when an employee is trained to run a more advanced piece of equipment, like a new robotics manufacturing system, the individual receives the appropriate recognition and certification. In the event that a position using that equipment becomes available, the individual can be given the opportunity to transfer, resulting in increased pay.

Try Rotation

Many who have worked in the same position a number of years experience what is called *burnout*. They've solved the same problems and performed the same tasks so many times that the job becomes routine and boring and performance can decrease. Rotating individuals to other assignments or positions may be all they need to become re-excited and re-energized. This doesn't mean simply moving employees from one location to the other, but rather allowing individuals to experience another position either on a temporary or permanent basis. Employees who rotate will not only enjoy the personal benefits of a changing job environment, but they will develop a better appreciation of the needs of other departments, learn skills that they can transfer to other positions, and get a better perspective of the overall needs of the company.

Consider Group Job Enrichment

Job enrichment can also be a department or group activity. You can enlist the support of everyone in the department or group to find ways to make the job better and more rewarding. The team approach is founded on the idea of improved communication and has been successfully used for years by many companies. The group can include everyone in the department, as well as outside individuals. The group can meet to discuss ways to improve the work environment, then evaluate and incorporate the suggestions to enrich the job experience.

Grow Employee Capability

Continuous learning is a hallmark of an innovative and improving company. Employees at all levels must continuously improve and expand their capabilities. The most innovative and productive companies continuously train to develop knowledge and skills as part of their regular routine.

Some companies take advantage of downtime during slack periods or off-season periods to focus on growing employee capability. Rather than cutting hours or laying off workers, try training them. Training should not just develop the basic skills necessary to perform a job, it should improve an employee's ability to accept greater responsibility, thus expanding their contribution to the company. Some organizations pay for outside seminars or college tuition, allowing employees to use time during the work day to complete degree requirements. While this may reduce profits during a slow period, it will create a more valuable employee who can perform at a higher level during peak periods.

Value Tenure

There must be a relationship between each employee and the employer. One way to publicly recognize this relationship is to celebrate anniversaries. Keep a calendar of each employee's starting date and do something special every year to recognize and reward tenure:

- Hang a simple sign over the door proclaiming, "Congratulations to John on his first anniversary."
- Have the employee stand at a meeting to receive a round of applause.
- Recognize milestone anniversaries with public recognition at family picnics or banquets.
- Give tangible rewards like a wristwatch or ring for milestone anniversaries.
- Give gifts of logo merchandise, such as T-shirts, sweaters, jackets, or even belt buckles to reward tenure.
- Send congratulatory cards, letters, or even flowers to employees at their homes.
- Include the news in the company newsletter.

This kind of special recognition of anniversaries lets the entire organization know that your company values loyalty and tenure.

Job enrichment is a retention tool. Keeping the job interesting, moving, challenging, changing, growing, and satisfying is vital to your efforts to reduce employee turnover.

FREQUENTLY ASKED QUESTIONS

Q. How much should the pay increase for skill certification be?

A. The increase should be significant enough to excite and motivate the employee, but not so much as to get wages out of balance with others or adversely affect profit. If an employee making ten dollars an hour were given a five percent raise because of increased skill and value to the company, it would benefit both the employer and employee.

Q. Isn't it best to assign employees to the tasks they can perform best rather than use job rotation?

A. Job rotation is not designed to create turmoil or reduce effectiveness. For example, if less than 10 to 20 percent of the employees are being rotated to another job at any one time, the organization should be able to make up for the lack of expertise by having a more satisfied and motivated workforce.

Q. Using teamwork and rotation sounds like a good idea. How can they be incorporated into a small business?

A. An easy way is for a rotating employee to work with one or two people from another department who are attempting to solve a problem or improve a process. Not only will the employee get a better perception of the department, but those working on the problem will benefit from a fresh perspective from another individual or department.

CHAPTER 18

Offering Financial Incentives and Other Perks

MONEY IS NOT THE ONLY REASON EMPLOYEES STAY,
BUT IT'S AN IMPORTANT ONE.

Financial incentives are important reasons why employees are attracted to companies and why they stay. Creating a financial package that attracts and motivates top employees is essential for a stable workforce. It enables you to retain top employees and reduce the cost and chaos of high employee turnover. The financial package should be explained in your employee handbook.

Financial Incentives

Dissatisfaction with pay has often been cited as a significant contributor to turnover. The story line in the Steven Spielberg movie *Jurassic Park* involves a computer programmer who feels he is not paid enough or recognized for the system he created. This employee decides to get even by stealing the trade secrets (in this case, dinosaur eggs) and selling them to a competitor. He decides to right the perceived wrong of not being compensated properly. Companies that experience significant theft and employee turnover should clearly examine their employees' perceptions of fair compensation based on the value of work compared to others.

Compensation includes not only salary, but all other benefits or financial incentives. It is important for management to monitor satisfaction with financial incentives, both internally and externally. Internally, you can determine employees' feelings and satisfaction levels through one-on-one communication or employee attitude surveys (see Chapter 15). Externally, you can measure against pay levels of similar employers in your industry. Many trade associations have salary surveys available.

To keep top employees, you need a strong, well-designed package of financial incentives that not only matches but leads the market, with innovative benefits and rewards, and the promise of a secure financial future. A poorly designed financial incentive package, even if it is costly, may not achieve positive results, while a well-designed package may accomplish the goals with less investment. The following sections examine how you can create a well-conceived financial incentive package that rewards tenure and provides motivation for performance.

Incentive Compensation

Incentives reward the achievement of the individual, group, and business targets. These incentives are normally categorized into the three elements of commission, bonus, and promotion.

Commission. Typically used with salespeople to reward sales achievement, commission plans must be well thought out and clearly tied to objectives. You can have

- straight commission which is income based on commission only—no salary.
- progressive commission that increases the percentage of payout as performance gets higher. This rewards the employee for exerting greater effort and producing more results.
- regressive commission that decreases the percentage of the payout as performance goes up. This keeps the payout from being excessive in case of a windfall or period of very high sales.

The type of commission plan you use depends on your company's objectives, the effort required by the employee, and the value of that effort to the organization.

Bonus. Generally, a bonus is used to motivate additional effort and cause the employee to strive to reach specific higher levels of performance. Today popular incentives are bonus plans for work groups or the entire company if pre-set targets are met. Work group bonuses promote cooperation between individuals or groups and increase motivation. Several levels of targets with increasing payoffs are generally more effective than one level. But be careful, too many levels can reduce the motivation to achieve specific levels or thresholds.

Promotion. Although used less frequently, especially in small companies, promotion is possibly the most valuable of the compensation elements. A creative and skillfully executed promotion can create excitement and motivation, and produce results far beyond its cost. Promotions can be used to generate excitement for a new product, push sales during a slow period, or even get employees focused on safety.

Incentive compensation that rewards performance is not only valuable in keeping employees, it is valuable in creating a positive, results-oriented workforce motivated to perform. Properly created, incentives can be easily funded by the additional performance they promote. While this may sound easy, it takes time, effort, and experience to create a plan that works. You can also use employee involvement to successfully create the specifics of incentive programs. Assemble a small group and give them an objective, such as increase sales by 10 percent. Provide the budget parameters, and then ask them to help design an effective incentive program. It is important to tell them how the objective will be measured and which compensation methods to use. Under your guidance, they can create an incentive program that fairly rewards individuals for performance. An additional benefit is that they have already bought into the program they created.

Skill-Based Incentives

As we continue to broaden the skills needed for today's workforce, the concept of skill-based pay becomes more and more appropriate. No longer can we expect individuals entering the workforce to have all the basic skills needed to be successful. As the complexity of tasks increases, such as continuing developments in information technology, existing employees have to learn new skills to remain productive and compete with the new employees entering the labor force. Some companies have provided the opportunity for employees to learn and based pay raises on each individual's ability to perform certain functions or pass a skills test. In this way, the employee determines the next raise by demonstrating increased value to the organization. For example, a delivery helper in a retail organization can increase his pay by learning the job of driver and being compensated for learning those skills. When he is promoted to driver the skill-based incentive he received as a delivery helper will be replaced by the promotional raise of the higher level position. Not only does this skill-based pay provide an incentive for employees to learn, it also automatically creates qualified candidates for higher positions within the company.

Employees who are rewarded for becoming more valuable to the company not only increase their value, but also remain where their value is appreciated.

Benefits

Benefits are becoming more important in the retention of employees. To be competitive in today's labor market, you must provide what are considered "essential" benefits. These include health care and paid time off. Other desirable benefits you should consider include: dental plans, educational assistance, pension plans, gain sharing, stock ownership, profit sharing, deferred compensation, and a variety of other innovative perks.

The following laws affect employee benefits: ADEA, ADA, ERISA, Civil Rights Act of 1964, Equal Pay Act, Unemployment Insurance, HMO Act, Older Workers'

Benefit Protection Act, TEFRA, Social Security Act, IRC, Federal Corrupt Practices Act, and state workers' compensation and temporary disability laws.

Health care. While the cost of health care benefits continues to rise, the advantage of providing it for employees is tremendous. It allows employees the security of knowing they will be protected from a catastrophic expense. To control medical costs, companies have reduced benefits and increased employee contributions, but realize that it is still important to make health care benefits available, even if employee contributions are needed.

Pension plans. Traditional pension plans bind the employee to the company. They provide a monthly payment after retirement for loyal employees who have been employed by the company for a specific number of years. Obviously, a good pension plan can act as an incentive for employees to remain with the company. Employees are motivated to perform so their efforts will be rewarded with increased salaries and promotions which will also increase their pension benefits at retirement. It is important to keep employees informed about pension plans and educate them on their terms and conditions

Gain sharing. Gain sharing is any company-wide pay plan set up to reward all employees in the company, or just specific work groups, for improving performance. The sharing of gain, either of operating profits or asset value, is an excellent approach to keeping talented employees, and focusing them and improving bottom-line results. Gain sharing is similar to profit sharing, but has more flexibility because it can be created to fit specific business objectives, not just profit.

Although it seems like it should be simple to designate a portion of a gain to be shared with all employees, there are strategic and legal entanglements to gain sharing that can actually adversely impact a company's financial performance. To set up a gain sharing plan, you should consult a professional who specializes in this area. The most commonly used gain sharing plans are the Scanlon, Improshare, and Rucker. One of these, or a derivative, may work well for your organization.

Stock ownership. One of the best methods to retain an employee is to treat the individual like an owner. This not only increases self-esteem, but also represents your long-term commitment to the employee typically reserved for only a select few. According to a recent survey of American workers, 85 percent rank stock options as a positive incentive.

Employees who own a part of the company have a say in how it is run, and are more likely to work harder than employees who are just working for a paycheck. Employee-owned firms consistently and significantly outperform competitors in both employment growth and sales growth.

At Wal-Mart, one of the key strategies from the beginning was for all employees to be shareholders in the company. As owners, employees (or associates as they are called) receive regular financial performance reports. This has been one of the main reasons Wal-Mart has grown from a small family-owned business to one of the most successful retail giants in the country.

You might think that an employee stock ownership plan (ESOP) is only appropriate for large companies. But in the article, "Ownership: ESOPs Motivate" in *Inc.* magazine, the author cites the successful use of an ESOP in a company of 11 employees. It increased the employees' wealth as their stock appreciated in value over the years, reduced the CEO's difficulty in managing, and increased sales significantly. If you would like more information on ESOPs, contact Employee Ownership for Small Business (National Center for Employee Ownership) at 510-272-9461.

Profit sharing. Profit sharing has become increasingly important in attracting and retaining employees. Employees consider profit sharing a valuable part of their compensation income and look forward to the statements showing how much their wealth is increasing. If you set up a profit sharing plan, be aware that there can be a significant setup cost and an annual charge to monitor regulatory changes and prepare employee updates and tax forms. It is also very important to stress to your employees that there is no obligation for the company to make any contributions if times get tough.

Deferred compensation. Many organizations use unique and creative deferred compensation packages to retain their employees. This concept of "golden handcuffs"—binding an employee to the organization by dangling future dollars—came into being around the mid-1960s in large corporations and was available only to high-level executives or key employees. But now it is being used more by smaller businesses for any employee who is valuable to the company. There are a variety of golden handcuffs, but all contain one or more of the basic ingredients of a deferred cash bonus and some type of investment vehicle.

True deferred compensation can be an excellent way to keep an employee long term. It is based on additional compensation above and beyond normal income that is deferred and invested for the employee until a maturity date. For example, if the company puts an additional 10 percent of an employee's earnings into a deferred compensation plan that matures in five years, the employee would have the equivalent of one-half year's income plus its growth in the plan after five years. While profit sharing is vested after a number of years and the employee can take all of the money at one time, deferred compensation does not allow this—an advantage for you. In our example, in the fifth year the employee would be eligible to get the first year's compensation, the sixth year the employee would be eligible to get the second year's compensation, and so on. As a result, the employee will always "leave money on the table" if he or she walks away from the company. Another advantage is that you can determine what you want to contribute to deferred compensation based on the position and the individual. According to IRS rules, this would be considered a non-qualified plan giving you significant flexibility.

In many smaller companies, employees may not be confident of the company's ability to pay the deferred compensation at maturity and will want to see tangible proof that compensation has been deferred and is available. An excellent way to provide tangible proof, and also increase assets, is to place the deferred compensation in an investment account managed by a professional. The agreement between you and the employee specifies the time and conditions under which the company will transfer ownership of the assets for that year's compensation to the employee. Having the deferred compensation contributed to an account not only allows the employee to feel protected against possible misfortune or bankruptcy of the company, but it allows the employee to participate in the management of the account, increasing the perception of the value. Using deferred compensation in smaller businesses is becoming a more viable alternative.

Flexible Benefits Plans

Today many employees do not fit the model of married with spouse and children, because they may be unmarried, single, or in nontraditional families. Because they have significantly different needs, there has been a rise in flexible or "cafeteria-style" benefit plans. These allow individuals to choose the benefits that are most advantageous for their particular situations. For example, a single mother may want child-care assistance much more than retirement benefits. The concept of adapting benefits to the employee not only assists the employee, but provides a very economical way for an employer to provide benefits. The numerous benefits options that are available, even to a small employer, include: medical insurance, long-term health care for the aged employee or employee's parents, dental plans, tuition reimbursement, and matching charitable contributions.

Professional Employer Organizations

Most small- to medium-sized businesses find the task of providing high-quality, up-to-date benefits at a reasonable cost a daunting one. This, and the fact that many companies do not want to be in the benefits business, has led to the emergence of a new type of company—the Professional Employer Organization (PEO). PEOs were created to leverage a company's position by providing better benefits at a lower cost and even offering additional human resource services. PEOs offer companies the opportunity to pool with other businesses to get the best rates, and they have professionals dedicated to creating benefit packages.

When payroll and benefit payments become too cumbersome for a company, employees may actually be fired and then hired back by the PEO. On the surface, nothing changes because the employee still works at the same company doing the same job, but now paychecks come from the PEO, which also handles the administrative filing of taxes and reports. While a PEO offers many benefits, small businesses have been reluctant to give up control of their employees and, as a result, have resisted this concept. But as your business grows, it is something you might want to consider.

Innovative Techniques

Much can be done to increase retention of top employees with innovation and creativity rather than cash.

- Spread rewards or bonuses for performance out over a longer period rather than dispensing them in a lump sum. General Motors typically spreads some bonuses over a three- to five-year period and if the employee leaves, the individual loses the unpaid portion.
- Give employees who work on new products a vested interest so they realize some of the gains the new product generates.
- Consider extending health coverage to all employees, including part-time workers. Starbucks Coffee Company gave part-timers health insurance and at the same time decreased their turnover to less than 50 percent in an industry where turnover runs 100 percent or more annually.
- Use noncash rewards as financial incentives, such as gift certificates that can be converted into merchandise. A cash reward is easily spent and gone, but merchandise will always be a reminder of the employee's performance and your recognition.

Communicate the Full Value of Financial Incentives

Often, especially in smaller companies, employers add a specific benefit assuming that employees will understand its real value. Unfortunately, without a detailed breakdown of the value of benefits, employees continue to view only their paycheck when evaluating the financial reasons to stay with a company.

Companies that realize this remind their employees of the real value and cost of company benefits and compensation. Periodically, the employees receive statements that detail the actual financial value of everything in their incentive package. In some instances, it even quotes the cost for the employee to secure the benefit on the open market. This statement includes not just salary and commissions, but other items such as automobile usage, health care coverage, retirement benefits, potential matching contributions to programs such as profit sharing, charity, education, and all other "cafeteria" benefits. The statement gives a total so that the employees understand the real value of their "pay." Figure 18.1 details the compensation for a sales clerk.

*F*REQUENTLY *A*SKED *Q*UESTIONS

Q. How often should an employee get a statement showing the real or full value of compensation?

A. The statement should be sent to the employees as often as needed to remind them of the real value of salary, incentives, and benefits. In most cases this is annually or semi-annually.

Q. Where do the dollars for deferred compensation come from?

A. It is not deducted or taken out of the employee's current pay. It is compensation budgeted and paid above and beyond the current or normal salary and bonus.

Q. What happens to the deferred compensation if the employee is terminated or leaves before the date agreed upon for receiving compensation?

A. It is specified in the agreement between the employee and the company that while the employee has the right to make limited investment decisions, the deferred compensation account is owned by the company until the employee satisfies the conditions of the agreement. In the event the employee leaves before that time, the ownership of the account stays with the company and the money can be used for a variety of needs including funding future deferred compensation.

FIGURE 18.1 • Total Compensation Summary

Sales Clerk: John Jones
SS# 222-22-2222
as of December 31, 1997

Compensation

Salary	$18,720.00 (@ $9.00 per hour)
Commission	5,861.00
Bonus	1,000.00
Subtotal	$25,581.00

Additional Financial Benefits

IRA matching	$ 360.00
Additional Life Insurance	275.00
Health Insurance	1,140.00
Dental Insurance	480.00
Child Care Allowance	600.00
Deferred compensation (@7%)	1,791.00
Subtotal	$4,646.00

GRAND TOTAL:
The financial benefit and compensation for the year 1997
$30,277.00

NOTE: You will be eligible to receive this year's deferred compensation of $1,791 plus any interest and appreciation on December 15, 2002. Your deferred compensation accounts grew 16.2 percent and have a total of $10,387 invested.

Q. If an employee does something that calls for immediate termination per our policy, can I make exception based on tenure?

A. Personnel policies stated in the employee handbook are a guide to handling situations. Circumstances and the employee's previous performance and activities must be considered in all actions. It is important to explain that the employee's tenure does not excuse the behavior and makes the conduct even more upsetting. However, in recognition of the years of positive service, additional leeway can be given if the employee wants to solve the problem. This does not lower expectations or standards.

Q. *Don't special perks for tenure, such as a better office or company car, create a sense of preferential treatment that can damage morale?*

A. It is very important to explain the reasons for the special treatment. If everyone knows it is in recognition and appreciation for previous contributions, it will motivate others to make similar contributions. Be sure that the reward is available to all and is not used as a vehicle for preferential treatment.

Q. *Do employees resent letters being sent home?*

A. As long as letters are positive and uplifting there should be no repercussions. The positives of letting family members know the value and contribution of the employee far outweigh any potential risk.

Learn from Your Losses

CHAPTER 19

Reviewing Why They Leave and the Costs Left Behind

YOU MUST KNOW THE FACTS
BEFORE YOU CAN IMPROVE IN THE FUTURE.

Even when you use the smart staffing hiring process and invest time and effort in keeping and rewarding top employees, some individuals will choose to leave your employ. This happens for many reasons that sometimes can't be prevented or foreseen. Still, many experts believe that the majority of employee resignations occur for common and avoidable reasons. Just as you invest time and effort in finding and keeping good employees, take some time to review the factors in the workplace and your employees' lives that have proven to cause turnover. Also take a good look at what it costs you every time an employee leaves. This review will renew your motivation to use smart staffing to begin with.

Ten Reasons Why Employees Leave

While there is no universal list of factors that pertain to every business, it is good to understand the most common reasons why people leave any place of employment so you can compare them to your own patterns of turnover. It will give you a starting point from which to respond to employees' needs, address common problems, and alleviate conditions that may be causing the resignation of people that you worked so hard to hire.

Basic Financial Needs

When earnings dip below the individual's minimum financial needs and the situation cannot be resolved at the current place of employment, the individual will look elsewhere for a job with better earnings. Because few people reduce their needs in order to stay with a company, care must be taken to ensure that the employee is able to live with the compensation. This is not to say you must increase pay levels to support whatever lifestyle an employee chooses, but be aware of the consequence of not meeting the employee's basic needs.

For the solution to this problem, see "Determine the Compensation" in Chapter 6.

Lack of Competitive Salary

In addition to meeting basic income needs, compensation must be at or above a competitive level for the geographical area and industry. Remember, even if you are paying what you consider to be a good salary and meeting the individual's basic needs, if employees hear of other people in similar positions making more money elsewhere, it will open the door to turnover. And don't just compare salary within your own industry. In the midwest, for example, retail organizations have tremendous problems keeping employees due to union wages in nearby manufacturing plants. Even if employees can't go to another company in your industry to make more money, the ability to make more outside the industry might cause them to consider leaving.

For a solution to this problem, see "Financial Incentives" in Chapter 18.

Inadequate Benefits

With the cost of health care and other life essentials rising, generous benefit packages are becoming more important as a retention tool, and inadequate benefit packages are often the reason for high employee turnover. As a sign of our times, day care benefits are heading the list of "must haves" in contract negotiations. (The cost of day care rose 202 percent from 1979 to 1994!) If you want to keep your young employees, you must help provide for the proper care of their children during working hours.

For solutions to this problem see "Flexible Benefit Plans" in Chapter 18.

Poor Communication

Poor communication causes many problems which reduce tenure. To begin with, it is essential that employees have a clear understanding of their jobs and what is expected of them. Employees who are criticized for falling short of unspoken expectations feel insecure and soon look elsewhere for work that will restore their confidence. Unspoken expectations can be easily prevented by giving each employee a copy of the job description and essential job functions.

Employees also begin to feel insecure when they hear information about their company or their position through the grapevine. In our fast-changing work world where jobs hang on mergers, acquisitions, and change, employees have a right to be very sensitive to poor communication from management. Candid and open communication will go a long way to reducing departures even in unstable times.

Surprisingly, formal communication programs that rely on office memos and e-mail are also often responsible for employee turnover. If one-to-one communication is abandoned in favor of mass high-tech communication, employees lose their feeling of connection with the company, the owners, and management. The loyalty and trust that keep employees on board are built during informal chats around the break table, at company picnics, and while working and talking shoulder to shoulder.

For solutions to this problem, see Chapter 15, "Communicating with Your Employees."

Negative Workplace Environment

Employees want a feeling of belonging and community—this feeling creates the workplace environment or climate. If there is a positive environment in which people have an affinity for those around them and each feels valued and liked, the employees stay. This becomes especially notable in the multicultural and multiracial workplace. When staffing people with diverse backgrounds, the owner/manager must be especially sensitive to the workplace environment that exists in the company. Few people give their best effort or stay in their job if the climate is negative.

For solutions to this problem, see Chapter 16, "Making Employees Feel Good about Themselves and Your Company."

Lack of Recognition

Lack of recognition translates to the employee as lack of success. Regardless of the level, position, or job, every employee wants to be recognized for a job well done. Companies that have recognition programs to reward effort and success have a much better chance of keeping their employees. These programs range from formal recognition events that cover the entire organization to very informal words of acknowledgment to an individual who is working hard. Employees need to feel successful, or they will seek change.

For solutions to this problem, see Chapter 16.

Unfair and Inequitable Treatment

All your positive efforts to keep and reward employees can be erased in a moment if employees feel that they are not being treated fairly and equitably. Especially in small businesses where there may not be formal policies and procedures, employees must be treated fairly and perceive that the rewards or penalties are equitable to the action and consistently applied to all employees. Otherwise owners/

managers open themselves to accusations of favoritism. The perception of unfair or inequitable business practices destroys trust and causes employees to leave.

For solutions to this problem, see Chapter 16.

Lack of Challenging Job Content

Positions with the greatest turnover tend to be those that are boring, repetitive, and not challenging. This is a problem that usually develops over time. A job that a person once found challenging may later become routine. When employees no longer have to think about the job, and it has become effortless and unexciting, they look for new challenges—sometimes outside of your company.

Plateaus, based on job content, are quite predictable if you're alert to them. They generally occur on three levels. The first is noticeable at about six months when employees decide whether or not they are happy doing the job. Next, between one-and-a-half to two years, employees develop knowledge and skill and begin to ask if they really want to do the job. At about the seven-year mark, if not promoted, they begin to ask if they could be happy doing the job for the rest of their career. At each plateau they are faced with the decision to go or to stay.

For solutions to this problem, see Chapter 17, "Providing Job Enrichment Opportunities."

Lack of Job Security

The landscape of American business has changed tremendously in recent years. Mergers, acquisitions, re-engineering, and downsizing have shown employees that their jobs are no longer entitlements. They have learned that excellent performance is not a guarantee of continued employment. When individuals feel continued employment is threatened and long-term job prospects are not good, they will take the initiative to find job security elsewhere. While no company can guarantee employment for life, all companies can reduce turnover by providing for the individual's need for employment security.

For solutions to this problem, see Chapter 15 and "Deferred Compensation" in Chapter 18.

Family/Work Conflicts

Organizations that are not aware of each employee's need to have a fulfilling personal life, especially in a two-income family, will continue to experience significant turnover.

Magazines such as *Fortune* spend a significant amount of time examining this situation. A recent cover story entitled, "Is Your Family Wrecking Your Career or Vice Versa?" reported revealing statistics. According to information provided by the Institute for a New Commonwealth, 84 percent of the couples surveyed reported that both spouses were working. This creates a radically different workplace than existed twenty or fifty years ago. It also creates a personal need for management to recognize the difficulties these families have in balancing their work life and their personal life, which can result in job dissatisfaction.

The younger "Generation X" employees also bring new family/work conflicts to the workforce. Personal satisfaction in their private life is very important to these workers. They will work hard, expect fair compensation, and require clear boundaries between work and the personal life. This may result from observing their parents or others who worked hard for many years for a company only to find themselves out of a job as a victim of corporate restructuring and downsizing. Many will leave companies that interfere with their family and personal life to take positions, even at lower wages, to satisfy the need for balance in their life.

For solutions to this problem, see "Career Counseling" in Chapter 16.

Termination Analysis

The reasons for employee turnover are quite consistent across businesses. But the reasons specific to your company are most important to you. To find out why your employees leave (so you can rectify the situation) you should examine voluntary terminations in the past twelve months. Using the "Voluntary Termination Analysis" form in Appendix M, group terminations by job title, months of tenure, the manager involved (if applicable), and the reason for leaving. Look for patterns. Do your employees leave because they were unqualified for the job? Because they were not trained properly? Because of poor management? Because of compensation disputes? Because of work/family conflicts? If you can determine a pattern, you can develop a plan using the information in this book to address these problems and reduce your turnover.

The Cost of Turnover

I've mentioned previously in this book that one of the most pressing reasons for using smart staffing is the high cost of poor hiring that results in employee turnover. But how much does it really cost to lose an employee?

Studies by industry associations, academic groups, and consulting organizations show the cost varies, depending on the position, from as little as a month's salary to one-and-one-half times the annual salary. This variation is so wide because of the diversity of situations, jobs, and companies.

Most people look at the real cost of turnover with wonder and amazement. Until they take the time and effort to truly calculate the cost they don't realize the effect. Most people don't even think about all the real costs, whether direct or hidden, when they think of turnover. Let's examine these real costs. (Figure 19.1 outlines the costs of losing a sales clerk.)

Turnover cost is divided into two distinct portions: direct costs and hidden costs. The direct costs are those that can be quantified by examining records and making good factual estimates of time and resources. These costs are sometimes difficult to measure exactly but, nevertheless, are very real. The following list details what organizations usually consider direct costs:

Termination costs:
- Additional administrative time required due to termination
- Separation or severance pay due to departure
- The cost of time conducting and tabulating exit interviews
- Increase in unemployment tax due to added turnover

Vacancy costs:
- Additional employee overtime
- Additional temporary help
- Additional work outsourced
- Less the wages/benefits not paid due to the vacancy

Replacement costs:
- Attracting and recruiting applicants
- Screening applicants
- Conducting employment interviews
- Pre-employment evaluations
- Drug testing, credit and criminal checks
- Checking candidates' references
- Additional staff time to process hiring paperwork
- Travel or moving expenses
- Permits, fees, or licenses for new employee
- Post-employment information gathering and dissemination cost
- Setup of benefits for employee
- Uniforms or special equipment

Training costs:
- Orienting employee
- Training literature and materials
- Formal class training, fees, and employee's time
- Time in informal training or coaching by manager
- Certification on equipment, systems or skills

FIGURE 19.1 • Cost of Turnover

The following is a calculation of the cost of losing a sales clerk.

Direct Costs
Termination Costs*:
❏ Administrative time
❏ Clerical time   3 hrs. @ $ 9.00/hr. $27.00
   Management time 3 hrs. @ $15.00/hr. $45.00
❏ Separation or severance 3 days @ $9.00/hr. $216.00
❏ Unemployment compensation increase   ?
❏ Benefits continuing after termination
   health/dental insurance $135.00
Vacancy Costs
❏ Additional overtime 3 hrs./day @ $13.50/hr. rate for 10 days $405.00
❏ Temporary help 2 weeks @ $12.50/hr. $1,000.00
❏ Reduction due to not paying departing employee's wages
   2 weeks @ $9.00/hr.   ($720.00)
* Hourly rates include benefits at a rate of 30 percent
Replacement Costs
❏ Attracting and recruiting (ads) $200.00
❏ Screening applicants 5 hrs. @ $15.00/hr. $75.00
❏ Conducting employment interviews 10 hrs. @ $15.00/hr. $150.00
❏ Pre-employment evaluations $50.00
❏ Background checks $25.00
❏ Reference checking 3 hrs. @ $15.00/hr. $45.00
❏ Staff time to process paperwork 2 hrs. @ $9.00/hr. $18.00
❏ Setting up employee benefits 2 hrs. @ $9.00/hr. $18.00
Training Costs
❏ Time orienting employee 4 hrs. @ $15.00 $60.00
❏ Training / literature / materials $90.00
❏ Formal class fees and employee's time
   Fee for workshop $75.00
   10 hrs. instruction @ $15.00/hr. $150.00
❏ Informal coaching / training 20 hrs. @ $15.00/hr. $300.00
Total $2,364.00

(continued)

FIGURE 19.1 • Cost of Turnover (continued)

Hidden Costs	
❏ Reduced productivity due to lower morale	?
❏ Reduced productivity due to lower skill of new employee	
0–30 days (salary of $1,584) @ 40% loss	$634.00
0–90 days (salary of $3,168) @ 15% loss	$475.00
❏ Potential loss of cash and assets	?
❏ Loss of customers or business transactions*	
One customer for life at gross profit	$5,000.00
❏ Lower sales effectiveness	?
Total	$6,109.00
Grand Total	$8,473.00

* It is difficult to determine the cost of losing a customer who will not return; however, it is a real loss. It varies by industry. This does not take into account the damage an unsatisfied customer could do by telling others about being treated poorly by an unhappy or unknowledgeable employee.

The hidden costs of turnover are said to be much greater than the direct costs. Studies indicate that as much as 80 percent of the cost of turnover is hidden. The following are hidden costs to consider:

- Reduced productivity of employees that remain after turnover
- Cost of inefficiency while replacement is learning
- Potential loss of cash and/or assets
- Loss of customers or business transactions
- Lower morale of employees left behind
- Lower sales effectiveness (Lower morale and lack of focus on aggressive sales can reduce overall sales per customer and take away from selling higher profit goods and services.)

Some question the actual cost of lowered morale and productivity when an employee leaves. *The Journal of Social Psychology* ran an article called, "The Effects of Turnover on the Productivity of Those Who Stay" that reported the results of a laboratory investigation into the effects of employee turnover on productivity. When groups were performing a proofreading task and one of the members quit during a break citing illness, dissatisfaction, or a desire for greater rewards elsewhere, there was a change in productivity among the remaining subjects on the next task. In the second proofreading task, those who were exposed to the dissatisfied group member proofread significantly less material. Losing employees not only affects the organization by putting a greater workload on the remaining employees, it also slows the output of those employees. This is a loss of productivity and profit that cannot be recovered.

Annual Turnover Costs

To get an idea of what it costs annually to lose employees in your organization, estimate the turnover cost of each position. Use the previous example of a sales clerk to help you estimate both the direct and hidden costs of losing an employee. Then figure out how many people, in each type of position, you have lost in the last year. Multiply the estimated turnover cost of each position by the number lost to get a total. This is the annual cost of turnover for your company. Figure 19.2 shows the turnover cost of a store.

If after you make this calculation you realize that you don't like the amount of money that's leaving your business with each departing employee, it's time to invest money in the smart staffing process. Imagine if your turnover drain was $99,972, as in the example. If you were able to cut the turnover of sales clerks in half, you would save $33,892. If you could also retain the store manager you would have an extra $66,080 of bottom-line profit to put in your pocket.

Many companies think the cost of running background checks, investing in higher pay, conducting attitude surveys, or hiring an employment consultant is prohibitive. But in actuality, it's the cost of investing too little in the hiring and retention processes that is prohibitive.

FIGURE 19.2 • Calculating Cost of Turnover

Position	#Left	×	Turnover Cost	=	Drain
Clerk	8	×	$ 8,473	=	$67,784
Store manager	1	×	$32,188	=	$32,188
_____	___	×	_____	=	_____
_____	___	×	_____	=	_____
_____	___	×	_____	=	_____
Total					$99,972

FREQUENTLY ASKED QUESTIONS

Q. *People cite "a better offer" many times when they are leaving the job. Does this mean they are getting more money?*

A. Not necessarily. Employees often use "a better offer" to avoid revealing why they are really leaving because they may not feel comfortable telling you the real reason. Even if the employee perceives that the offer is better it may not be more money. It may be a better opportunity, position, or even location.

Q. *We are a small company and cannot afford formal recognition programs like Fortune 500 companies. What can we do?*

A. Even if you can't have an extensive program similar to those of Fortune 500 companies, you can institute a routine, systematic program recognizing performance and tenure. Many times informal programs are more meaningful.

Q. *As a small company we have several employees who have different benefit needs. How can we adjust our benefit package to them?*

A. Some companies create cafeteria-style programs that allow employees to pick the benefits they need from a pre-approved list with a preset benefit allowance.

Q. *How can I find out the average turnover rate in my industry?*

A. Most industries have associations which make detailed studies of different business practices including turnover. The associations that serve your industry are listed in *National Trade and Professional Associations* published by Columbia Books, Inc. You can call 202-898-0662 for more information.

CHAPTER 20

Conducting the Exit Interview

DON'T BE AFRAID TO DIG
FOR THE REAL REASONS YOUR EMPLOYEES LEAVE.

Until you pinpoint the specific causes of turnover in your company, you can't eliminate the problems or reduce turnover cost. The best source for this information is from departing employees. They can provide valuable information that can help your company reduce turnover and improve operations. You can obtain in-depth, candid, and accurate information from employees who are leaving your company through an exit interview. The objective of this kind of interview is to obtain accurate and specific information concerning what caused or motivated the employee to leave, and point out needed changes in the company's policies and management style.

Preparing for an Exit Interview

There are specific steps you should take to prepare for an effective exit interview so that it will not be a futile exercise. You want to obtain real information you can use to increase employee satisfaction and reduce turnover.

Determine if You Will Immediately Accept the Resignation

Before the exit interview occurs, you or the individual's immediate supervisor should try to uncover the specific reasons the employee is leaving and determine if the situation can, or should, be salvaged. As soon as this information is gathered, you should review the employee's work performance, discuss why the individual is leaving, decide if you should try to retain the individual, and possibly determine what can be done to prevent it from occurring again.

Then, decide if you want to try to keep the employee in the company or if you will accept the resignation. Either way, it is time to move on to an exit interview.

Scheduling the Interview

The timing of the exit interview depends on your objective. If the objective is to retain the employee, the quicker it is conducted the better your chance of success. Once an employee gives notice and tells coworkers and friends, the individual is mentally committed to the decision.

If the objective is to gather the greatest amount of information with the most specific details, it is best to conduct the exit interview at the end of the individual's employment, but before the individual receives a final pay check. When conducted at that time, the departing employee will not be worried about the reactions of others and may even want to give information that will help those who remain.

If the objective is to gain objective and unbiased information that you can use to keep current employees from leaving, the exit interview should take place about three months after departure. By this time, negative feelings will have cooled off, minor irritations will have disappeared, and only real concerns will remain. While still in your employ, the individual may have discounted a lot of the good aspects of the position and painted an overly optimistic picture of the new job. After working in the new position for three months, the individual will have a more balanced perspective.

Deciding Who Should Conduct the Interview

Unfortunately, the typical exit interview involves an employee, who is disgruntled enough to leave, talking with the immediate supervisor, who is emotionally involved in the situation. Neither may be motivated to be candid. The employee may want a reference from the supervisor and doesn't want to "burn any bridges." On the other hand, the employee may be angry and outspoken, but not objective. The supervisor may not want to dig to determine specifics, fearing he or she is part of the problem. As a result, the exit interview is comprised of a polite conversation that benefits no one. A good exit interview should be more than an obligatory meeting between the departing employee and the immediate supervisor.

The immediate supervisor should be consulted, but not directly involved. You should ask the supervisor to submit a report outlining any understanding of the circumstances surrounding the resignation. Why is the employee leaving? How has the employee performed? Has discipline been a problem? What should be done to prevent this type of turnover in the future? The Exit Interview Worksheet in Appendix N will help the supervisor report this information.

With this information in hand, you now need to locate an objective person to conduct the interview. It should be someone the employee will be open and candid with—an individual the employee perceives as fair and impartial. If the departing employee is willing to be open and candid without repercussions, you will obtain accurate and valuable information. Many times the employee talks openly with someone higher in the organization and details the real reasons for termination. If there is no one higher than the immediate supervisor, you should find an outside party or consultant who can conduct the exit interview. It requires an objective person who can filter out biased information and identify the real reason the employee is leaving.

Before the interview, be sure to provide the interviewer with helpful information, such as a statement of the employee's salary and history, prior performance appraisals, career goals (from the counseling sessions), and any past problems that have occurred. Also, give the interviewer a completed copy of the Exit Interview Worksheet.

Conducting an Exit Interview

Guarantee Confidentiality

Whether the interview is conducted in person or by phone, the departing employee needs to be immediately assured of confidentiality. The interviewer should explain that the employee's comments will be confidential, the specifics will not be communicated to the supervisor, and most importantly, the information will not affect any future reference for the employee. When the employee feels there will be no reprisals, you get honest information.

Probe to Determine Reasons for Leaving

The interviewer should make an effort to find out specifically why the employee is leaving. As discussed in Chapter 19, the ten most typical reasons are: (1) basic financial needs, (2) lack of competitive salary, (3) inadequate benefits, (4) poor communication, (5) negative workplace environment, (6) lack of recognition, (7) unfair and inequitable treatment, (8) lack of challenging job content, (9) lack of job security, and (10) family/work conflicts. The employee might be leaving for health or personal reasons or just to relocate.

If the employee states "low earnings" as a reason for leaving, don't automatically conclude that lack of competitive salary is the problem. The interviewer should probe deeper. This reason may really be a symptom of something else, such as lack of sales due to inadequate skills, low sales activity, or inadequate sales potential. You need the real reason to make changes that will positively affect turnover.

The interviewer can record his or her findings on the Final Exit Interview Form in Appendix O.

Determine Employee's Feelings About the Company

To determine the employee's feelings about the company and the job, the interviewer can ask questions to gauge satisfaction levels. The excerpt in Figure 20.1 from the Final Exit Interview form lists the kinds of things you can subjectively measure.

Look at the Supervisor/Employee Relationship

The interviewer should look into the employee's relationship with the supervisor to determine if problems or complaints were communicated to the supervisor, or even caused by the supervisor. If the complaints were taken to the supervisor, the interviewer should find out how they were handled. If they were not, the interviewer needs to find out why. The Final Exit Interview form has a section for recording this information.

Exit Questions

Make sure your interviewer has questions that will give you the answers you need to eliminate problems and reduce turnover. You may tailor these questions to meet your own very specific needs, or you can choose from the sample ques-

---

FIGURE 20.1 • Employee's Feelings

	Very Satisfied	Satisfied	Dissatisfied	Very Dissatisfied
Nature of the job	❑	❑	❑	❑
Salary treatment	❑	❑	❑	❑
Benefits programs	❑	❑	❑	❑
Training and development	❑	❑	❑	❑
Utilization of skills	❑	❑	❑	❑
Performance appraisals	❑	❑	❑	❑
Opportunities / advancement	❑	❑	❑	❑
Overall	❑	❑	❑	❑

tions in Figure 20.2. In either case, make sure you provide your interviewer with a list of the questions you need answered.

Written Questionnaire Interviews

Rather than conducting in-person exit interviews, some organizations interview by mail. You can send the former employee a letter expressing your regret and ask the individual to complete a confidential written questionnaire. Enclose

---

FIGURE 20.2 • Sample Questions for Exit Interviews

- How do you feel about the job you're leaving?

- How do you feel about the company?

- How do you feel about your supervisor?

- When you joined the company, you must have felt you could meet your career objective here. What has caused you to change your mind?

- Did you take problems or complaints to your supervisor? Were they handled to your satisfaction?

- What caused you to consider leaving?

- Did you get enough training to do your job?

- How often did you get feedback on your performance?

- Was the appraisal of your performance fair and accurate?

- Were there enough opportunities for professional growth?

- How did you feel about the compensation?

- How do you feel about our benefit program? What needs improvement?

- What could have been done to change the situation so you would still be with us?

- Did the company you will be working for recruit you or did you seek them?

the questionnaire and a self-addressed, stamped envelope. Figure 20.3 shows a sample letter.

Keep in mind that, as with any mail survey, the percentage of responses will be quite low. A 2 to 10 percent response is normal for most direct-mail surveys. You should have a much better response to an exit interview survey, but it will vary depending on the employees' attitudes and the company climate.) You may be able to increase the response by offering anonymity. You can give the individual the option of leaving off his or her name, you can have the questionnaire mailed

---

FIGURE 20.3 • Sample Cover Letter for a Written Interview

Date

Mr. Steve Cullen
111 Main Street
Mt. Pleasant, SC

Dear Steve,

Our employees and their contributions are important to us. As a former employee, you can assist us in determining why valued employees leave our company and how we can improve our work environment.

Your candid comments on the attached questionnaire would be appreciated. If you would like to make additional comments or suggestions, please feel free to use the reverse side. We have provided a self-addressed, stamped envelope for your convenience in returning the questionnaire to us.

We sincerely appreciate your time and effort in assisting us to create an environment where employees can reach their fullest potential and enhance our success.

Sincerely,

Company Owner
Enclosures

to an impartial third party, or you can explain that the information will be tabulated and reported to management in summary form.

The questionnaire should seek the same type of information you would gather through an in-person interview. Ask the reason for leaving, the type of new position taken and the salary at this job. You should also ask what the new position offers that your company does not. You will find a Confidential Questionnaire Form in Appendix P.

Analyzing the Results of Exit Interviews

You should analyze and tabulate the information from all exit interviews on a quarterly, semi-annual, or annual basis. This kind of overview summary gives you an objective look at patterns, trends, and consistent factors that are causing turnover in your business.

Check for Validity

The information from exit interviews can't be taken at face value alone. Many departing employees will not be honest about their motives. Before you act to make changes based on exit interviews, check the information against other sources to verify validity. You can compare what employees say at their exit interview to what they have stated on their attitude surveys (Chapter 15) about problems like low compensation and their relationship with the supervisor. You can also use their performance appraisal forms (Chapter 14) to double-check problem areas that may have been observed and see if they have been addressed. If, for example, you previously noted that the employee did not seem to have the skills to perform the job, the real reason for the resignation may be lack of adequate training rather than the employee's statement of finding a better career opportunity. You can also double-check areas of concern by talking to the departed employee's peers. If you find a pattern of terminations based on working conditions, you might talk to the remaining employees to get their feedback and suggestions for future improvements.

Implementing an Action Plan

The exit interview will point out the reasons individuals leave your employment, but having this information will not reduce your rate of turnover or decrease the cost of employee turnover. You must take this information and do something with it.

For example, if you find that the majority of your sales clerks were very happy with the working conditions and their managers, but left because they could not meet their living expenses on the hourly wage you pay, then action needs to be taken. Go back to Chapter 18 to find creative financial incentives and perks you can afford that will satisfy your employees. Or, if you find a pattern of resignations due to lack of challenging job content, try a program of employee rotation as explained in Chapter 17.

The problems you uncover through exit interviews bring you full circle in the hiring process. To reduce turnover, you need to hire intelligently, reward good employees, and learn from your losses.

*F*REQUENTLY *A*SKED *Q*UESTIONS

Q. *In a small company where can we get someone who is unbiased to conduct an exit interview?*

A. Anyone can be authorized by the company to conduct an exit interview. Consultants are a key resource and often used for this purpose. Or, if funds are tight, you might arrange a reciprocal agreement with another company. You will conduct an exit interview for them, and they will conduct yours.

Q. *If the problem is money, should I increase the salary to keep the departing employee?*

A. In the short term, it seems less costly to keep a good employee by increasing the salary. However, it can create a long-term problem or negative impact on other employees. It is not wise to increase a salary out of the normal range just to keep an employee.

Q. *Is it a good idea to conduct an exit interview in the workplace?*

A. You can meet in the workplace if you have a neutral and private area. The most valuable information will be obtained from an exit interview only if the employee feels comfortable.

Conclusion

Some people say that knowledge is power. I disagree. Power comes from what you do with that knowledge. You may have had the experience of reading a book or attending a seminar and knowing that the information applied to you and your needs. You may have even decided that you really wanted to implement the suggested changes into your life or your business. And then the day ended, and the next day, and the next and nothing happened. You were not empowered by that knowledge.

In this book, I have given you information that all small business owners/ managers vitally need. I have no doubt that you understand the value of hiring intelligently. I have no doubt that you realize the impact your employees have on your bottom-line profits. But I also know that this knowledge won't affect your business unless you put it to work for you.

It's true that smart staffing takes time, thought, effort, and even some cash—but so does every aspect of your business that's vital to its success. Commit right now to taking steps toward improving the way you find, hire, and retain your employees. Don't put it off.

When you make this commitment, sit down and decide where you will start. If you are in need of new employees right now, start at the beginning and create a new, smart hiring process. If your priority right now is keeping the top employees you have, begin by focusing your actions on Step 4: Keep and Reward Top Employees. If you've just lost a top employee and want to use this experience as a learning tool, start with Step 5: Learn From Your Losses. The key point is this: Do something. Today, start changing the way you handle the most valuable asset you have—human capital. This, above all other business strategies, is the one that will have the most direct positive effect on your company's reputation, productivity, growth, and profits.

Job Definition

Title: _____ Date: _____

Reports to: _____ Defined by: _____

RESPONSIBILITIES (rank in order of importance):

1. _____

2. _____

3. _____

4. _____

5. _____

6. _____

7. _____

8. _____

DUTIES (rank in order of importance):

1. _____

2. _____

3. _____

4. _____

5. _____

6. _____

7. _____

8. _____

9. _____

10. _____

11. _____

12. _____

13. _____

14. _____

15. _____

ESSENTIAL JOB FUNCTIONS:

Examine the job to determine the minimum level of mobility, visual ability, hearing ability, learning and mental capacity that a person must have to meet the standard for the position.

Function   **Standard**

_____   _____

_____   _____

_____   _____

_____   _____

_____   _____

_____   _____

EXPECTED LEVEL OF PERFORMANCE STANDARDS:

_____

_____

_____

_____

_____

COMPENSATION: _____

_____

_____

_____

GROWTH OPPORTUNITIES: _____

_____

_____

Hiring Criteria

Title: _____   Date: _____

Reports to: _____   Defined by: _____

MUSTS (job cannot be done without):

1. _____

2. _____

3. _____

4. _____

5. _____

6. _____

7. _____

8. _____

PREFERREDS (rank in order of importance):

1. _____

2. _____

3. _____

4. _____

5. _____

6. _____

7. _____

8. _____

9. _____

10. _____

11. _____

12. _____

NOTE: Consider factors such as education, experience, knowledge, skills, personal traits/behavior, mental ability, appearance, physical ability, communication, and other requirements to successfully perform the job.

Application for Employment

We encourage applications from qualified individuals with disabilities.

Name of applicant

First name   Middle name   Last name   Date of application

_____   _____   _____   _____

Current mailing address   **Telephone number**

Number and street   City   State   Zip   Area   Number

_____   _____   _____   _____   _____ - _____ - _____

Permanent mailing address   **Telephone number**

Number and street   City   State   Zip   Area   Number

_____   _____   _____   _____   _____ - _____ - _____

Type of work for which you are applying   **Type of employment you want**

First choice   Permanent ☐

_____   Part-time ☐

Second choice   Summer ☐

_____

Any preference or restriction regarding work location

_____

Minimum salary requirements   Date available for work

_____   _____

Personal

Social Security Number

_____

Are you eligible to work in the
United States?   Yes ☐   No ☐

Are you at least 18 years old?
Yes ☐   No ☐

Are you able to work flexible hours?
Yes ☐   No ☐

Have you ever been convicted of a felony? If yes,
list date and place   Yes ☐   No ☐

Do you have a relative
employed with ABC Company?
Yes ☐   No ☐

_____

Have you applied before, if so when?

Yes ☐   No ☐   _____

Military

Branch of U.S. Service

_____

Date entered

_____/_____

Date discharged

_____/_____

Highest rank attained

_____

Do you have U.S. Armed Forces Reserve obligations?   Yes ☐   No ☐

List any special training received: _____

Education

Last high school and address

Highest grade completed

_____   _____

Did you graduate   Yes ☐   No ☐   Course or field of study _____

Business or Technical school and address

Years completed   Certificate obtained

_____   _____   _____

College   School location (city & state)   Major field of study   Credits   Degree

_____   _____   _____   _____   _____

_____   _____   _____   _____   _____

Employment Record

List most recent employment first. Include all former employers and self employment.

Employer's Name and Phone number   Supervisor's name   Supervisor's job title

_____ _____   _____ _____

Employer's Address, City, State   Start pay / End pay   Reason for leaving

_____   _____ _____

Describe duties _____

_____

Job title _____   From _____ / _____ To _____ / _____

Employer's Name and Phone number   Supervisor's name   Supervisor's job title

_____ _____   _____ _____

Employer's Address, City, State   Start pay / End pay   Reason for leaving

_____   _____ _____

Describe duties _____

_____

Job title _____   From _____ / _____ To _____ / _____

Employer's Name and Phone number   Supervisor's name   Supervisor's job title

_____ _____   _____ _____

Employer's Address, City, State   Start pay / End pay   Reason for leaving

_____   _____ _____

Describe duties _____

_____

Job title _____   From _____ / _____ To _____ / _____

Employer's Name and Phone number   Supervisor's name   Supervisor's job title

_____ _____   _____   _____

Employer's Address, City, State   Start pay / End pay   Reason for leaving

_____   _____   _____

Describe duties _____

_____

Job title _____   From _____ / _____   To _____ / _____

Employer's Name and Phone number   Supervisor's name   Supervisor's job title

_____ _____   _____   _____

Employer's Address, City, State   Start pay / End pay   Reason for leaving

_____   _____   _____

Describe duties _____

_____

Job title _____   From _____ / _____   To _____ / _____

References

Please provide the names of five references who know you in a work environment who are not listed above as supervisors.

1 Name   Telephone number   Occupation or position

_____   _____   _____

Company, institution, or organization _____

How long has reference known you?   Under what circumstances has reference known you?

_____   _____

2 Name   Telephone number   Occupation or position

_____   _____   _____

Company, institution, or organization   _____

How long has reference known you?   Under what circumstances has reference known you?

_____   _____

3 Name   Telephone number   Occupation or position

_____   _____   _____

Company, institution, or organization   _____

How long has reference known you?   Under what circumstances has reference known you?

_____   _____

4 Name   Telephone number   Occupation or position

_____   _____   _____

Company, institution, or organization   _____

How long has reference known you?   Under what circumstances has reference known you?

_____   _____

5 Name   Telephone number   Occupation or position

_____   _____   _____

Company, institution, or organization   _____

How long has reference known you?   Under what circumstances has reference known you?

_____   _____

I certify that the above information is true and complete to the best of my knowledge. I understand that misrepresentation or omission of facts requested on this application is cause for rejection of this application or for subsequent dismissal from employment. I authorize an investigation of any of the facts set forth in this application. I give permission to check my educational background, references, professional license, criminal record, driving record, and credit record and release any and all persons, companies, or agencies responding to such investigation from any liability for any damage due to releasing information pertaining hereto. I understand I will be required to provide information for compliance with the Immigration Reform and Control Act. I understand that I may be required to have a physical examination, drug test, and pre-employment evaluation. I understand and agree that my employment with ABC Company is entered into voluntarily and I may resign at any time.

Signature _____ Date _____

Application will be active for ninety (90) days.

If driving required:

Driving Information

Driver's license number   State   Expiration date

_____   _____   _____

   A. Is the above a valid driver's license?   Yes ☐ No ☐

   B. Have you ever been denied a license, permit or privilege
      to operate a motor vehicle?   Yes ☐ No ☐

   C. Has any license, permit or privilege ever been suspended or revoked?   Yes ☐ No ☐

If the answer to either B or C is YES, attach a statement giving details.

Have you had an accident in the past 5 years? (Attach sheet if more space is needed.)

Nature of accident (head-on, rear-end, etc.)

Last accident date _____   _____

Injuries Yes ☐ No ☐   Fatalities Yes ☐ No ☐

Nature of accident (head-on, rear-end, etc.)

Next previous date _____   _____

Injuries Yes ☐ No ☐   Fatalities Yes ☐ No ☐

Traffic convictions and forfeitures for the past five years (other than parking violations)

Location (city and state)	Date	Charges	Penalty
_____	_____	_____	_____
_____	_____	_____	_____
_____	_____	_____	_____

Additional Information for Sales Position:

Describe your typing or keyboard skills.

_____

_____

Explain situations where you have had to demonstrate your mathematical ability such as calculating payments and handling cash.

_____

_____

Are you able to lift 40 lbs. and move it 40 feet unaided?   Yes ☐   No ☐

Can you reach and answer the phone by the third ring
from any place in the store?   Yes ☐   No ☐

Recruiting Plan

Position: _____

Date of projected opening: _____

Reason position open: _____

Date the position must be filled: _____

Staffing Options:

____ full-time   ____ part-time

____ permanent   ____ temporary

____ outsourcing

Job Definition:

current one: ____ accurate   ____ needs revision

new position: ____ create one

Hiring Criteria List:

current one   ____ accurate   ____ needs revision

new position   ____ create one

Compensation:

hourly: _____   salary: _____

commission: _____   bonus: _____

incentive perks:

_____

_____

Applications:

No. needed: _____

Submission form: ____ mail   ____ e-mail   ____ fax   ____ in-person

Locations to apply: _____

Telephone calls (time/day): _____

Action	Individuals Responsible	Target Date
Creating/placing ads	_____	_____
Networking	_____	_____
Other applicant sources	_____	_____
Screening applications	_____	_____
Screening interviews	_____	_____
In-depth interviews	_____	_____
Pre-employment evaluation	_____	_____
Reference checking	_____	_____
Creating and making offer	_____	_____
Sending reject letters	_____	_____
Orienting new employee	_____	_____
Training new employee	_____	_____

End Evaluation:

What did I learn that can apply in the future to get a higher quality candidate, reduce the effort needed, or shorten the time required? What valuable lesson did I learn?

_____

_____

_____

_____

_____

_____

Employment Ad Placement Log

It is important to keep track of our employment advertisements in all areas. By knowing the responses to the ads and their placement, the best decisions can be made for future use of resources.

Location/Position	Ad#	Paper	Placement	Cost	Response

Location/Position	Ad#	Paper	Placement	Cost	Response

Employee Referral Form

Help Us Grow
I Have Identified a Winner!

Referral Name: _____

Phone Number: _____ Company/Location _____

Address (if known): _____

Information about the referral:

_____

_____

_____

_____

What position do you think they fit best?

_____

Why?

_____

_____

Send original to Owner/Manager and retain copy for your records.

Your Name: _____ Date: _____

Manager Followup: _____ Date: _____

Results of Referral: _____

Pre-Employment Evaluation Sources

INSTRUMENTS:

OUTLAW GROUP, Inc., P.O. Box 661, Mt. Pleasant, SC 29465. Web site: www. outlawgroup.com. Customized Hiring Systems, including Job Matching using pre-employment assessments and integrity testing.

Profiles Technology, 2100 Hwy 360, Suite 400B, Grand Prairie, TX 75050, 972 988 3725. Profile Evaluation for Sales and Management Candidates.

Reid Psychological Systems, 2687 McCollum Parkway, Kennesaw, GA 30144, 770-428-1448. Paper and Pencil Honesty Test for new employees and existing employees.

The HR Chally Group, 500 Lincoln Park Blvd., Suite 204, Dayton, OH 45429, 513-299-1255. Evaluation Systems for Management, Sales, and Technical Candidates.

Center for Creative Leadership, P.O. Box 26300, Greensboro, NC 27438, 919-288-7210.

Gallup Research, Inc., 301 South 68th Street, Lincoln, NE 68510, 402-489-9000.

London House, Inc., 9701 West Higgins Rd., Rosemont, IL 60018-4720, 800-221-8378.

Caliper Management, 741 Mt. Lucas Road, Princeton, NJ 08540, 609-924-3800.

Pinkerton Services Group, 6100 Fairview Rd., Suite 900, Charlotte, NC 28210, 704-552-1119.

Wonderlick Personnel Testing, Inc., 1509 North Milwaukee Ave., Libertyville, IL 60048, 800-323-3742.

American Society for Training and Development, 1640 King Street, Box 1443, Alexandria, VA 22313, 703-683-8100. Partial listing of Pre-Employment Instrument providers are available by contacting ASTD.

BACKGROUND INVESTIGATION:

Informus Corporation, 2001 Airport Road, Suite 201, Jackson, MS 39208, 800-364-8380.

Employment Screening Service, 207 East Bay Street, Suite 306, Charleston, SC 29401, 803-853-7243. Employment verification, education verification, credit reports, driving records, and criminal record searches.

Choice Point, (formerly Equifax), 1000 Alderman Drive, Alpharetta, GA 30203, 770-752-5681. Offers pre-employment screening: criminal record checks, credit and motor vehicle reports, verification of education and credentials; drug testing: specimen collection, lab and medical Review Officer services.

DRUG ABUSE/TESTING:

Center for Substance Abuse Prevention Hotline, drug testing, 800-843-4971.

CREDIT REPORTS:

Local Credit Bureau

CRIMINAL HISTORY:

Local Courthouse

Applicant Reference Data Sheet

Work References

Name _____ **Date** _____

Instructions: Please give complete information. List the last four positions, starting from the most recent position. Give the names of all those who were your direct supervisors while at the company and those who best knew the quality of your work. If you are still employed at your last position, please provide others, such as those who have left the company or will respect your confidentiality.

Company _____ Your Position _____

Last Supervisor _____ Phone _____

Supervisor's Title _____ How long supervised? _____

Other Supervisor _____ Phone _____

Supervisor's Title _____ How long supervised? _____

Other Supervisor _____ Phone _____

Supervisor's Title _____ How long supervised? _____

Other Supervisor _____ Phone _____

Supervisor's Title _____ How long supervised? _____

Company _____ Your Position _____

Last Supervisor _____ Phone _____

Supervisor's Title _____ How long supervised? _____

Other Supervisor _____ Phone _____

Supervisor's Title _____ How long supervised? _____

Other Supervisor _____ Phone _____

Supervisor's Title _____ How long supervised? _____

Other Supervisor _____ Phone _____

Supervisor's Title _____ How long supervised? _____

Company _____ Your Position _____

Last Supervisor _____ Phone _____

Supervisor's Title _____ How long supervised? _____

Other Supervisor _____ Phone _____

Supervisor's Title _____ How long supervised? _____

Other Supervisor _____ Phone _____

Supervisor's Title _____ How long supervised? _____

Other Supervisor _____ Phone _____

Supervisor's Title _____ How long supervised? _____

Company _____ Your Position _____

Last Supervisor _____ Phone _____

Supervisor's Title _____ How long supervised? _____

Other Supervisor _____ Phone _____

Supervisor's Title _____ How long supervised? _____

Other Supervisor _____ Phone _____

Supervisor's Title _____ How long supervised? _____

Other Supervisor _____ Phone _____

Supervisor's Title _____ How long supervised? _____

The information furnished is accurate and complete, and is furnished in the pursuit of employment. Any misrepresentation or omission in providing information to verify employment and work history is cause for rejection of the application or for subsequent dismissal from employment.

I authorize the investigation of all statements contained in my application and this reference worksheet.

Date _____ Signature _____

Applicant's Information Release Statement

Date: _____

To: _____

_____

_____

Applicant: _____

Social Security Number: _____

Applicant's Statement of Release:

"I have read this evaluation form and hereby give my former employer permission to complete it based on my former employer's evaluation of me. I understand the information is confidential. I hereby waive all rights to see or review the comments furnished by my former employer."

Applicant's Signature _____

The above applicant has listed your firm as a previous employer. Please verify by answering the following:

Dates Employed _____ to _____

Position Held _____

Attendance Record _____

Job Performance _____

Personal Appearance _____

Reason for Leaving _____

Eligible for Rehire _____

Remarks, If Any _____

Information Furnished By:

_____   _____   _____
Signature   Title   Date

The above information will be held in strictest confidence. Thank you for your cooperation.

Sincerely,

Applicant Reference Summary Sheet

Reference Worksheet:

Name: _____ **Date Reference Completed** _____

Start Date: _____ End Date: _____ Position: _____

Quality of work?	Poor	Good	Excellent
Gets along with people?	Poor	Good	Excellent
Attendance/Tardiness?	Poor	Good	Excellent
Personal problems at work?	Poor	Good	Excellent
Attitude/Work habits?	Poor	Good	Excellent
Loyalty/Honesty?	Poor	Good	Excellent
Need for close supervision?	Poor	Good	Excellent

Specific reasons given by supervisor for termination

_____

Would company rehire?   Yes ___ No ___ Explain _____

Strengths (List Three)	Weaknesses (List Three)
_____	_____
_____	_____
_____	_____

I received information from direct supervisor and fully understand the applicant's performance in this position. Yes _____ No _____

How would I rate the applicant's performance in this job compared to standards/others?

Poor   Good   Excellent

Is the reference check consistent with applicant's view of his performance and work habits?

What concerns do I have that need further investigation?

_____

_____

Based on job performance, would I recommend hiring the applicant?
Yes _____ No _____

Hiring Check Sheet

Candidate Name: _____ Date Applied: _____

Initial Screening: Date: _____

    resume? _____ yes _____ no

    phone contact? _____ yes _____ no

    application complete? _____ yes _____ no

Screening Interview: Date: _____

Interviewer: _____

    _____ Phone _____ In-Person

Recommendation or notes: _____

_____

In-Depth Interview: Date: _____

Interviewer: _____

Recommendation or notes: _____

Pre-Employment Evaluations:

References:

Checked by: _____

Notes: _____

_____

Background check:

Areas investigated: _____

_____

_____

_____

Notes: _____

_____

Tests:

Name of Test   Results

_____

_____

_____

_____

_____

Hired:

Date Offered: _____ Date Started: _____

Location: _____

Final Evaluation Form

Factor	Weight	Rating		Final Points
_____	_____	× _____	=	_____
_____	_____	× _____	=	_____
_____	_____	× _____	=	_____
_____	_____	× _____	=	_____
_____	_____	× _____	=	_____
_____	_____	× _____	=	_____
_____	_____	× _____	=	_____
_____	_____	× _____	=	_____
_____	_____	× _____	=	_____
_____	_____	× _____	=	_____
Total	100			

Summary:

_____

_____

_____

_____

_____

Hire:

Date Offered: _____ Date Started: _____

Location: _____ _____

Voluntary Termination Analysis Form

Name	Job Title	Months Tenure	Manager	Reason for Termination

Name	Job Title	Months Tenure	Manager	Reason for Termination

Exit Interview Worksheet

To be completed by interviewer after discussion with immediate Supervisor.

Employee Name _____ Title _____ Location _____

Interviewer's Name _____ Title _____

Type of separation:

❏ Resignation   ❏ Mutual Agreement   ❏ Dismissal   ❏ Other

Date notice given ____ / ____ /____   Hire date ____ / ____ / ____

Last scheduled working day ____ / ____ /____   How notified _____

Would Supervisor recommend for rehire?   ❏ Yes   ❏ No   Explain _____

_____

Supervisor's understanding of why employee is leaving: _____

_____

_____

Supervisor's evaluation of employee's work performance: _____

_____

_____

What is the Supervisor's opinion of the real cause of the individual's departure?

❑ Poor hiring decision ❑ Poor supervision

❑ Inadequate orientation/training ❑ Other (explain) _____

_____

What should be done to prevent this type of turnover in the future? _____

_____

If Resignation

Check the primary reasons for employee's dissatisfaction

❑ Type of work   ❑ Working conditions   ❑ Personal reasons

❑ Fellow employees   ❑ Supervision reasons   ❑ Company policies

❑ Obtain better position ❑ Relocation   ❑ Health reasons

❑ Pay   ❑ Work hours

❑ Other _____

Final Exit Interview Form

To be completed after interview.

Real Reason If Terminated:

❏ Unsatisfactory performance   ❏ Unacceptable conduct

❏ Unacceptable attendance record   ❏ Violation of policy

❏ Failure to follow procedure   ❏ Other

Explanation: _____

_____

At exit interview, the interviewer should determine the employee's feelings about the following aspects of his or her employment experience. Check what best describes employee's feelings.

	Very Satisfied	Satisfied	Dissatisfied	Very Dissatisfied
Nature of the job	❏	❏	❏	❏
Salary treatment	❏	❏	❏	❏
Benefits program	❏	❏	❏	❏
Training and development	❏	❏	❏	❏
Utilization of skills	❏	❏	❏	❏
Performance appraisals	❏	❏	❏	❏
Opportunities / advancement	❏	❏	❏	❏
Overall	❏	❏	❏	❏

Supervision

Relationship with supervisor? _____

Were complaints taken to supervisor? ❏ Yes ❏ No Handled promptly?

_____

Please describe: _____

_____

General Comments _____

_____

Recommendations to prevent future turnover _____

_____

Interviewer _____ *Title* _____ *Date* _____

Confidential Questionnaire

Name _____ Position _____
     (optional)

Location _____ Length of Employment _____ Salary _____

Reason for Leaving

Dissatisfied with:

_____ Salary   _____ Type of Work

_____ Working Conditions   _____ Supervisor

_____ Advancement Opportunities   _____ Other*

*Please explain _____

_____

_____

Reasons other than dissatisfaction:

_____ Mutual Consent   _____ School

_____ Relocation of Spouse   _____ Military

_____ Health   _____ Other*

*Please explain _____

_____

_____

_____

If another position, where? _____

Type of Firm? _____

Type of Work? _____ Salary _____

How did you learn about the position?   ____ Ad   ____ Agency

                                          ____ Friend   ____ Other

What does your new position offer that our company did not offer?

_____

_____

_____

Glossary

acclimation plan A plan designed to help new employees feel welcome and incorporate them into the organization.

accountable guarantee A minimum earnings level during a specific period, such as one month, designed to protect an individual's cash flow without increasing the company's liability. Individuals must earn more than the account able guarantee before they receive additional compensation.

applicant Any person who completes a job application or formally submits a resume in pursuit of employment with a company.

application The form or document specifically designed to obtain the necessary information from an applicant for the company to make a well informed employment decision.

attitude surveys Surveys designed to assess and identify specific attitudes of employees regarding the organization, the work, management, and the way they are treated.

background checks Investigations into areas such as driving history, felony conviction record, credit check, credentials, and education.

behavioral style instruments Tools to identify and measure qualities of the individual to assist in matching the individual to the job.

benchmarks The observed traits and behaviors of successful and unsuccessful employees used to create a basis for measuring a candidate's potential for success.

candidate An applicant who has progressed through the hiring process by meeting the hiring criteria's musts for the position.

career counseling The process of helping an employee evaluate career goals and desires, and compare them to the opportunities in the organization to assist in developing a more satisfying career.

closed question A question that can be answered with one word or a limited response.

contingency search A candidate search in which a fee is only paid if the firm's suggested candidate is hired for the position.

counter offer A response by a candidate's current employer to meet or match conditions or entice the employee to refuse an offer of employment.

defining the job Also called job definition, it includes the responsibilities, duties, essential functions, and expected level of performance in a job.

employment agreements Agreements that set conditions or impose limitations on employees after termination.

essential job functions The minimum levels of physical actions, such as lifting, mobility, hearing, mental capacity, and communicating, necessary to do the job. These are defined by the Americans with Disabilities Act.

executive interview A meeting between employees and executives in which top management can ask questions and collect information, and employees can express their feelings and concerns.

exit interview The process of obtaining information from departing employees to learn the reasons and conditions that caused the employee to leave.

halo effect Allowing one positive characteristic or situation to become so overwhelmingly important that weaknesses are overlooked and problems are excused.

hiring criteria Specific requirements to be successful in a job, including the education, experience, knowledge, skills, behavior, personal traits, mental ability, appearance, physical ability, and values. These requirements are divided into musts and preferreds.

hiring process A series of steps used to fill a position, including identifying the job, locating applicants, and interviewing and evaluating candidates.

in-depth interviews Meetings with candidates designed to uncover the information necessary for the interviewer to make a hiring decision.

initial performance period Probationary period before the employee reaches regular employee status.

integrity instruments Tests to help determine applicants' values and attitudes about theft, admission of employee theft and other work-related wrongdoings.

job enrichment A purposeful process designed to capitalize on an individual's ability and personal skills and allow an industrious employee to focus on something other than a narrow job description.

job performance The quality and quantity of work along with the other habits, attitudes, and values displayed in carrying out the duties and responsibilities of the position.

job match Making sure a person's natural behavioral style and tendencies are similar to the requirements of the position to increase the likelihood of success with the employee.

musts The minimum requirements of a candidate necessary for a reasonable chance of success in the position.

negligent hiring Failure to discover negative information about a candidate, such as incompetence or criminal activity, that may affect job performance and endanger clients and coworkers. Liability can be imposed on the acts of employees, even outside the scope of employment, if the employer has been negligent in exercising their responsibility during hiring.

open-ended question A question to which there is no one-word answer or limited response.

orientation The process of communicating to a new employee what to do and how to do it, including both written and unwritten rules.

panel interview A meeting with a candidate in which multiple interviewers take turns asking prepared questions.

patterned interview A meeting with a candidate in which the same specific structured questions are asked of each individual so answers can be compared.

pre-employment evaluation The use of instruments, tests, background checks, reference checks, credit checks, and any other form of evaluation designed to allow the organization to make a better hiring decision.

preferreds The characteristics the company would like an ideal candidate to have that are not necessary to performing the job.

recruiting plan A method designed to ensure the organization is fully staffed at all times, which includes hiring targets, hiring criteria, candidate sources, recruiting methods, compensation, and a list of the individuals involved and their responsibilities.

red flag Any situation or information that causes a degree of concern, which should be examined and resolved before moving forward in the hiring process.

retained search A candidate search performed by an executive recruiter who earns the fee whether the position is filled or not as long as the contracted assistance is delivered.

screening applicants Reviewing applications or resumes to determine if the individuals appear to have the musts and deserve an invitation to a screening interview.

screening interview A meeting designed primarily to determine if the applicant meets the musts and is a candidate for further consideration.

serial interview An interview technique in which several meetings take place in sequence and each follows up or builds on the previous one.

stonewall reference A reference that provides little or no information.

structured on-the-job training A planned methodical approach to teaching job skills through demonstration, lecture, coaching, written instruction, or other programs when formal classroom training is not possible.

unaccountable guarantee A minimum earnings level, including salary, incentives, and promotional compensation, during a specific period, that the employee does not have to pay back with future earnings.

value instruments Tools designed to identify the candidate's drive for recognition, economic benefits, power, and the need to follow rules and procedures, as well as other key values.

work reference An individual whose knowledge and judgment is based primarily on a work relationship, such as a supervisor or coworker.

Index

About the Author

Wayne Outlaw is president of the Outlaw Group, Inc., of Mt. Pleasant, South Carolina, a speaking, training, and consulting firm that focuses on improving sales and services through better hiring and management of people.

Outlaw graduated from The Citadel, served as a Captain in the Infantry, and spent 13 years with Xerox, where he held the record for the quickest promotion to branch Marketing Manager. As a Sales Manager, he took the last place sales team to first place in just one month, with the same staff. Outlaw developed the benchmark sales strategy used worldwide by Xerox to beat lower-priced competition. He founded his own firm, which began as an executive search firm, in 1984.

Wayne Outlaw holds the designation of Certified Speaking Professional, awarded by the National Speakers Association, and Certified Management Consultant, awarded by the Institute of Management Consultants. He was the seventh person to be awarded both designations. He is a speaker with content and depth to his program, and a consultant with a great presentation. He was a nominee for the Entrepreneur of the Year Award presented by *Inc.* magazine two years in a row.

Increasing results through people's performance is the theme of hundreds of articles Outlaw has written for business and trade publications on sales, service, performance improvement, and management. He has learning systems on time management, customer service, people management, and hiring. He publishes "The Outlaw Report," a bimonthly newsletter that focuses on increasing results through people's performance with a focus on hiring, training, managing, and retaining employees that sell and serve customers.

About the Outlaw Group

The Outlaw Group, Inc., is an international management consulting firm that focuses on assisting corporations to increase their results by not only hiring and retaining better people, but by creating a positive work environment and increasing employee performance. The Outlaw Group identifies the real barriers to higher performance and develops specific solutions designed to meet the unique needs of each situation and company.

The Outlaw Group assists clients through employee and customer surveys, customer service systems, performance management systems, hiring systems, candidate evaluation, sales and marketing audits, and organizational development. Wayne conducts seminars, workshops, and keynote speeches for associations and corporations. Clients include ComputerLand, Dale Carnegie, Folgers/Proctor & Gamble, Exxon, IBM, Toshiba of Canada, Val-Pak, and various national and regional associations.

If you'd like to learn more about how these workshops and consulting services can increase results by improving people's performance, or to receive a free sample of "The Outlaw Report," please contact:

Outlaw Group, Inc.
P.O. Box 661
Mt. Pleasant, SC 29465
Phone: 843-884-9361
Fax: 843-881-1758
E-mail: wayne@outlawgroup.com
www.outlawgroup.com

658.31   Outlaw, Wayne.
O

        Smart staffing.

$19.95

DATE			

11-4-98